THE SAN FRANCISCO MIME TROUPE READER

The San Francisco
Mime Troupe Reader

SUSAN VANETA MASON

The University of Michigan Press   ANN ARBOR

Copyright © by the University of Michigan 2005
All rights reserved
Published in the United States of America by
The University of Michigan Press
Manufactured in the United States of America
♾ Printed on acid-free paper

2008   2007   2006   2005   4   3   2   1

A CIP catalog record for this book is available from the British Library.

Library of Congress Cataloging-in-Publication Data

The San Francisco Mime Troupe reader / edited by Susan Vaneta Mason.
       p.   cm.
    Includes bibliographical references.
    ISBN 0-472-09842-X (cloth : alk. paper) — ISBN 0-472-06842-3
(pbk. : alk. paper)   1. San Francisco Mime Troupe—History.
I. Mason, Susan Vaneta, 1946–   II. Title.

PN2297.S25S26 2005
792.3'09794'61—dc22   2004022451

During the life span of the Babyboomers now turning 40, the United States plus all countries within our reach have come to be ruled by a shadow (now no longer a secret) government of spy agencies, right-wing billionaires and military fanatics. Our oceans have been turned into chemical dumps, half the world's rain forests have vanished, holes have appeared in our ozone layer, and our hopes for the future have been buried under a steadily mounting pile of unimaginable weapons. During the same period, a single topic has dominated the American stage: personal relationships.

—Joan Holden, 1988

In our society we have things that you might use your intelligence on, like politics, but people really can't get involved in them in a very serious way— so what they do is they put their minds into other things, such as sports. . . . it occupies the population, and keeps them from trying to get involved with things that really matter. In fact, I presume that's part of the reason why spectator sports are supported to the degree they are by the dominant institutions.

—Noam Chomsky, 1989

We live in a society that rewards and honors corporate gangsters—corporate leaders who directly and indirectly plunder the earth's resources and look out for the shareholders' profits above all else—while subjecting the poor to a random and brutal system of "justice."

—Michael Moore, 2001

Foreword

Encompassing more than four decades of political satire, the San Francisco Mime Troupe's longevity is itself a political and artistic triumph; this theater ensemble, like a character Brecht's Herr Keuner described, has now outlived many of its enemies. Presidents, dictators, and corporate executives who inspired the Mime Troupe's satire are now out of power, and survive in some cases only as footnotes to history. By contrast, the Mime Troupe is still actively entertaining audiences, as its comic opposition to abuses of power and wealth goes on in its fifth decade, with free performances in city parks and annual tours across the country.

Tyrants and plutocrats come and go; but then so does topical theater. Satire is not often staged with posterity in mind; play texts like the Mime Troupe's often go uncollected, nuances of humor and physical comedy in the plays vanish along with the actors after the last curtain call, and once-timely plays are rarely revived, unless Aristophanes wrote them. This might explain why some of the San Francisco Mime Troupe's most popular plays could not be found in print until now. Fortunately for posterity, and for those now reading the book, Susan Mason has assembled some of the Mime Troupe's finest texts, and provided engaging introductions to the history behind the plays, so their context can be more fully appreciated.

Though on the page they inevitably lack the full humor and body of a live performance, these plays remain important and enriching documents of American theater history, models of satire from which new generations can learn much about art and politics. In the United States there have been few satire ensembles comparable to the San Francisco Mime Troupe—none with a comic body of work seen as widely as these plays have been through years of national and international tours. If the Mime Troupe's theater collective, critical of its own country's military and economic programs, had originated forty years ago in the Soviet Union, American critics probably would have been praising its "dissident" humor and defending its free speech to the skies during the Cold War. Our government's officials and their friends in the corporate world cherish comic criticism as long as it is not directed at them. Then again, perhaps a theater of dissent should not be too well received.

The worst that can be said about the Mime Troupe is that it has been warmly welcomed by audiences around the world. It was and is a popular theater company, far better known onstage than in print. If you have not had the pleasure of seeing the San Francisco Mime Troupe live, on one of its outdoor platform stages, with lighting provided by the sun (and occasional fog in the hometown of San Francisco), with hundreds and sometimes thousands of people fervently cheering anticapitalist heroes and laughing at foolish tyrants, this book will provide some compensation, as it sets the scene with photographs, eyewitness accounts, and sensitive background briefings. If you have seen the Mime Troupe perform these plays, you know why you are here.

The publication of this volume gives the San Francisco Mime Troupe's plays a new life, allowing the company to outlast even more of the enemies it satirizes. Unfortunately, the injustices and outrages attacked by the plays have successors, too. The newest eruptions of war, unemployment, and recession increase the need for plays like the Mime Troupe's in our cultural discourse. At the 1968 Radical Theatre Festival in San Francisco, troupe founder R. G. Davis expressed a hope that in the future there would be "one, two, three, many radical theaters." His call for more radical theater has not been wildly successful; the troupe, alas, has few rivals and fewer equals in the United States, although many artists who have left it for other venues continue to create innovative and committed theater. In a sense the San Francisco Mime Troupe itself has been one, two, three, many radical theaters, as it changed, accepted new challenges, and trained new artists over four decades. All of those theaters and their history can be found here, although by the time you read this, two or three new plays will have been added to the repertoire, and, audiences permitting, there is no end in sight.

Joel Schechter

Acknowledgments

I want to acknowledge the support and assistance of the former and current members of the San Francisco Mime Troupe. I am especially grateful to Bruce Barthol, who gathered material and offered his help for four years. His patient encouragement, observations, suggestions, and corrections were invaluable. Joan Holden met with me, read two drafts, checked facts, and gave me useful feedback and valuable insights. R. G. Davis told me wonderful stories about the troupe in the 1960s and answered numerous email inquiries. Other current and former troupe members who gave me their time, information, and memories of productions include Joaquin Aranda, Sandra Archer, Peter Berg, Wilma Bonet, Lee Breuer, Dan Chumley, Steve Friedman, Lonnie Ford, Marga Gomez, Miche Hall, Arthur Holden, Ed Holmes, Barbara Jeppeson, Saul Landau, Ed Levey, Barry Levitan, Sharon Lockwood, Anke Mueller, Esteban Oropeza, Patrick Osbon, Denny Partridge, Henri Picciotto, Eduardo Robledo, Peggy Rose, Audrey Smith, Andrea Snow, Michael Gene Sullivan, and Isa Nidal Totah. I am so grateful for their time.

Thanks to Peter Coyote and Peter Berg for permission to publish *Olive Pits,* to R. G. Davis and Saul Landau for permission to publish *Minstrel Show,* to Steve Friedman for permission to publish *Telephone,* to Andrea Snow for permission to publish "The Big Picture," to Bruce Barthol for permission to publish "Jingo Rap," "Dictators' Song," "80–20," and "We're Rich Folks," and to the San Francisco Mime Troupe for permission to publish plays from the 1970s, 1980s, and 1990s. Thanks also to longtime Mime Troupe critics Robert Hurwitt, Welton Jones, and Nancy Scott, who talked to me about their four-decade relationships with the company and the shows. Thanks to Tom Hayden for connecting the past to the present.

I want to acknowledge Barbara Mason's work as editor of illustrations.

Her computer skills were absolutely essential in acquiring and copying poster artworks, several of which were graciously provided by Lincoln Cushing. Her advice about photographs and graphic images was invaluable. Thanks to the photographers and artists whose work is individually acknowledged within.

I am grateful to the people who have helped me with research and writing: Jan Breslauer, Domnita Dumitrescu, Marian Faux, John Flynn, Karen McKevitt, Eric Noble, Levi Phillips, Joel Schechter, Ted Shank, Susan Suntree, and Susan Swanson.

California State University, Los Angeles, gave me a ten-week creative leave in 2000 and a ten-week sabbatical in 2002 without which I could not have completed this work. I want to thank my colleagues José Cruz González, Judith Hamera, Shiz Herrera, and Hae Kyung Lee for their support and my students for their constant encouragement.

I am very grateful to LeAnn Fields at the University of Michigan Press, for believing in this project and for her calm support.

I want to thank many friends and family members who encouraged, supported, and advised me: Hilda Ayala, Molly Engle, Josh Gerth, Elisa Marina Gonzalez, Shin Lee, Debra Moore, Janelle Reinelt, Michele Worthington. A special thanks to Eugene van Erven, who urged me to undertake this project.

Contents

Productions by the San Francisco Mime Troupe

This chronology includes all major and some minor productions.

1959   *Mime and Words*
1960   *Eleventh Hour Mime Show*
1961   *Act without Words II* (Beckett)
       Purgatory
       Krapp's Last Tape (Beckett)
       Event I
1962   *The Dowry*
       Act without Words II
       Who's Afraid
1963   *Plastic Haircut* (film)
       Event II
       The Root
       Ruzzante's Maneuvers
       Ubu the King (Jarry)
1964   *Mimes and Movie (Plastic Haircut, Act without Words II)*
       Event III (Coffee Break)
       Along Comes a Spider
       Tartuffe (Molière)
       Chorizos
1965   *Tartuffe*
       The Exception and the Rule (Brecht)
       A Minstrel Show or Civil Rights in a Cracker Barrel
       O Dem Watermelons (film)
       Il Candelaio
       Chronicles of Hell (Ghelderode)
1966   *Minstrel Show*
       Act without Words II
       The Exception and the Rule
       What's That? A Head?
       Jack Off!
       Mirage (film)

Centerman (film)
Olive Pits
Search and Seizure
The Miser (Molière)
Output You
1967   *The Condemned* (Sartre)
The Vaudeville Show
L'Amant Militaire
Olive Pits
1968   *Olive Pits*
Gorilla Marching Band Debut
Ruzzante or The Veteran
Meter Maid
Little Black Panther
The Farce of Patelin
1969   *The Third Estate*
Congress of Whitewashers (Brecht)
The Farce of Patelin
1970   *Congress of Whitewashers*
Independent Female, or a Man Has His Pride
Telephone
Seize the Time
Ecoman
1971   *The Dragon Lady's Revenge*
Highway Robbery
1972   *High Rises*
Frozen Wages
San Fran Scandals of '73
1973   *The Mother* (Brecht)
The Great Air Robbery
1974   *The Mother*
The Great Air Robbery
1975   *Frijoles or Beans to You*
Power Play
1976   *False Promises/Nos Engañaron*
1977   *Hotel Universe*
1978   *Electro Bucks*
1979   *TV Dinner*
We Can't Pay, We Won't Pay (Fo)
Electro Bucks
1980   *Factperson*
Squash

Introduction

I first saw the San Francisco Mime Troupe perform at the outdoor Saturday market in Eugene, Oregon, in the late 1970s. The production, *Hotel Universe,* seemed right at home among the tie-dyed clothes, produce, and handcrafted goods for sale in the stalls there. At the back of the small portable stage, a colorful curtain bearing a cartoon painting of a hotel hung from a pole. The props and costumes were simple. The cast, comprised of seven actors, black, white, and Latino, played quirky caricatures of the elderly inhabitants of a low-income residential hotel and the nasty landlord trying to evict them. The style was broad and farcical. Actors sang and danced and talked to the audience while a small band played upbeat music. Spectators booed the landlord's threats and cheered when Gladys, Myrna, and Manuel decided to fight back, singing what would become one of the troupe's most popular songs: "We Won't Move." The performance was free, and spectators, some with noisy, excited children, crowded around the stage. The spectacle gave me a new understanding of the power of "rough theater," British director Peter Brook's term for performances where audience and cast alike become participants in a raucous celebration of resistance.

The San Francisco Mime Troupe is not silent. "Mime" in their title refers to ancient Greek and Roman mime—scenes and characters from everyday life performed in a ridiculous manner. Although the company has experimented with a variety of styles during its forty-five-year history, ancient mime, with its exaggerated, highly physical acting style, has been a constant. Shows are colorful, noisy, and festive, often touching the same nerve that gives spectators the urge to run away and join the circus. Some have. Throughout the troupe's history, their performances around the country have attracted new members.

During the 1960s, the Bay Area was the heart of the American counterculture movement, with flower children in Haight-Ashbury, the Free Speech Movement in Berkeley, and rock concerts in the Fillmore Auditorium. The San Francisco Mime Troupe was the movement's theater. By the end of the decade, two national tours extended the troupe's increasingly radical reputation across the country, where, in addition to performing, members participated in antiwar demonstrations and led protests. On two occasions, actors were arrested during performances, acts of censure that only added to the troupe's reputation.

The troupe is the longest-running political theater company in U.S. history, and their tenacity is part of their message. The company's very existence is emblematic of their determination to keep on fighting for human principles in a world that values profit over people. Theater historians generally group the San Francisco Mime Troupe with other mid-twentieth-century ensembles producing original work: Living Theatre, the Performance Group (later the Wooster Group), Open Theatre, Bread and Puppet, El Teatro Campesino, and Mabou Mines, and in fact, three of these companies are closely related to the Mime Troupe. Mabou Mines, founded in 1970 by former troupe members Lee Breuer, Ruth Maleczech, and Bill Raymond, was influenced by the troupe's early aesthetic experimentation. Bread and Puppet, an East Coast contemporary of the Mime Troupe founded in 1960, exchanged staging techniques with the group at the Radical Theatre Festival in San Francisco in the late 1960s. The third participant at this festival, El Teatro Campesino, had already been deeply influenced by the troupe's style and politics. El Teatro founder Luis Valdez joined the Mime Troupe in 1965 after seeing them perform at San Jose State College. Valdez left later that year to work with Cesar Chavez organizing farmworkers in Delano, California, where El Teatro Campesino became the theater arm of the United Farm Workers union.

The Mime Troupe takes its message of political empowerment and social change directly to the people. Their free performances in parks in and around San Francisco every summer since 1962 have become an institution, attracting as many as three thousand spectators to a single performance. Many audience members return year after year to have their politically progressive ideals reinvigorated. Some have grown up with the Mime Troupe, and now bring their children and grandchildren.

Troupe founder R. G. Davis always insisted on theater unencumbered by ties to government and corporate funding, so after performances he would pass the hat for donations, a custom that has persisted to this day. For most of the 1960s the troupe survived solely on these personal contributions, and proceeds from college appearances. However, staging free theater in an increasingly costly world became difficult, and these lofty standards eventually gave way to economic necessity. In the 1970s the troupe applied for and received local grants; in the 1980s, national grants; and, in the 1990s, corporate grants, representing a final surrender of the company's original commitment to economic autonomy.

The troupe's internal structure changed at a much more accelerated pace, with radical alterations at the end of the first decade. From the company's founding in 1959 until 1969, R. G. Davis was artistic director and made all final artistic decisions, as do most artistic directors in American theaters. However, because of the company's evolving Marxist ideology, members began questioning the organization's traditional hierarchical structure and wanted more participation in decisions. In December 1969, when members voted to reorganize as a collective, Davis resigned. While many signature elements remained after collectivization, including the broad acting style, free admission, and productions in the parks, the split was traumatic, causing long-term emotional aftershocks. Given the enormity of this organizational change, its ideological ramifications, and the resulting loss of the single artistic vision of the company's creator, it is necessary to consider two distinct troupes: that of the R. G. Davis decade (1959–69) and that of the collective (1970 to the present).

One fundamental change in the troupe's ideology after 1970 was its definition of the target audience. To whom was their message of social change addressed? While Davis's mission had been to challenge the assumptions of liberal, educated, white spectators, the post-1969 collective determined to build a multiethnic working-class audience. They quickly realized that in order to accomplish this, they had to change the demographics of an organization that was, in 1970, primarily white and college educated. In 1974 they took the unusual step of no longer hiring white actors, and by 1980, had achieved an ethnic diversity that predated the multicultural trend in the arts so prevalent in the later 1980s. Then the troupe, as a microcosm of our racially charged American society, had to grapple with internal conflicts that inevitably arose, especially when working on plays that focused on racial issues. In addition, the use of stereotypical ethnic characters, a stock feature of many productions, has not always been well received by the public. Representations and other questions of race have been a minefield throughout the troupe's history. The descriptions in this book attempt to portray these conflicts accurately. As a pioneering multicultural company, the troupe's challenges and how they dealt with them can be instructive.

In general, the collective organization of the troupe has changed over time from utopian to pragmatic. Practical elements of running the business (such as hiring a professional office staff) and outside forces (especially establishing a contract with Actors Equity, the stage actors' union that presupposes a traditionally structured theatrical organization) have tempered the troupe's original collective design, but they remain a worker-owned organization. This commitment, in the face of all obstacles, has kept their work vital and honest. A visit to the troupe's studio in San Francisco's Mission District reveals a small theater company much like others struggling to survive the hostile economic climate of the twenty-first century. An assortment of volunteers, interns, part-time and a few full-time workers staff the small office, which for a few years in the first flush of collectivization was run by company members.

Their commitment to a collectivist ideal has been tempered not only by practical business concerns, but also by the troupe's primary dedication to creating good theater. Although the collectivist ideology has usually served and informed their art, at times collectivism and good theater have been at odds. Casting in particular has presented challenges, when, for example, a past policy of rotating leading roles among the members conflicted with a director's casting choice. One of the company's strengths has been their determination to work through such struggles by spending hours and days in meetings trying to resolve internal conflicts and reach consensus. In general, however, when conflicts occur, art prevails over ideology.

The troupe has experimented with collective playwriting since 1970, and although there is no formula, today most shows are created in a quasi-collective process. Topics are usually agreed upon at the company's January retreat, when members discuss issues they feel are most pressing. The topic chosen often suggests a particular style, such as science fiction or film noir. All company members research the topic, and most shows are written by more than one person, sometimes a team of five or more, working with one or more lyricists. This process typically takes up to three months. A show generally has one director, who as in traditional theater has complete artistic authority over it. Because productions are created for the existing company, casting is often implicit in the script, but, as in traditional theater, the director makes the final choices. The rehearsal period is often little more than a month and follows a pattern familiar to anyone mounting a new play. Rewriting continues throughout rehearsals and into the summer performances. Performances in public parks open on or about the Fourth of July and continue until Labor Day.

Shows rarely observe stylistic purity, although a Mime Troupe style has evolved over the years. Because most shows are performed outside for a huge crowd, they are highly physical and involve interaction with the audience. All shows use at least some epic techniques derived from the theater of Bertolt Brecht, such as double and triple casting, signs, songs, and direct audience address. Comedy has dominated the troupe's repertory, but there are notable exceptions. During the troupe's first decade, commedia dell' arte, the highly physical improvised form of street theater from the Italian Renaissance, was the signature style; melodrama replaced it in 1970. All shows since the mid-1970s have been musical theater.

A distinctive feature of the troupe's shows after collectivization has been the comparatively high number of leading female characters. Joan Holden, the troupe's principal playwright for over three decades, created many of these roles for Sharon Lockwood, whose stage persona of earthy indomitability became a salient feature of these characters. It was Lockwood's feisty Myrna in *Hotel Universe* who kept the other residents resolute in their fight to save the hotel, and whose optimism electrified me at my first San Francisco Mime Troupe performance. Her characters were a beacon for more than twenty-five years during the Reagan, Bush, and Clinton years in the 1980s and 1990s.

My original plan was to publish a volume entirely of San Francisco Mime Troupe plays, but no comprehensive history of the troupe from 1959 to the present exists, and I have oriented the book to fill that gap. It attempts to place the plays in their historical and company context, while accommodating a maximum number of scripts.

This book draws heavily on conversations with, and writing by, people with a long history with the troupe. Because few theater companies persist as long as the Mime Troupe, critical longevity can offer insights that short-term acquaintance might overlook. Founder R. G. Davis is the authority on the troupe in the 1960s, and the author of *The San Francisco Mime Troupe: The First Ten Years*, published in 1975. Joan Holden emerged as the company's spokesperson during the 1970s. She has been interviewed frequently by critics and has published numerous articles on the troupe.

Several San Francisco critics important to the research for this book are longtime Troupers. Nancy Scott was an enthusiastic early fan who reviewed troupe shows in the *People's World* in the 1960s and remained a steadfast supporter of their work through her tenure until 1986 as theater critic for the *San Francisco Examiner*. Robert Hurwitt, a writer for the *Berkeley Barb, East Bay Express, San Francisco Examiner,* and currently the *San Francisco Chronicle* who received the George Jean Nathan Award for dramatic criticism in 1995, was an actor with the troupe from 1966 to 1967. He often places his reviews of the troupe within the context of the company's entire history. Bernard Weiner, theater critic for the *San Francisco Chronicle* from 1974 to 1990, worked with Hurwitt to have the troupe chosen for the special Tony Award for regional theater in 1987. Steven Winn, current Arts and Culture critic for the *San Francisco Chronicle*, began reviewing the troupe in the 1980s. Welton Jones, former theater critic of the *San Diego Union* (later *San Diego Union-Tribune*), is possibly the only out-of-town critic with a long track record with the troupe, from the mid-1960s to 1994.

This book is divided into decades starting with the 1960s, with the story of each decade in the troupe's history followed by representative scripts from the era. Also included is diverse commentary on the plays from the press and from artists who participated in the productions, in an effort to bring the scripts alive for the reader.

In assembling a book chronicling the long-lived and prolific San Francisco Mime Troupe, selecting a limited number of representative scripts presented a challenge. With topical political plays it is particularly difficult to predict which will remain relevant after their historical moment has passed. The final selection criteria included critical acclaim, historical relevance, popularity, stylistic and thematic diversity, and availability. *Hotel Universe* (1977), the most often produced show in Mime Troupe history, examines urban renewal and the loss of low-income housing, the subject of at least five troupe shows. *A Minstrel Show, or Civil Rights in a Cracker Barrel* (1965), an exposé of white liberal racism, became the troupe's most notorious creation. *Ripped van Winkle* (1988), a satirical look at a 1960s hippie lost in the consumer-driven 1980s, is probably the most popular of all troupe shows and one of the most blatantly self-referential. The troupe took on the Vietnam War in a comic-strip style in *The Dragon Lady's Revenge* (1971). *Factwino Meets the Moral Majority* (1981), modeled on Marvel comics, challenges right-wing Christian fundamentalism. *Back to Normal* (1991) skewers the public's vulnerability to the jingoistic hype over the Persian Gulf War. *Olive Pits* (1966) is a one-act from the troupe's commedia dell'arte era, and the short sketch *Telephone* (1970) demonstrates some of the troupe's puppet techniques.

Two plays in particular it pained me to exclude because of space limitations: *Steeltown* (1984), the troupe's examination of unemployment in the industrial Midwest, is now represented by a photograph; *Offshore* (1994), the result of a pan-Asian collaboration critiquing globalization at the end of the twentieth century, is represented by one scene and one song.

I have included lyrics, photographs, and graphic designs from a forty-year span, chosen to illustrate stylistic diversity and to invoke the presence of some other productions. A few photographs include spectators, illustrating the spatial relationship between the stage and the audience; some demonstrate Mime Troupe techniques. Michael Bry's photograph from 1985 shows how the troupe staged a nightmare Reagan Supreme Court with giant puppets. Marian Goldman's photograph from *False Promises* illustrates the troupe's use of Brechtian staging techniques. Poster designs can also capture the essence of a show. Fortunately, much poster art from the troupe's previous productions can be tracked down, as many were printed by Inkworks Press in Berkeley and are still sold in the "boutique" at troupe shows. Five posters are reproduced in this book.

Spain Rodriguez has designed troupe graphics for over twenty years. He created most of the illustrations that appear in letters to potential contributors in the 1990s. Five of his designs, including a comic strip he published in the *San Francisco Bay Guardian* advertising *Factwino vs. Armageddonman,* are included in this book.

Grassroots organizations such as the Mime Troupe often work with numerous people in the local community. The troupe's fortieth anniversary program includes a list of about four hundred people who have worked with the company since its inception. Those mentioned in the following pages will have to stand for the rest.

The San Francisco Mime Troupe has been underestimated in American theater history, where the East Coast gets most of the attention. I have tried to correct that imbalance by writing about a company that has been influential in keeping alive an ancient theater tradition that is at home in the west, where there are fundamental aesthetic differences from the east. West Coast theater is more physical and less intellectual—more grounded and less conceptual. This could be the legacy of our Wild West history, but I think it's the weather. It seems no accident that three existing California theater companies (Dell'Arte Players, the Actors' Gang, and the San Francisco Mime Troupe) are rooted in Italian commedia dell'arte, a form of theater best realized in the open air. Free theater in American parks has its historical roots in a warm Mediterranean climate with a sociable culture.

However, the San Francisco Mime Troupe's tradition reaches even further back, beyond the Italian Renaissance to Greece, where ancient audiences made pilgrimages to Athens to see how Aristophanes would satirize their community. Similarly, every summer thousands of contemporary spectators pack lunches, children, and sunscreen and head for San Francisco parks to see the Mime Troupe lampoon current events and ridicule public figures. Although it's been years since the company was charged with obscenity, and the shows rarely shock or astonish anymore, there are ancient echoes in the ways the troupe brings the community together each year to celebrate the possibility of social change.

1. The 1960s: Mime to Guerrilla Theater

The San Francisco Mime Troupe was in the vanguard of the alternative theater movement in the United States, helping shape the Bay Area's cultural
life during the transition between the Beats of the 1950s and the Free Speech
Movement of the 1960s, when San Francisco was the "Athens of the counterculture."[1] Ronald Guy Davis founded the troupe in 1959, and within five
years major features that still define the company had been established: its
name, free shows touring in local parks, and a broad performance style
drawn from easily accessible forms of popular theater. Major challenges
faced by the troupe included grappling with the economics of free theater
and creating a precedent for performing in public places. The major changes
during the decade included company membership and the development of
a radical political ideology.

The troupe's first decade corresponded to a time of explosive social and
political change in the United States beginning with the assassination of
President Kennedy on 22 November 1963. As the unofficial "theater of the
movement," troupe shows tackled the decade's major issues, especially civil
rights and the Vietnam War. Martin Luther King Jr. was awarded the Nobel
Peace Prize for advocating nonviolence in 1964, but over one hundred riots
erupted in major American cities between 1965 and 1968 and King was assas-
sinated on 4 April 1968. Youth rallied against the draft, and by the end of the
decade Americans of all ages participated in massive demonstrations against
the Vietnam War. Campuses were in revolt: the Free Speech Movement at
the University of California, Berkeley, in the fall of 1964 and Columbia University's insurrection in the spring of 1968 toppled conventional notions of
authority.

The Company

R. G. Davis was twenty-four years old when he arrived in San Francisco in 1958. He had just completed a six-month Fulbright studying with mime artist Etienne Decroux in Paris. Although New York was then the undisputed heart of the American theater, Davis wanted the less commercial and more European cultural environment that San Francisco offered. Allen Ginsberg had defined the beat generation, reading "Howl" at San Francisco's Six Gallery three years before; Lawrence Ferlinghetti, Jack Kerouac, and Gary Snyder were also there. As part of this literary renaissance, San Francisco possessed at least one theater to compare with experimental companies in Europe such as the Royal Court in London and the Berliner Ensemble: the San Francisco Actors' Workshop.

The workshop had been created in 1951 by Herbert Blau and Jules Irving, then professors at San Francisco State College, with director Alan Mandel. They introduced their small, elite audience to the work of writers such as Edward Albee, Harold Pinter, and Samuel Beckett, making a place for themselves in Western theater history with their production of *Waiting for Godot* at San Quentin in 1957. Davis had heard about the workshop in Europe. He auditioned and was selected as an assistant director in 1958.

Two years later, as the regional repertory movement gained momentum, a Ford Foundation grant permitted the workshop to expand into a resident equity company. The Kennedy administration made the arts fashionable, and in 1965 government support for the arts would be institutionalized with the creation of the National Endowment for the Arts (NEA). The proliferation and decentralization of professional theaters accelerated. When Blau and Irving accepted offers to manage Lincoln Center in 1965, several leading actors from the company followed them. The Actors' Workshop struggled and then closed one year later, but was immediately succeeded by a bigger resident repertory company: American Conservatory Theatre.

Shortly after he joined the Actors' Workshop, Davis created his own ancillary project, the R. G. Davis Mime Troupe, with some of his students and workshop members. They premiered *Mime and Words* at the San Francisco Art Institute on 29 October 1959. The following year they performed at the Pacific Coast Arts Festival at Reed College, organized by Reed student and future troupe member Arthur Holden, at the Monterey Jazz Festival, and in the Actors' Workshop's Encore Theatre on Sunday nights at 11:00 P.M., the only time the stage was available. The *Eleventh Hour Mime Show* opened 11 December 1960. Although no admission was charged, contributions were encouraged. The first night an audience of 120 people contributed seventeen dollars.

In January 1962, the troupe premiered *The Dowry* at the Encore and that summer returned theater to the open air with two performances in parks.

The following January, due primarily to Davis's contempt for corporate funding and the resulting business model adopted by the San Francisco Actors' Workshop, the R. G. Davis Mime Troupe severed "all connections with Actors' Workshop, abandoning security, renouncing establishment success, and losing most of the company."[2] Their new home was Davis's studio in an abandoned church at 3450 Twentieth Street, at the corner of Capp Street, in the Mission District. That May they premiered *The Root*, at the Capp Street Studio prior to five park performances.

While rehearsing *Ruzzante's Maneuvers* in 1963, the company became the San Francisco Mime Troupe. Davis described the rationale: "I couldn't see my name on a banner above the commedia stage. 'Mime' stayed in the title because it was closer to the dance troupes yet apart from the regional theatres. We were to travel light and move around—thus, 'Troupe.' 'San Francisco,' naturally."[3]

Before their first outdoor performance of *The Dowry* in Golden Gate Park, they applied to the Park Commission and were issued a permit for two performances. The following year they successfully applied for additional dates for *The Root* and *Ruzzante's Maneuvers*. However, permission was accompanied by the unconstitutional warning, ignored by the troupe, that the content of their shows would need approval.

In 1964 they successfully applied for more park performances for *Chorizos*. However, "the artistic and political unrest that had been simmering in San Francisco . . . began to boil in 1964" and, as the troupe's antiestablishment rhetoric escalated onstage and off, so did the old guard's desire to silence them.[4] Censorship had been an issue in San Francisco at least since the obscenity trial of "Howl" in 1957. Then the House Un-American Activities Committee hearings in San Francisco in 1960 galvanized and united the Bay Area's Left. In July 1964, at the Republican Convention in San Francisco, Barry Goldwater accepted the nomination with the pronouncement: "Extremism in defense of liberty is no vice." As if in response, the Free Speech Movement erupted in Berkeley that fall.

Consequently, when the troupe applied for park permits to perform *Il Candelaio* (adapted from the play by sixteenth-century Italian philosopher Giordano Bruno), in 1965, they were granted forty-eight performance dates on condition that the production used no obscene words or gestures. Civil liberties lawyers invited to preview the show found nothing offensive and "warned the commissioners not to become censors."[5] However, the company's most notorious show of the 1960s, *A Minstrel Show, or Civil Rights in a Cracker Barrel,* had opened indoors the previous month, so the commissioners were on the alert. After the third performance of *Il Candelaio* they revoked the permit, describing the play as "indecent, obscene and offensive."[6]

The fourth performance had been scheduled for 2:00 P.M. in Lafayette Park on 7 August. The actors handed out flyers urging the public to attend and drew a crowd of about a thousand. Davis took the role of Brighella, usually played by Luis Valdez (who had just joined the troupe), which opened the show. After explaining the permit situation and involving spectators in an increasingly animated discussion, Davis moved into the performance area (the troupe had not erected a stage that day), greeted the crowd, and announced: "Ladieeeeees and Gentlemen, Il Troupo di Mimo di San Francisco, presents for your enjoyment this afternoon . . . AN ARREST!"[7] With that, in a perfectly executed leap into the air, Davis was grabbed by a police officer and arrested. In that moment, what the troupe would call "guerrilla theater" was born.[8]

Davis was released on bail, park performances continued uninterrupted, and on 1 November 1965, he was tried and convicted of performing without a permit. *Ramparts* writer David Kolodney noted with sarcasm that Davis had been arrested for "free entertainment in the public parks without a Ford Foundation grant."[9] Meanwhile the Park Commission had turned down the troupe's request for a permit to perform *The Miser* the following summer and created new restrictions for performing in the parks, including preapproval of play summaries. The American Civil Liberties Union filed a suit against the Park Commission on behalf of the Mime Troupe in February 1966, and in July argued in court that the commission's rules were unconstitutional. Judge Joseph Karesh agreed, and the troupe won the right to perform in the parks uncensored.

Although they performed indoors as well, the troupe's park shows returned theater to its essential community role. The *San Francisco Examiner's* Kenneth Rexroth, whom Jack Kerouac had dubbed the "father of the Frisco poetry scene," recalled the function of theater in ancient Greece and Renaissance Italy while praising the troupe's 1963 park appearances: "Let's hope this is an entering wedge, and that eventually we will have all sorts of musical and dramatic activity in the parks. I can think of few better ways to raise the muscle tone of a flabby community."[10]

An unpublished troupe document from the end of the decade notes that "the 'liberation' of the parks set a precedent for theatres in other cities to go outdoors without fear of arrest, and this test case opened the door for most of the free activities that burst upon the San Francisco scene in the next few years."[11] The most memorable heir was probably the San Francisco Diggers, an anarchistic paratheatrics group begun as an offshoot of the Mime Troupe in September 1966. They expanded the concept of performance by taking theater beyond the parks and directly into the streets of the Haight. Several troupe members including Emmett Grogan, Kent Minault, Peter Coyote, Peter Berg, and Judy Goldhaft went with them.

Once San Francisco parks were liberated, the troupe determined to take on other Bay Area communities. Two in particular, Mill Valley in 1968 and Hayward in 1969, led to legal skirmishes. In both cases the ACLU successfully intervened.

To pay legal fees from Davis's arrest, Bill Graham, who had been hired as the troupe's promoter in 1965, held what became the first of four appeals to raise money. Appeal I took place in the company's loft on Howard Street on 6 November 1965. Charles Perry describes it in *The Haight-Ashbury: A History:* "The censorship issue rallied the art world and Graham was showered with names of people who wanted to be involved." They included the Committee, folksinger Sandy Bull, Allen Ginsberg, the Fugs, and Jefferson Airplane.[12] The line of people waiting to get in stretched around the block.

Appeal I raised about two thousand dollars and was so successful Graham planned another for 10 December and, at jazz columnist Ralph Gleason's urging, rented a large auditorium on Geary near Fillmore. The poster (by Wes Wilson, who began creating the classic psychedelic rock posters the next year) read: "Appeal II, for Continued Freedom in the Arts." Performers at this Mime Troupe benefit included the Jefferson Airplane, the Great Society, Big Brother and the Holding Company, Quicksilver Messenger Service, the Charlatans, John Handy Quintet, Mystery Trend, Gentlemen's Band, and the Grateful Dead (formerly the Warlocks), using their new name for the first time that night. Over thirty-five hundred people paid $1.50 to attend. At 1:00 A.M. a double line a block long still waited to get in. With Appeal III, at the Fillmore on 14 January 1966, Graham paid the bands, launching his enterprise, Bill Graham Presents. He left the Mime Troupe that February after the troupe voted against becoming rock producers.

In 1967, Davis, Lee Vaughan, Kent Minault, and Ron Stallings were busted for possession of a few marijuana seeds and stems in Calgary, Alberta, on 14 March, while touring *A Minstrel Show.* Just one year before, Davis had written: "Never be caught in a politically aesthetic skirmish with grass in your pocket."[13] Appeal IV, to cover legal fees, was staged on 12 April with Jefferson Airplane, Moby Grape, the Grateful Dead, Quicksilver Messenger Service, Loading Zone, and Andrew Staples Group. Produced by troupe member Robert Hurwitt, it raised six thousand dollars.

In spite of the financial support from bands in the 1960s, by the end of the decade the Mime Troupe was fervently opposed to the capitalist enterprises most bands had become. In a company document from 1969, the troupe denounced the change in rock music since the mid-1960s: "What is now the hottest of commercial properties was still a communal art form." The troupe defined its own mission as convincing artists "to stop working for art's or money's sake and to start working for the people and social change . . . distinguishing the true cultural revolution, which aims to change the institutions, from the fashion 'revolution' as represented by hip capitalism and *Hair*."[14]

The company's aesthetic and political ideology evolved during the 1960s in response to vast social changes, the civil rights movement, the war in Vietnam, and the public's increasingly aggressive opposition to the government. By the middle of the decade they were committed to "guerrilla theater," a term coined by troupe member Peter Berg after Davis's staged arrest. From challenging aesthetic conventions—by performing free and outside of conventional theater spaces—the troupe naturally moved into challenging social and political institutions.

In his first essay on guerrilla theater, published by the *Tulane Drama Review* in 1965, Davis described it as the opposite of bourgeois theater—a portable theater with neither elaborate materials nor a big budget, which has a social obligation: "to teach, direct toward change, be an example of change."[15] After this essay was published, theaters and scholars quickly co-opted the term. It is even parodied (or travestied, as Peter Coyote writes) in a scene in the film *Easy Rider* set in a commune where "dodos clump through a mindless commedia-type stage play announced by a crudely lettered sign as 'Gorilla Theater.'"[16]

Davis wrote three essays from 1965 to 1968 addressing the concept of guerrilla theater and differentiating the troupe's goals from the radical chic trend. After a heated company debate, the troupe self-published these as *Guerrilla Theatre Essays: 1* in 1970. They affirm the troupe's commitment to a radical leftist ideology: "This is our society, if we don't like it it's our duty to change it; if we can't change it, we must destroy it."[17] In another article in 1967, Davis wrote that the message of troupe shows was that "the U.S. must be destroyed."[18]

From 1968, the company required reading in political theory and scheduled group seminars. At least two contentious issues arose out of the readings of Mao and Marx. Because the troupe's mission was "to teach, direct toward change, be an example of change," the first question is: teach and change whom? From Mao they learned that the answer was working people.[19] Davis, on the other hand, believed that guerrilla theater's personnel "must come from the class they want to change. If you are middle class dropouts, you then play for middle class dropouts."[20]

In *Theatre for Working-Class Audiences in the United States, 1830–1980*, Daniel Freidman described the troupe in the 1960s as "*the* theatre of America's left-wing community," which was, at that time, primarily "white students and counter-culturists," not the working class.[21] Moreover, with college and university tours, the troupe continued building an educated, white, middle-class audience. Shifting their focus to the working class as the source of social change would become one of the first issues the troupe resolved to accomplish in the 1970s.

The other controversy involved the third part of the troupe's mission, to be an example of change. Although membership changed often and performance styles adapted to the different demands of the plays, from 1959 until 1969 the company was structured hierarchically, as were most, if not all, theaters in the United States. From their reading about collective ownership, company members began questioning their internal structure and asking for more voice in the artistic process. Most productions had been created with a high degree of collaboration, but Davis had the final word. This ideological struggle would lead to Davis's resignation at the end of the decade.

The company's business organization developed along traditional lines, although until 1964, Davis handled most everything. After Sandra Archer joined as an actress in 1964, she began keeping the books, though she was unsalaried throughout the decade. By the mid-1960s the paid office staff consisted of a secretary, a tech team of two, and a business manager–booker. Ann Reilly was secretary, followed by Louise Aliamo. Bill Graham was hired as the business manager–booker in 1965 and stayed about a year. Peter Solomon and Roy Dahlberg worked as bookers in 1968 and 1969, and Solomon continued booking for the troupe on and off into the 1980s. Lew Harris was the company manager in 1967 and 1968, then Bob Slattery. Bruce Bratton did publicity late in the decade.

Because the troupe defined itself in contrast to commercial theater, and, with *The Dowry*, began an unrelenting critique of profit, they needed to devise nontraditional means of generating income. "How does one keep alive doing independent, radical, chaotic, anarchic theatre?" Davis asked in a 1964 essay comparing alternative theater to commercial. "We did it by accepting donations after the performance, borrowing trucks to get stuff to and from the performing area, and by giving a percentage of the take to the performers themselves."[22] From the very beginning, in order to differentiate his actors from amateurs, Davis insisted that the company minimize material expenses so that the actors could be paid, even if only a dollar per performance, as in 1964. The *Ubu King* program in 1963 emphasized this position: "Donations at the door. . . . Minimum production costs. People, not machines."[23]

The first outdoor performance of Machiavelli's *The Root* in 1963 generated donations of twenty-eight dollars. By the midsixties donations averaged seventy-five to one hundred twenty-five dollars per performance. A park season of about one hundred performances over three months could net over ten thousand dollars.

Soliciting contributions at the end of the performance was and is called "the pitch." One of the performers steps up to the edge of the stage after the show and tells spectators what they can do about the social issues raised in the play. He or she then explains how the company is funded and asks for money, adding that members of the company are positioned throughout the audience. Since the 1990s the pitch also reminds spectators to sign the mailing list: "The FBI knows where we are, you should too."

Another means of soliciting donated income, then and now, is through "appeals," usually in the form of a letter from the company, but sometimes media generated, or advertised fund-raising events such as Graham's. In September 1968, when troupe members were earning five dollars per performance, they sent a letter to one thousand potential supporters asking each to contribute ten dollars. This appeal generated about twenty-five hundred dollars, and soon after, troupe members, then numbering about twenty, were paid a weekly salary of twenty-five dollars.

In 1966 the company began touring as a means of generating income and spreading the word. For touring performances at colleges and universities, the troupe generally charged $750 plus about 75 percent of the gate. Activist organization benefits typically cost the sponsoring group $250 per performance plus about 50 percent of the profits.

By the late 1960s the company was making $60,000 to $75,000 a year, enough to pay the office staff and, in 1968, to move from 924 Howard Street (where they had rented a loft next to the offices of the Students for a Democratic Society in 1965), to a larger building at 450 Alabama Street in the Mission District.

Federal and corporate grants were the most contentious potential source of income. The troupe finally decided against applying for an NEA grant in the 1960s, primarily because of the potential damage to the company's reputation by association with the U.S. government at the height of the Vietnam War. They did, however, apply for funds from San Francisco's Hotel Tax Fund and received $1,000 in 1964 and again in 1965, although the latter was withdrawn when Davis was arrested in the park.

In 1967 Davis explained that the turnover in membership was high: "We burn people up."[24] At about that time, he dismissed thirty-five members of the unwieldy fifty-nine-member company. Davis was dedicated to building up a core of artists committed to changing the system (capitalism and American imperialism) and eliminating the amateurs. The remaining fourteen full-time members really began to think of themselves as a company.

In 1968, against Davis's wishes, the company began experimenting with various "organizational schemes" including "loose leadership, company meetings, gerontocracy and finally an elected Inner Core of five members."[25] Toward the end of 1969, long meetings were devoted to structural reorganization, and one night, as Davis tells it, because the Inner Core was deemed not workable, "the first impulse was to create a loosely ordered 'collective.'"[26] Davis believed fervently that collective governance was politically and artistically ineffective, and so, in December 1969, he took a leave and then resigned from the troupe in 1970. His resignation stunned company members. Sandra Archer recalls that she and Joan Holden "were devastated."[27] In the program for its Fortieth Anniversary, the company wrote: "The Troupe became a collective partly by ideology: members who were reading Marx and Mao argued that workers should control the means of production; and partly by default: no one could take R.G. Davis' place."[28]

In his book, Davis lists 319 names of "people who were responsible for the creation" of the company.[29] Of those only Sandra Archer, Joe Bellan, Lorne Berkun, Dan Chumley, Randy Craig, Steve Friedman, Jason Harris, Joan Holden, Melody James, Sharon Lockwood, Joan Mankin, Patricia Silver, Peter Snider, Jael Weisman, and Jack Wickert remained at the end of the decade.

The Productions

Davis describes the experimental nature of the Mime Troupe's early work in his first chapter. Beckett's *Act without Words* (April 1961) was Grotowski-style poor theater borrowing the concept of "nothing in the hands, nothing in the pockets" from Davis's training with Decroux in Paris.[30] *Event I* (November 1961), at the Encore Theatre, was a happening with sound and music developed out of improvisation: "a madman show for insane people who were struggling to present all of the world in one hour."[31]

Lee Breuer, who worked with Davis on these early "Events" at the Encore wrote in 2000 that these shows "were thirty years ahead of their time and unchanged they could open at the Kitchen or P.S. 122 today."[32] Breuer, actress Ruth Maleczech, and Bill Raymond left the troupe around 1963 and soon after founded Mabou Mines in New York.

Although the troupe's earliest work did not include spoken words, by 1962 improvised dialogue had been added. Davis later explained: "Mime is the point of departure for our style, in which words sharpen and refine, but the substance of meaning is in the action."[33] Davis's emphasis was never on silence but on physical expression, and on minimizing material elements: sets, lights, costumes.

The word *mime* in the company's name has been a source of confusion for over forty years because spectators and sponsors unfamiliar with the troupe's work imagine silent performers in white gloves and invisible boxes. It has also become a way to determine the era of one's association with the company since members from the first decade use the French pronunciation ("meem"), while those after 1970 use the American ("mime").

With *The Dowry* (a Molière-Goldoni composite) in January 1962, the troupe began experimenting with commedia dell'arte by improvising scenes and studying pictures and descriptions. Davis recalls their first outdoor performance that summer; after actress Yvette Nachmias ran offstage she announced: "The reason for the large movements and gestures is because they performed outside." They trusted the exaggerated style they learned through research, but they had only performed inside. "Once outside," wrote Davis, "theory and reality crashed together into a screaming joyous perception."[34]

The troupe honed its craft in a series of commedias. The most successful was *L'Amant Militaire* (1967), adapted by Joan Holden from Carlos Goldoni's antiwar play by the same name. Adaptation for the troupe, defined in the *L'Amant Militaire* program, always meant "exploiting" the original, "using what we can and discarding the rest, writing in new scenes and characters, to say nothing of new emphases."[35] They mined popular culture and contemporary politics, inserting anachronistic elements into the shows.

In *L'Amant Militaire*, the Spanish have intervened in a civil war in Italy. The troupe made certain spectators would understand that their production was really about the war in Vietnam by adding the puppet Punch to comment on the action and draw contemporary parallels. Punch even led spectators in chanting, "Hell no, we won't go." Besides the war, the play also takes jabs at religion, capitalism, and politics. Des Moines critic Donald Kaul described the effect of the production: "It was shocking. It was unpatriotic. It was blasphemous. I don't know when I've enjoyed an evening of theatre more."[36] As a result of the successful New York performances of both *L'Amant Militaire* and *Olive Pits*, the one-act it toured with, the troupe received its first Obie in May 1968 for "uniting theatre and revolution and grooving in the park."

L'Amant Militaire also marked Joan Holden's first play for the troupe. Her husband, Arthur Holden had joined the troupe in 1963. In 1966, Davis mentioned he was looking for someone to adapt a commedia, and Arthur suggested Joan. The following year, with her first play, she began a thirty-three-year career as the troupe's principal playwright.

The civil rights movement inspired another major show of the decade: *A Minstrel Show, or Civil Right in a Cracker Barrel*. It became the most infamous production in troupe history. The play uses the format of a minstrel show and racial stereotypes to expose racism and white liberal hypocrisy. Davis explained that the show transformed "a stereotypical image into a radical image."[37] Where spectators expected a show about integration, they got one celebrating difference: "We poked not at intolerance, but toleration."[38] Two scenes in particular, "Chick and Stud" and "Old Black Joe," incited accusations of obscenity because of simulated sex acts (a white "liberal" female and a black "buck" feigning intercourse in the former, and "I'm coming" with masturbation gestures in the latter). The San Francisco production opened in June 1965 and created an uproar at UC Berkeley that September.

A Minstrel Show, developed and rehearsed over a nine-month period, includes material excerpted from extant minstrel shows and improvised by the cast, with some original scenes, such as "Chick and Stud," written by Saul Landau. Representatives from the Congress of Racial Equality (CORE) and Student Nonviolent Coordinating Committee (SNCC) were invited to attend previews and give feedback. The cast of six was divided evenly between black performers and white, all in blackface and blue satin minstrel suits. The race of individual performers was intentionally withheld from spectators "to fuck up their prejudices."[39] The seventh cast member, the interlocutor, represented white authority. The show used live banjo music and tambourine, composed by Steve Reich, and mixed media with Robert Nelson's film *O Dem Watermelons* preceding the intermission. Although the show usually met with critical praise, it was often described as "disturbing." It walks a fine line in its use of stereotypes, and Davis believes the manner in which it is performed can make it a racist show or one challenging racism.[40]

The month before *A Minstrel Show* opened, Davis directed *The Exception and the Rule*, Brecht's morality play on the nature of capitalism. This four-character one-act about man's exploitation of man was presented on a double bill with journalist Robert Scheer's lecture about the war in Vietnam. Critics suggest Davis's direction of Brecht was meticulous, in contrast to the expansive, rough style of the commedias.[41]

Scheer used epic techniques in his Vietnam lecture, juxtaposing his commentary with contradictory taped statements made by President Johnson. Most troupe shows used a variety of epic techniques: masks, cross-gender casting, double and triple casting, direct audience address, music, songs, puppets, and a highly physical acting style.

Davis's next experiment with Brecht was far more ambitious, and much less well received. *Turandot—or The Congress of Whitewashers* was Brecht's last play and turned out to be Davis's last with the company. Davis chose Chinese opera for the production's style: masks, dragons, stylized movement, and Chinese costumes. As with *The Exception and the Rule*, the production was apparently flawless, and photographs in Davis's book attest to its striking visual images. Critic Martin Gottfried described it as "exquisite" and "beautiful." However, he added that spectators should ignore the confusing dialogue.[42] The text was apparently complex and unwieldy and the production's message unclear. Davis later admitted that "there are limits to theatrical complexities in the open air."[43]

The Gutter Puppets were among several subtroupes within the company, developed to perform skits along with major productions or separately at rallies and protests. Gutter Puppet shows, which first appeared in April 1968, employed puppets, clowns, and crankies (a horizontal rolling scroll that creates settings or tells a story visually). "Their strings are severed . . . disconnected from the powers at the top and answerable only to those on the bottom, the Gutter Puppets, unlike their 'responsible' counterparts are thoroughly irreverent, impeccably honest and brimful of information on how to succeed as a revolutionary in the midst of the labyrinth."[44] Gutter Puppets were usually the small handheld variety interacting with actors, but for the anti–Vietnam War skit *Eagle Fuck* (1967), they were nine feet tall.

Gutter Puppet skits such as *Telephone, Meter Maid, Meat,* and *Eagle Fuck* were agit-prop, designed to get spectators to take action. *Telephone* taught spectators how to charge long-distance phone calls to major corporations. *Meter Maid* encouraged the use of pop-top tabs in parking meters. *Meat* and *Eagle Fuck* used shocking imagery to provoke protests against the Vietnam War. Peter Coyote, who was a member of the troupe in the midsixties, described *Eagle Fuck:* "gigantic puppets, draped in black shroud and topped with mournful skull-white paper-mâché heads, representing Vietnamese women. The 'women' walked around carrying little puppet babies and going about their bucolic business for a few minutes before an equally gargantuan eagle puppet with an enormous pink penis entered, fucked them, and killed them. End of Show. Five minutes tops."[45]

Davis noted turnover of members in the company was high, as the chronology of productions in his book reveals.[46] Some early members who remained for much of the decade included Sandra Archer, who was the leading lady, Joe Bellan, Peter Coyote, Judy (Rosenberg) Goldhaft, Jim Haynie, Arthur Holden, Joan Holden, Jerry Jump, Saul Landau, Joseph Lomuto, and John Robb. Many members were college students who joined after seeing the troupe perform on tour. A wave of members left after the *L'Amant Militaire* tour, and several newcomers stayed on into the 1970s: Dan Chumley, Steve Friedman, Melody James, Sharon Lockwood, and Jael Weisman.

Music has been a part of troupe shows since the beginning. Lee Breuer designed sound for *Event I,* and Steve Reich designed sound and composed music for several shows from 1963 to 1965, including *Minstrel Show.*

The troupe's Gorilla Marching Band, created by Charles Degelman in 1968, followed anti-Dow marchers on campuses and frequently accompanied tours along with the Gutter Puppets. A short-lived guerrilla theater invention, the Ladies Drill Team, performed military exercises to urge women to rebel against traditional gender roles. Another subtroupe, the Gargoyle Carolers, consisted of several troupers dressed as ghoulish characters from Hieronymous Bosch and Brueghel paintings, adapting Christmas carols to annoy consumers around Christmas in 1966. They were arrested for begging but got off because no one could identify the actor in the bear head who held the tin cup.[47] Davis recalls that these guerrilla actions were often an attempt to do something illegal.[48]

The troupe was active in local issues, one of which lead to the formation of the Artists Liberation Front (ALF) on 10 May 1966. When San Francisco Mayor Jack Shelley created an Art Resources Development Committee and neglected to invite the participation of many local artists, troupe members crashed the 2 May luncheon meeting and a week later created the ALF. As an added impetus, they were denied funding by the Hotel Tax Fund again two days after their surprise appearance at the luncheon.

Coyote writes that the ALF "intended to bypass 'official' city-sponsored art and bring recognition to the work of community-based artists and people of color who were being ignored."[49] One third of the forty-five members of the organization were from the Mime Troupe; others included Bill Graham, Lawrence Ferlinghetti, Kenneth Rexroth, Ralph Gleason, and Hunter Thompson. In the fall of 1966, ALF held a series of street fairs in various neighborhoods with music, puppets, and assorted forms of entertainment. A benefit for the ALF at the Fillmore on 17 July was so successful that the line of those waiting to get in stretched around the block. A highlight of this Mardi Gras masked ball was the troupe's Gorilla Marching Band performing "I Got Fucked in Vietnam" to the tune of the "Ballad of the Green Berets."

Other troupe political activities included picketing the Crown Zellerbach headquarters in San Francisco; performing at the Traps Festival benefit for the Bob Scheer for Congress Campaign on 16 April 1966; participating in "Teach-On LSD," a benefit for the Timothy Leary Defense Fund on 19 July 1966; protesting the war in Vietnam by hanging animal parts from a slaughterhouse on a fence at the Human Be-In in Golden Gate Park in 1967; and the Gorilla Band leading a parade of strikers at Harvard attempting to cut the university's ties with ROTC in 1969.

In 1968 the troupe organized the Radical Theatre Festival, sponsored by the Associated Students at San Francisco State College, 25–29 September 1968. The participants, Bread and Puppet Theatre, El Teatro Campesino, and the Mime Troupe, came together "to identify what radical theatre means" and to share ideas.[50] The four-day conference included parades, films, panel discussions, performances and workshops in commedia, mask making, music, improvisation, and political theater. The troupe sold twelve hundred copies of the festival proceedings in the six months after the volume was printed, affirming the powerful impact that radical theater made on scholars and artists.

During the latter half of the 1960s, touring helped the troupe gain a national reputation, and led to their first Obie. The first tour took the controversial *Minstrel Show* to the Pacific Northwest in April 1966. A performance at St. Martin's College in Olympia, Washington, was abruptly terminated with a blackout during the "Chick and Stud" scene. The story of this incident and the production's alleged obscenity was picked up by Associated Press. Fame followed. The report spread quickly and put campus and community authorities on their guard. As a result, the show was always well attended and frequently began with one of the actors announcing that spectators would be shown a "modified" version of the production. However, no modifications were actually made, and the rest of the Northwest tour was highly successful.

During the Southern California leg of the tour, the UCLA performance was canceled, apparently due to the well-publicized controversy. A performance at UC Irvine, preceded by the bogus promise of a modified version, generated letter writing and complaints. One outraged Irvine audience member signed and notarized an affidavit wherein she described every single simulated act and four-letter word she had found objectionable in the production.

In Denver three actors were arrested and charged with obscenity after their second performance on 28 September. The ACLU posted bail, and the actors continued the tour to excellent reviews on campuses and in commercial venues. They were acquitted after a trial in February 1967. The New York production, presented by Dick Gregory, who also introduced performances, drew praise from the *New York Times, Village Voice,* and *New Yorker.* Richard Shepard even wrote in the *New York Times* that publicity from the Denver bust "may replace being banned in Boston as a press agent's dream."[51]

The troupe's second national tour took *L'Amant Militaire* and *Olive Pits,* both which had opened in San Francisco the summer of 1967, to the Midwest, East Coast, and Southern California. On this tour, a major commotion occurred at Fullerton State College, where the Jack London Society booked *Olive Pits* for 7 February 1968. Remembering the ruse of a "modified" performance of *Minstrel Show* at UC Irvine, college president William Langsdorf and the Faculty Council judged the troupe "unreliable" and banned them from the campus. The trustees of the college filed an injunction against the troupe's appearance; the ACLU filed a countersuit. Drama professor George Forrest thought he could get around the ban by having the show performed in his class. The administration countered that only three classes would be allowed to observe, the troupe would be issued a restraining order, and a police officer would be stationed in the room. The troupe finally performed in an orange grove immediately east of the campus to a huge crowd of students and teachers who had just held an anticensorship rally.[52] In the aftermath, Professor Forrest resigned, and the college created new policies for approving events. In April the troupe was welcomed to the campus with a performance of *Ruzzante,* on tour with *Patelin* and Gutter Puppet skits.

On a Southwest tour in 1969, a performance of *Meat* upset administrators at Navajo Community College in Arizona, and the company was escorted off the campus. That October they made their final tour of the decade with *Congress of Whitewashers* in the Pacific Northwest.

The logo Davis chose for the Mime Troupe was a griffin holding a banner reading, "Engagement, Commitment, Fresh Air." It came from a drawing by Jacques Callot, famous for his commedia drawings, studied by the troupe. The three words defined the direction the company would take into the twenty-first century. Although Davis left the company in 1970, members from the first ten years speak about his role with a kind of reverence, and Nancy Scott commented that Davis cast a long shadow. Arthur Holden, who joined the troupe in 1963 and retired in 1996, said: "We've been overly meticulous in giving Davis the credit—and he deserves it—for starting the Troupe, and starting it with the right idea, which is that theatre had achieved a level of sacred temple art. . . . So, in taking it away from the hall and bringing it to the park, that was a very important fundamental basis on which we have worked ever since."[53]

Notes

1. Jack Kroll, "Pratfalls and Politics," *Newsweek,* 22 January 1973, 65.

2. R. G. Davis, *The San Francisco Mime Troupe: The First Ten Years* (Palo Alto, Calif.: Ramparts Press, 1975), 197. Hereafter cited as *First Ten Years.*

3. Ibid., 18.

4. H. C. Petley, "The San Francisco Mime Troupe," *Cavalier,* May 1967, 99. For more discussion of the political climate in San Francisco at this time, see Eric Noble, "The Artists' Liberation Front and the Formation of the Sixties Counterculture," Diggers website, 16 December 2001, http://www.diggers.org/alf_version_1996.htm. Lenny Bruce's obscenity trial in New York City that June also heightened tension about censorship.

5. Davis, *First Ten Years,* 66.

6. Lloyd Zimpel, "Surprise in the Wings," *The Nation,* 7 March 1966, 276.

7. Davis, *First Ten Years,* 67.

8. Peter Berg, a member of the troupe, coined the term *guerilla theater.* He says he thought of the concept when Davis was arrested. Peter Berg, telephone interview by Susan Vaneta Mason, 18 May 2002.

9. David Kolodney, "San Francisco Mime Troupe's *Ripping Off Ma Bell,*" Ramparts, August 1970, 26. Davis had been outspoken in his opposition to the collusion between corporations and repertory companies.

10. Kenneth Rexroth, "Performing in City Parks," *San Francisco Examiner,* 21 July 1963. Kerouac calls Rexroth "Rheinhold Cacoethesthe." Jack Kerouac, *The Dharma Bums* (New York: Penguin, 1976), 14.

11. "San Francisco Mime Troupe," n.d., n.p. This document on troupe letterhead may have been a press release. It was probably written late in 1969 because it mentions the planned 1970s season of shows but does not mention the collective.

12. Charles Perry, *The Haight-Ashbury: A History* (New York: Random House, 1984), 31–32.

13. R. G. Davis, "Guerrilla Theatre," *Tulane Drama Review* 10 (summer 1966): 135. Peter Coyote, who was on this tour, tells the story in hilarious detail. Coyote, *Sleeping Where I Fall* (Washington, D.C.: Counterpoint, 1998), 51–55.

14. "San Francisco Mime Troupe," n.d., n.p.

15. Davis, "Guerrilla Theatre," 130.

16. Coyote, *Sleeping Where I Fall,* 102.

17. R. G. Davis, "Cultural Revolution U.S.A.," in *Guerrilla Theatre Essays: 1* (San Francisco: San Francisco Mime Troupe, 1970), n.p.

18. R. G. Davis and Peter Berg, "Sartre through Brecht," *Tulane Drama Review* 12 (fall 1967): 132.

19. The troupe's required reading included Mao Zedong, *On New Democracy: Talks at the Yenan Forum on Literature and Art.*

20. R. G. Davis, "Guerrilla Theatre: 1967," in *Guerrilla Theatre Essays,* n.p.

21. Bruce McConachie and Daniel Freidman, eds., *Theatre for Working-Class Audiences in the United States, 1830–1980* (Westport, Conn.: Greenwood Press, 1985), 201.

22. R. G. Davis, "Radical, Independent, Chaotic, Anarchic Theatre vs. Institutional, University, Little, Commercial, Ford and Stock Theatres," in *Guerrilla Theatre Essays,* n.p.

23. Davis, *First Ten Years,* 26.

24. Petley, "San Francisco Mime Troupe," 67.

25. Davis, *First Ten Years,* 124.

26. Ibid., 126.

27. Sandra Archer, telephone interview by Susan Vaneta Mason, 28 June 2002.

28. "The San Francisco Mime Troupe: The First Forty Years," n.p.

29. Davis, *First Ten Years,* 127–28.

30. Ibid., 20.

31. Ibid., 24.

32. Lee Breuer, essay for Susan Vaneta Mason, 14 May 2000. When I asked Breuer for a few sentences on the San Francisco Mime Troupe, he wrote the following:

> When Susan asked me to write three or four sentences about Ronny Davis I thought about it all afternoon—and then told her it was impossible—for the longer I thought the more I wanted to say.
>
> I wanted to say that R. G. Davis was my first teacher. That if it were not for him and the Mime Troupe, I would never have directed a play. That to him I owe my introduction to both the motivational and the formalist schools of theatre in this century and that his efforts to find the bridges between them have inspired me for forty years.
>
> It was through Ronny that I met composer Bill Spencer who hooked me on music theatre and Judy Collins the painter and designer who hooked me on Performance Art. His "events" at the Actor's Workshop Encore Theatre in which I had the honor to collaborate were thirty years ahead of their time and unchanged they could open at the Kitchen or P.S. 122 today.

Three of six founding members of Mabou Mines—Ruth Maleczech, Bill Raymond and myself worked with and learned from Ronny in these formative years. His myth as a Bill Graham produced counter cultural political activist and centerpiece of 60s San Francisco has obscured the fact that RG Davis was an inspirational artist. Ronny—I blatantly write you a true homage. No one I know has ever deserved one more.

33. Clay Geerdes, "S.F. Mime Troupe: Do It in the Road," *LA Free Press*, 11 July 1969.

34. Davis, *First Ten Years*, 35.

35. *Guerrilla Theatre Essays*, n.d., n.p.

36. Donald Kaul, "Mimes Grace U. of I.," *Des Moines Register*, 26 October 1967.

37. Davis, *First Ten Years*, 57.

38. Ibid., 63.

39. Ibid., 50.

40. R. G. Davis, interview by Susan Vaneta Mason, 10 May 2002.

41. Paine Knickerbocker, "Morality Play on Vietnam," *San Francisco Chronicle*, 28 January 1966.

42. Martin Gottfried, "The Theatre," *Women's Wear Daily*, 22 August 1969.

43. Davis, *First Ten Years*, 124.

44. R. G. Davis, "On the San Francisco Mime Troupe," *Arts in Society* 6 (1969): 411.

45. Coyote, *Sleeping Where I Fall*, 58.

46. Davis, *First Ten Years*, 195–214.

47. Ibid., 71.

48. Davis, interview, 10 May 2002.

49. Coyote, *Sleeping Where I Fall*, 77.

50. "Radical Theatre Festival, San Francisco State College, 1968" (San Francisco: San Francisco Mime Troupe, 1969), 7.

51. Richard Shepard, "Mr. Interlocutor, Updated, Arrives," *New York Times*, 22 October 1966.

52. Randy Grater, "London Society Presses Battle against Mime Ban," *Titan Times* (California State College at Fullerton), 13 February 1968.

53. Nancy Scott, "Celebrating the Presence of Mime," *San Francisco Examiner*, 5 July 1992.

A Minstrel Show, or Civil Rights in a Cracker Barrel

1965

Script by R. G. Davis and Saul Landau

Introduction

When the troupe set out to do a play about the civil rights movement, they mined one of the most racist entertainment forms in American theatrical history, then infused it with a contemporary critique. While creating *A Minstrel Show,* Davis, Landau, and the cast of black and white actors talked about racial issues, and built the show around them. Representatives from CORE and SNCC were invited to previews and asked for feedback. Although *A Minstrel Show* received great reviews in major papers, and Dick Gregory presented the show to acclaim in New York, it was denounced by some black organizations and individuals. Bill Bradley, then with CORE, refused to see it. Reactions to the show were always mixed, but everyone agreed it was disturbing. During the two years *A Minstrel Show* toured, the troupe's reputation for irreverence and obscenity brought notoriety and a huge following. This show put the troupe on the national map.

Commentary

Saul Landau

The *Minstrel Show* tried to use humor to open up issues around race at a time when it had become difficult to talk about certain racial themes in certain correct circles. The skits tried to bring the issue of class into the dialogue over race and to get beyond peoples´ fixation on using correct language. It wasn't the use of the "N" word that was keeping the majority of black people in poverty; it was an economic and social system that had hopelessly entwined race and class. Laughter, even black humor, can help liberate or at least release and through satire, parody, slapstick, song and dance and just plain old bad jokes, we hoped to get people to laugh about issues that ordinarily were not funny as a means to thinking critically about them, releasing them from their correct and often sterile forms of thought. Did we succeed? I don't know. But people laughed—or walked out in disgust if they lacked a sense of humor. But it was theater and how do you get ideas and politics into play in a play except by burlesquing them? (Email to Susan Vaneta Mason, 20 June 2002)

Joan Bazar

The skits force a reexamination of attitudes underlying much of the hypocrisy confusing relations between the races. ("Civil Rights Minstrel Skewers Racial Poses," *Berkeley Daily Gazette*, 28 July 1965)

R. G. Davis

The coon is a racist stereotype. These are masks, showbizness stereotypes, thus not to be acted "truthfully." They are to be presented as caricatures. The original cast of performers, Jason Marc Alexander and Willie Hart, were not actors at all. They were not entertaining the audience, but necessarily dedicated to what Heiner Muller used to say his purpose was: "to exacerbate the class relations in the audience." In this case, we had to exacerbate the deepest racist notions in the audience, even those who thought they were not racists (most liberals and soft headed leftists). We worked on the racist elements in popular culture; the actors knew it and played with it, conscious and critical of it, so they could parody it. One has to play it with critical affection but within a contemporary social context. The toughest stance we took was our criticism of integration without substantive political economic change. (Letter to Susan Vaneta Mason, 18 June 2002)

Claudia Orenstein

The combination of both blacks and whites in blackface also emphasized the fact that the stereotype was essentially a mask that anyone could wear. (*Festive Revolutions: The Politics of Popular Theater and the San Francisco Mime Troupe* [Jackson: University of Mississippi, 1998], 110–12)

Student Nonviolent Coordinating Committee

The minstrel show was an indigenous American art form, which intentionally and by acquiescence contributed to the humiliation of the American Negro. For Ronnie Davis and the Mime Troupe to take this form and attempt to make it a vehicle for the pride, anger, and satire of the "new" Negro is a courageous and creative act. ("Mime Troupe Minstrel Show," *The Movement*, published by the Student Nonviolent Coordinating Committee of California, July, 1965)

Lloyd Zimpel

The myths, fears and distortions—from both Negro and white viewpoints ... are stripped away with varying degrees of satirical cleverness, insight, and brash humor. ("Surprise in the Wings," *The Nation*, 7 March 1966, 277)

Nancy Scott

It does not conform to anybody's notion of "good taste." There's no comforting messages of brotherly love. ("The Mime Troupe 'Puts It on the Line,'" *People's World*, 19 June 1965)

Richard Shepard

What starts out to be a standard minstrel show, Mr. Bones, Mr. Interlocutor, old-line gags, soon turns into a gloves-off joust with society, no holds barred. ("Mr. Interlocutor, Updated, Arrives," *New York Times*, 22 October 1966)

Peter Coyote

A rare cultural epiphany perfectly in sync with the historical moment. (*Sleeping Where I Fall* [Washington, D.C.: Counterpoint, 1998], 39)

The Production

A Minstrel Show, or Civil Rights in a Cracker Barrel opened on 17 June 1965 at Commedia Theatre, Palo Alto, with the following cast:

Inkspot	*George Mathews*
Gimme	*John Broderick*
Klinker	*Kai Spiegle*
Hokus	*Willie Hart*
Snowball	*Julio Martinez*
Bones	*Jason Marc-Alexander*
Interlocutor	*Robert Slattery*

Directed by R. G. Davis. Music by Steve Reich. Musicians: Carl Granich, Chuck Wiley. *O Dem Watermelons* filmed and edited by Robert Nelson. Presented by Bill Graham.

Characters (in order of appearance)

6 Minstrels (3 white, 3 black)
Gimme
Bones
Klinker
Hokus

Inkspot
Snowball
Interlocutor (white)

A Minstrel Show, or Civil Rights in a Cracker Barrel

Two Banjo players enter, set up stage behind seven chairs in a half circle. Begin to play.

Act One

Enter MINSTRELS *in sky blue tuxs, cakewalk and play tambourines while singing "At a Georgia Camp Meeting."*

A camp meeting took place, by the colored race;
Way down in Georgia.
There were folks large and small, lanky, lean, fat and tall,
At this great Georgia Camp Meeting.
When church was out, how the sisters did shout,
They were so happy.
But the young folks were tired and wished to be inspired;
Hired a big brass band.
Chorus
When that big brass band began to play
Pretty music so gay, hats were then thrown away.
Thought them foolish people their necks would break,
When they quit their laughing and talking and went to walking
For a big chocolate cake.

End standing on chairs. Throw tambourines in the air. Catch them. Jump off chairs and bow.

INTERLOCUTOR: Gentleman, be seated. *(All sit except* GIMME.*)*

GIMME: Wish I was rich, wish I was rich, wish I was rich.

INTER: I heard you the first time, Mr. Gimme.

GIMME: Did you? But de fairy gimme three wishes, and dem was it.

INTER: Where did you see a fairy?

GIMME: On a ferry-boat.

All chuckle.

INTER: Mr. Bones, are you a Republican or a Democrat?

BONES: *(Rises.)* Oh, I'm a Baptist.

INTER: You misunderstood me, Mr. Bones. What I mean is, what are you doing for a livelihood?

GIMME: *(Interrupts.)* Oh, I'm a floorwalker in a drygoods store. A lady come in dere de other day, say she wanted to buy a pair of garters. I ask her what kind and she say "rubber." And I say, if I do, I get discharged.

All chuckle, laugh.

INTER: Come, come, whom did you vote for last time?

BONES: Robinson Crusoe.

INTER: What did he run for?

BONES: Exercise.

All laugh.

INTER: Now cut out the foolishness. Are you a Republican or a Democrat?

BONES: Democrat.

INTER: And your wife is also a Democrat?

BONES: She was, but she bolted.

INTER: Bolted the party?

BONES: No, just me. When I come home late, she bolts de door.

All chuckle, laugh, jest.

INTER: Mr. Inkspot, were you ever in Canada?

INKSPOT: No, Sah. I ain't never been no place in China.

GIMME: I been in Canada, Mistah Interlocutor. I almost flew there.

INTER: What do you mean, you almost flew there?

GIMME: If I'd had a couple feathers in mah hands I'd a flew. Dere was sebenteen sheriffs after me.

INTER: What part of Canada were you in?

GIMME: In de wheat belt. Almost got married dere, too.

INTER: Indeed?

GIMME: Uh-huh. Met a grass widow with hay fever, an'a woman can't get rid of hay fever dressed like dat.

INTER: Dressed like what?

GIMME: In a wheat belt. She always had a head cold.

INTER: Where did she get her cold?

GIMME: She didn't know. Said if she did, she'd take it back.

INTER: What I mean is, how did she catch her cold?

GIMME: Her nose ran after it.

INTER: You said she nearly married you.

GIMME: No, I said I nearly married her. I would of married de ol girl too, cept for somethin she said.

INTER: What did she say?

GIMME: "No." It was at a summer resort beach and the sun was awful hot and shinin.

INTER: And she gave you the cold shoulder?

GIMME: Naw, she couldn't do that; it was too sunburned. But was dat woman eber cold. Why, she could freeze a piece of ice out of hot water 'fo de water got cold.

INTER: It isn't much fun making love to a cold woman, is it?

GIMME: You gets about de same satisfaction you gets tryin to play a ukulele wid a sledge hammer. *(Laughs.)* Den I come home. Know how long I was in Canada?

INTER: No, how long were you in Canada?

GIMME: Same as I is here: six foot three.

All laugh raucously.

INTER: Mr. Klinker, I honestly believe that you are the most intelligent person I've ever seen.

KLINKER: *(Posing)* Yes sah, I accepts de nomination. Lotsa folks has tol me dat, but I ain't tol none of em mah secret for bein so wise.

HOKUS: Tell me, boy. I need some surplus wisdom. Tell me how do you get so wise?

KLINKER: I eats a certain kinda fruit dat make me wise.

HOKUS: Golly. I wish I had me some of dat fruit.

KLINKER: Sure cost a heap of money. *(Takes a fake large cloth prune from his pocket.)* I got one right here. Mmm-hmm. De wise fruit. Cost two half dollah each.

HOKUS: You mean anybody eat dat, dey get wise?

KLINKER: Sho' nuff. Just account you is my friend, I lets you have dis one here fo one dollah!

HOKUS: Doggone if it ain't worth a dollah to get wise. You got change fo a eight dollah bill?

KLINKER: Got a seven dollah bill.

HOKUS: Here am de money. Gimme de fruit dat'll make me wise. *(Takes a fake bite from the prune and looks puzzled.)* Hey Klinker!

KLINKER: *(Goes to exit.)* Huh?

HOKUS: You's a crook. Dis ain't nothin but a dried prune you sell me!

KLINKER: See? You getting wise already! *(All crack up.)*

INTER: And now ladies and gentlemen, Brother Inkspot Johnson will give a dramatic recitation of the famous theory of Darwinian evolution. Brother Johnson.

Reshuffle chairs: the line becomes a classroom.

INKSPOT: Fellow sufferers and backbiters!

KLINKER: Dat's what we sufferin from, all right!

INKSPOT: Mah text for dis evenin am taken from dat passage of nonsensical trash in de book ob Darwinian theoryism: dat we am de descendants ob de monkey!

KLINKER: De Rhesus?

INKSPOT: De racist. We have been insulted without our own consent, and are we, freeborn sons of slavery, gon to stand by and hear our rights being run down by a foreigner?

ALL: No!

INKSPOT: Is we monkeys, or is we not?

KLINKER: We snot!

INKSPOT: If all de race were at one time nothin but monkeys, den I ask you, in de name of *[local authority]*, where did dey get dere organ-grinders from?

ALL: OH, DAT'S DEEP! HALLELUJAH, BROTHER! TELL IT!

KLINKER: We will admit, when necessity compels us to, dat over dere in *[scene of Troupe's most recent bust]* we often come into contact wid de monkeys, but am dat our fault? No man am a monkey as long as he don't have an appendage hangin from him like de Ole Boy! (GIMME *checks his crotch.*)

ALL: HALLELUJAH! AMEN!

INKSPOT: When Darwin claim dat we am de descendant ob de monkey he places hisself into a ridiculous position to be sued for libel!

ALL: YEAH! YEAH!

INKSPOT: Fo when he say dat, he call *(to girl in first row)* your father an orangotang, honey, and *(in tears)* my dear sweet mama a baboon! *(Group cries ad lib.)* Shall we stand by and listen to dat defamin insinuation without arisin upon our indignation and hurlin, I say thrustin, dem bery words back into de traitor's teef? If you are men, arise to the pedal extremities and swear it am a lie!

GROUP: *(Rising.)* IT AM A LIE!

INKSPOT: But if you are monkeys, den sit down like gibberin bullfrogs and croak!

KLINKER: *(Sitting.)* Eat it, beat it, eat it!

INKSPOT: My bery blood boils when I notemplate de exaggeraity ob such a delusionary, impedemiracal, hallucinginic—

GROUP: WHOO EE! BOO!

INKSPOT: —phantasmagorical, cro-magnin trip! It am a well authenticated fact dat Darwin were a bachelor all his life.

GIMME: *(As queen.)* Oh, he had to be, honey!

INKSPOT: Fo no true woman would lie dere and allow herself to be put down by such a contaminatin philosophire.

GROUP: AMEN!

INKSPOT: Have I vindicated de race in de sight ob dose who am assembled here?

GIMME: Sho nuff, honey.

INKSPOT: Or shall I have to go further into de mathematical problem ob humanity, and dereby show clearly to your prejudiced minds—

HOKUS: And dere are a lot ob you out dere

INKSPOT: —dat no man am a monkey as long as he behave himself?

BONES: Take it one step further, brother.

INKSPOT: When one ob de race goes up in de big rocket ship into de stratosphere, I as you, am he a astro or not?

HOKUS: He astro all right.

INKSPOT: When de human bein goes flyin round up dere in de thin air he gets nominated for de U.S. Senate when he come down. Now I reminds you de monkey went up dere first, so by all common logic and justice he ought to be president.

ALL: *(Rising.)* HE IS!

INKSPOT: I shall now bring my discourse to a close

BONES: Close your discourse, baby.

INKSPOT: —but still adhere to de predictions ob my own conscience and never allow any man to stuff me with de idea dat I descended from de monkey, or any other wild animal for dat matter!

GROUP: YEAH! YEAH!

INKSPOT: So I leave you with dese parting words: ar-ri-ba-doo-chi.

ALL: What?

INKSPOT: Which mean, when translated into de English lingua: *(intones)* my Cadillac double-parked, de rioters are working overtime, ad de back ob de bus am pullin up, so I repeat, arribadoochi, soul brothers.

ALL: *(Crack up.)* HALLELUJAH!

Reshuffle: chairs back to original half circle.

INTER: And now, Ladies and Gentlemen, a famous Stephen Foster song: "Old Black Joe."

GROUP: *(Singing "Old Black Joe.")*

I'm coming, I'm coming, for my head is bending low.
I hear those gentle voices calling, "Old Black Joe."

Group stands, backs to audience, hums while INTERLOCUTOR *turns to audience and recites.*

INTER: Gone are the days, when my heart was young and gay,
 Gone are my friends from the cotton fields away
 Gone from the earth to a better land I know
 I hear those gentle voices calling, "Old Black Joe."

Group sings and interlocutor is silent.

GROUP: I'm coming, I'm coming, for my head is bending low.

One of the cast, back to audience, simulates masturbation. Group hums while INTERLOCUTOR *recites.*

INTER: I hear those gentle voices calling,

GROUP: *(Sings.)* Old Black Joe.

Group stands on chairs in Spanish pose and hums while INTERLOCUTOR *recites.*

INTER: Se fueron los días buenos

Cuando mi corazón era joven y feliz

Se fueron también mis amigos buenos

De los suelos de algodón.

Se pasaban, se pasaban para una tierra mejor, eso lo sé.

Escucho las voces suaves llamándome

VIEJO NEGRITO JOSÉ.

Group turns singing.

GROUP: I'm coming, I'm coming, for my head is bending low. *(Hum the rest.)*

INTERLOCUTOR: *(Recites.)* Escucho, escucho las voces suaves llamándome *(sobbing with tears)* VIEJO NEGRITO JOSÉ. *(Overcome.* BONES *steps off chair, takes* INTERLOCUTOR *to side. Others step off, march to center facing each other.)*

KLINKER: Grammerphone gesellshaft. Volkswagen uber alles. Von volkswagen zu General Motors. Hansel and Gretel in der Schwartzwald. Jessie Owens ve vill get you! *(Etc., ad lib.)*

ALL: Gone are the days, when my heart was young and gay,

Gone are my friends, from the cotton fields away,

Gone from the earth to a better land I know,

I hear those gentle voices calling, "Old Black Joe."

All stop downstage.

KLINKER: *(Steps in front of group.)* Alte schwarzer Juden! *(*MINSTRELS, *surprised, drive him back to chair.)*

ALL: *(Snapping fingers and jigging.)*

Eeney, meeney, miney, mo

Catch a nigger by the toe

If he hollers, let him go

Eeney, meeney, miney, mo.

BONES: Mr. Interlocutor, I's got somethin to tell de folks.

INTER: Yes, Bones, what is it?

BONES: Somethin important.

INTER: Well, go ahead and tell it then.

BONES: Thank you. I am here, my friends, to speak before you one and all to honor a very festive occasion.

GROUP: Yeah. Ho hum. (*Yawn.*)

BONES: For it has been proclaimed throughout this land by the President hisself, as sure as he is the leader of this humble band of people, that one week will be set aside every year at the same time so that we call all take pride in the accomplishments of the past. So we for you are going to trace back through the years and the ages the history of the colored race as glorious as the Bible's pages. Yes, at times things looked very bleak for the black man—

GROUP: And very black for the bleak man!!

BONES: But it is changed, for Negro History Week will tell you all how it really happened. How we balance out on the great ledger book of time, and who was who in literature, so that we looks mighty fine, and deserving of a week unto ourselves.

KLINKER: Oh no, we ain't gonna share it with nobody.

BONES: —de first man to be killed by de redcoats in de war for Independence: Crispus Attucks. (*Reshuffle: re-assemble chairs in view of audience.*) We takes you now to a historic street in Boston, the very street where the first shots heard round the world rang out.

GIMME *and* INKSPOT *as colonists, in periwigs;* WASP *accents overlaid on dialect.*

1: What do you think about joining Sam Adam's gang?

2: Dey is too far to de left for me.

1: I personally favor dat Virginia revolutionary, Patrick "Give me liberty or give me death" Henry.

2: My friend, THIS IS REVOLUTION.

1: Revolution? Shi-i-it.

2: No, I'm serious. I'm tired of talking. We have to act, to mobilize every man, woman and child. Make ready for another tea party.

1: That's right. We have to find the right tactics to deal with—

BOTH: THE RED COATED MENACE! (*Enter* HOKUS *as* CRISPUS, *sweeping. Colonists ad lib to seats, spit on floor for him to sweep up.*) Wanta take care o dat, nigger? (*Enter* KLINKER *as* HORSEMAN.)

HORSEMAN: DE REDCOATS IS COMIN! De Redcoats is comin! HERE COME DE REDCOATS! RE-E-E-E-ED COATS! (*The two revolutionaries rise and grab* CRISPUS.)

1: Crispus, do you believe in equality?

CRISPUS: Yeah.

2: Do you believe in justice?

CRISPUS: Yeah.

1: Do you believe in brotherhood?

CRISPUS: Sure!

2: Do you believe in taxation without representation?

CRISPUS: Yeah, yeah! I believe in everything. What's wrong with everybody? *They leave him standing there to be shot by the redcoats.*

SNOWBALL *takes off shoe and raps seat of chair simulating rifle shot.*

BONES: But dat sad story ingrained in de very history of dese United States has a happy ending. While de founding fathers was debating whether de nego counts one-third, one-half, or three-fifths of a whole person, for votin purposes only of course, God in heaven above was rewardin ol Crispus as he rewards all de heroes of American history, by grantin dem everlastin immortality in de grade school history books. So we goes now to do heaven above where de soul of our hero is alive and flyin. *(CRISPUS eats watermelon. BONES calls.)* Crispus, you's a hero, baby. Tell us your story—would you give your life again for the cause of freedom?

CRISPUS: Lawsy, Mass'r, I'ze just mindin my own business, cleanin up, when dese two mothers throw me into de middle of de street and dem redcoated cats shoot me. Leave me alone, man, I'm eatin!

BONES: Remember de first nego republic, in de isle of Haiti, de first republic dat became all black? A revolution occurred dere, led by dat great black revolutionary, Tousant Loveture, the great organizer, theoretician, obstetrician of de black republic in Haiti. Tousant set out to free all de black slaves and to make dem citizens. First he fought de British Army, den de British Navy, den he fought de French Army, den he fought de French Navy. From dese experiences he derived new and original tactics of de revolution. To enliven our history we takes you back to de organizin days, de beginnin, de very beginnin struggle of de revolutionary heroes in dat Haiti. Here we present Tousant speakin to his men about the tactical stratagems of de revolution. *(Reshuffle: all set up chairs facing* TOUSSAINT, *played by* GIMME, *who is mounted on a chair. Group ad libs argument: what is needed is a. voodoo! b. Xerox machine! c. picket line! d. bananas!)*

TOUSSAINT: Men. Men. Men! *(Group quiets slowly.)* Now I want you to go out dere and kill every one of dem white mother-fuckers!

GROUP: *(Rising.)* YEAH! *(Freeze.)*

BONES: De progress of de black man's rise to equal status in dis hyer great country was marked by a singular event. De first nego to be invited to de White House was dat great educator of de middle mind, I mean de man who set up a school and led his people to de crafts of technology, to de door of de factory, to de workbench, to de workhouse, to de back door of de corporation: our own Booker T. Washington, Jr. *(Action.)* President Theodore Roosevelt invited Mr. Washington to de White House and historical meetin of de first nego to come to de White House we innacts for you now. We take you to de Teddy Roosevelt office in de White House.

INTER: *(Playing T.R. seated at desk. Knock on door.)* Come in, come in.

SERVANT: *(Enters shuffling, played by HOKUS.)* Missa President, Mr. Booker T. Washington, Sir.

BOOKER: Mr. Pres.

SERVANT: *(Searches him.)* He clean, boss, he ain't got nothin on him.

BOOKER: Mr. Booker T. Washington, Jr. at your service sir!

T.R.: *(Still seated.)* What agency sent you over, son? You forgot your mop and bucket.

BOOKER: No, Mr. President, you don't understand. I am the Booker T. Washington, acknowledged leader of the great nego people—

T.R.: Tsk, tsk.

BOOKER: *(To audience.)*—who advocates that the nego withdraw from partisan politics and make himself useful in this great nation, so that society will need him and he will find his rightful place in the great industrial complex.

T.R.: Oh, well. In that case I appoint you my official adviser for all problems involving the nego race. You certainly shall have your place in the White House. As a matter of fact there's a small maid's room vacant in the attic.

BOOKER: Thank you, Mr. President.

T.R.: And on the way out you'll find the broom closet at the foot of the stairs.

SERVANT: What you want to give him my job for?

BOOKER: Don't worry my man, we can divide the work equally. You can polish the big stick, and I'll walk softly.

BONES: De contribution of de nego to dis here country has to be reckoned with. There are many instances in which de nego has given of his imagination, his sweat, his feet, his baseball glove to de intellectual and cultural life of dis great land. A unforgettable moment in de history of the nego people was the discovery of peanut oil by de professor of science, George Washington Carver. *(Action.)* We takes you now to dat very laboratory in 1921 at de very day, de very hour, de very moment ob dat great discovery which has given so much to de cause ob humanity. George Washington Carver creatin, discoverin, discoverin for all humanity! *(Reshuffle: INKSPOT plays CARVER.)*

JANITOR: *(Played by GIMME, enters—shuffling and sweeping, whistling "We Shall Overcome.")* Missa Carver, you been here all night, you just squeezin your life away for humanity.

CARVER: *(Head in hands.)* Dat's it! *(He begins to squeeze parts of himself, finally getting to his peanuts.)* Oil! Oil! You squeezes dem and you gets little drops of oil! Fetch me some more peanuts!

JANITOR: Laawsy, Missa Carver, dat's a real discovery. You is a genius, you's a real humanitarian, us can fry chicken in dat oil, potatoes, hush puppies. We can employ de bloods from coast to coast, we can start of chain ob Hickory Pits, we can elevate de nego, we—

CARVER: *(Wasp accent.)* Precisely what do you mean by we? Now get me the President of Skippy on the phone—Boy.

JANITOR: Boy? *(Throws CARVER a bird. Freeze.)*

BONES: We have shown you a few moments in de past of de nego in History. But now let us bring you to dis very season, dis decade. Where de nego has stood up for his rights, and as a freedom loving but determined citizen has contributed to Democracy and Justice. No matter bout how much talk dere is of negos having smoldering resentments burning deep down inside dem, the white man knows dat in time of crises he needs the nego. And he sure does use him, especially in wartime.

Remember the war betwixt and between the states? Dere was whole nego regiments dat fought dose cracker troops, and in one great battle an entire black company was wiped out clean. General Ulysses Grant hisself said dat everyone of dose boys was fit and deserving to wear de blue uniform. During World War II, despite a small racial riot in Australia—you know, boys will be boys—the nego won fame for hisself by driving trucks on de Red Ball Express. On dose battle-front highways, he ran over more white Germans dan he did white Americans. For his powerful performance in all dose wars Uncle Sam rewarded de nego by integrating him with de white man in de army.

Nowadays, de nego soldier is de very backbone of our fight for freedom in Vietnam. Thousands of mammies all over de U.S. has photographs of their little boys proudly displayin their uniforms. De veterans of Little Rock and Selma and de guerrilla troops from Watts has forgotten their bad feelings about de ol white power structure and has taken out all their hostility on de common yellow enemy again. In no other country could de poor black man rise from de cotton fields and de poolrooms to become one of our boys in uniform. In fact, de army has been so good to de nego that de whole world acknowledges it as de blackest institution we has.

We takes you now to de fightin fields of Vietnam where de nego soldier is applying de skill dat he has learned so well livin in de old U.S. of A.: De use of fire to gain his ends. As de scene opens, *(enter KLINKER and SNOWBALL as Vietnamese)* we see two of de enemy subvertin their own country by plantin rice to feed de Viet Cong.

VIETNAMESE PEASANTS: We is plantin rice.

1: Dis is hard work. I wish I was in Saigon.

2: Yeah, my cousin works dere as a house boy for de Ass't Ambassador and while his excellency is out shtuppin de local girls, my cousin is shtuppin his excellency's wife.

1: Where you learned dat word, "shtuppin"? Dat an American word?

2: Oh yeah. My cousin gets it off a record made by some high official name Lenny Bruce.

Enter INKSPOT *as Viet Cong holding paper gun. First day in uniform.*

1: Look at him. First day in uniform, he think he Ho Chi Minh. How you doin, kid?

VC: Not bad. *(Pulls out copy of "Mohammed Speaks.")* Look what we found on body of dead American soldier. Ain't dat somethin? Dey reads on battlefield.

GIMME *jumps up as* NEGRO SOLDIER *with bomb in both hands.*

NEGRO SOLDIER: Awright, you dirty commie rats, you back slidin no good motherfuckin, bolshevick, brainwashed, propagandistic low life, humpin bumpin, pot head glue sniffers!

PEASANTS: Who dat?

VC: *(Dropping rifle.)* I don't know. He sure ain't one of us, and he ain't white man neither.

1: Maybe he Russian.

2: Could be UN has sent peace-keeping team and one ob de troops from Tanganyika.

NEGRO SOLDIER: Just keep em up. I know you little yellow rats are sneaky—

VC: I don't understand him, but I know a few words in English. "Mother fucker! You colored, we colored. We friends. Both hate white man." *(Smiles as others admire him.)*

NEGRO SOLDIER: Don't give me that shit, man. We lets you live and you become dominoes. Goddam yellow peril. You's a threat to my freedom. You ain't gonna turn me around. You think we wants to live like ants? Man, you ain't even got no TV.

1: You understand him, Ho Chi Minh?

VC: No, but it sure don't sound like English. Let me try again. "We want peace. We brothers, don't want no trouble, only want own country back."

NEGRO SOLDIER: Damn slant eyed gooks. You want me to let my country down, after all it did for me and my people. I'm gonna kill all of you to do my part for freedom and democracy. *(Gestures with bomb at them. Says "booomm!" They all fall. Freeze.)*

BONES: Yes, friends, dere is de proof. Every day in Vietnam a nego soldier is de best carrier of de American way of life.

On de home front, we are all familiar with de taxin labors of one ob de finest ob nego leaders, Reverend Doctor Martin Luther King, Jr.

Recently, one of de most important tributes to the Great Black Massas, uh . . . Masses, was de awardin of the Nobel Peace Prize to Reverend Brother King, Martin Luther, Jr. We now take you to a jail cell where Reverend King is serving time for his part in a sit-in demonstration. Brother Martin, you's won de Peace Price—50,000 dollahs. I guess you feels pretty good, now dat you's top man on de totem pole?

KING: Yes, boy, I feel proud, just like a new man.

BONES: But what you gonna do with all dat money?

KING: I'm gonna use dat money to erect a new symbol for our people. We are gonna walk in de footsteps of de greatest pacifist of all time, Jesus Christ. We must learn to love de white man, we must pray *(all enter as if praying)* for de white man, for dat is our only salvation, de only way to achieve Justice under God. For it is written in de Good Book that he who lives by de sword shall die by de sword, and he who wreaks vengeance, shall too feel de sharp blade of vengeance . . . *(Continues ad lib.)*

MINSTRELS: *(Segue into Muslims chanting and stomping.)* 1—We're brave; 2—We're strong; 3—We're killers; 4—Black is beautiful; 5—Violence; 6—Blood in de streets; 7—Revolution; 8—Revenge; 9—Blood in de gutters. *(Continue ad lib in chaos of chanting and stomping.* INTERLOCUTOR *enters to stop them.* MINSTRELS *begin finger-popping,* KING *goes to* INTERLOCUTOR, *tries to face up to him, fails and joins* MINSTRELS. MINSTRELS *go into "Easter Time.")*

LEFT GROUP: *(Including* KING) Easter time is de time for eggs,
And de time for eggs is Easter time.
Easter time is de time for eggs,
And de time for eggs is Easter time.

RIGHT GROUP: Easter time and de honey is fine,
And de honey is fine at Easter time.

All sit. Crossfire.

SNOWBALL: Mr. Interlocutor, a Black Cat crossed my path de other day.

HOKUS: A black cat? Don't dat mean bad luck?

SNOWBALL: Uh-uh, not unless dere's a whole bunch of white cats followin him. *(All crack up.)*

KILINKER: Mr. Interlocutor, dere's a man in my home town dat tried to pass for white.

INTER: Tried to pass for white?

KLINKER: He used a hair straightener, lip thinner, skin bleach, nose remover and try to pass, but dey always catch him every time.

INTER: How come?

KLINKER: He couldn't hide his natural sense of rhythm. *(All crack up.)*

GIMME: Speakin of natural sense of rhythm: congratulations, Inkspot!

INKSPOT: Huh?

GIMME: You just been nominated Catholic Mother of the Year! *(INKSPOT chases GIMME off stage.)*

GIMME and INKSPOT re-enter.

INKSPOT: It's okay, I gave him a white eye.

INTER: Boys, boys, I want you to play a little scene for me. Snowball, I want you to go off-stage and get a girl's mask and a skirt. You will play the Chick.

SNOWBALL: Squawk! *(Like a chicken, exits.)*

KLINKER: His name's Snowball, not No Ball.

INTER: And Mr. Gimme, I want you to play the stud. This will be a scene between a Chick and a Stud. Gentlemen, arrange the chairs. *(INTER-LOCUTOR exits.)*

Reshuffle: set up chairs for band stand, cabaret. Pantomine and mime: group becomes Dixieland band (no sound). SNOWBALL enters as girl, in white dollface mask and skirt over his costume. Walks to chair, swinging hips. GIMME (trumpeter) comes off stand, approaches girl, buys her drink, she is coquettish, he ask her to leave, she does. They circle the stage, go to his pad, he opens door, she enters, he locks door, bolts, latches, and bars it. She sits on edge of bed (two chairs). He sits, puts hand on her knee, she takes it off. He puts hand around her shoulder, she cuddles; grabs for her breast, she takes hand off; for crotch, she stops him; for breasts again, she stops him; for leg, she stops him; he uses two hands, grabs leg and breast at once, she gets confused, finally gives in. He lays her out, screws her mimetically. She pulls skirt down, sits up on edge of bed, wrings hands; disturbed. He gestures, "what's the matter?" Both move to spot. Left stage CHICK; right stage STUD. Both in single spot. Finally speaks.

STUD: For Christ's sake, if you got something to say, say it.

CHICK: What's wrong?

STUD: Nothing's wrong, baby. You got a problem and I was just solving it for you. Felt pretty good, didn't it. Yeah, de white man invented that problem for the black man to solve.

CHICK: You really can't have a relationship with me just as a person.

STUD: Baby, you came up here with me willingly, and lay down on that bed and spread your white legs, and humped up and down and moaned in my goddam ear. You was horny for a black, baby, a black body on top of you, and now you think it's disgusting and cheap.

CHICK: Well, I didn't need you!

STUD: What? What was all that moaning and groaning and oh how I love it about? Tell me you didn't like that.

CHICK: I wanted you to feel good, but you're not man enough to accept it. You can't even be a good lover: if you can't take you can't give.

STUD: That's a cliché. You don't know who I am.

CHICK: And you! You may have the body of a man, but emotionally you're a child. You can't know me as a woman.

STUD: Woman! Ain't nobody tole you baby? You ain't nothin but a white chick. You're status and satisfaction and revenge. You're pussy and pale skin and you know no white man can satisfy you like I can. Now me, I'm different; I'm all Negro, with the smell of Negro, and the hair of Negro, and all the goddam passion of Africa and wild animals. I haven't got the same hang-ups, have I?

CHICK: I feel sorry that so many bad things have happened to you. I really want to love you, because you need love.

STUD: You're a whore.

CHICK: Don't say that!

STUD: You're a whore. You're trying to sell me something. You want me to buy what you've got. You've got guilt and you're selling it to me under a different label. You love Negroes but I'm a man, and you can't love me if you love Negroes.

CHICK: But I can. I want to. I lied. You did satisfy me. You were majestic and you were tender. Did you think I wouldn't notice your tenderness? You do want to love me.

STUD: Shit, you been readin too much James Baldwin.

Mimetic reaction: she takes off skirt and mask, holds them before her and moves tenderly, pleadingly toward him, offering herself sacrificially. He becomes cool, lecherous. She continues toward him, holding the mask in front of her. He strangles the mask as she holds it, his hands circling an imaginary throat just below the mask. The mask and skirt are dropped to the floor. He looks at it, kicks it tentatively, then she picks it up and starts laughing at him. Blackout.

Screen descends. MINSTRELS *sit in front of screen and sing while silent film rolls. Movie: "O Dem Watermelons" (by Robert Nelson, Saul Landau, and R. G. Davis). Song continued as below until bouncing watermelon comes on screen. Then a yell to the audience: "Come on everybody, follow the bouncing watermelon!" Song: "Massa's in the Col, Col Groun."*

Round de meadows am a ringing
De darkies' mournful song
While de mockin bird am singin
Happy as de day am long.
Where de ivy am a creepin
O'er de grassy mound,
Dere ol' massa am a sleepin
Sleepin in de col, col, groun.
Chorus

Down in de corn fiel
Hear dat mournful soun,
All de darkies am a weepin
Massa's in de col, col, groun.

Massa make de darkies love him
Cause he was so kind
Now dey sadly weep above him,
Mournin cause he leave dem behind.

I cannot work before tomorrow,
Cause de tear drop flow,
I try to drive away from sorrow,
Pickin on de ol banjo.
Chorus
(fast) Den oh, dat watermelon
Lamb ob goodness you must die,
I'm gwine to join de contraband children
Gwine to get a home bye and bye.
(slow) Watermelon, watermelon, watermelon
O dat watermelon, o dat watermelon
Watermelon, watermelon, etc.
Chorus minimal repeat. By Steve Reich.

INTER: And now, ladies and gentlemen, there will be a 15-minute intermission, during which time we will have dancing on the stage. The Minstrels will go among you and take a partner and do a dance up here on the stage. House lights and music, please. Gentlemen, find your partners.
MINSTRELS *go out into the audience, find blonde girls to dance with. Music: Muslim song: "White man's heaven is a black man's hell."*

Act Two

Banjo strikes up tune, bringing MINSTRELS *back to stage.* MINSTRELS *sing and play tambourines: "Georgia Camp Meeting."*

A camp meeting took place, by the colored race;
Way down in Georgia.
There were folks large and small, lanky, lean, fat and tall,
At this great Georgia Camp Meeting.
When church was out, how the sisters did shout,
They were so happy.
But the young folks were tired and wished to be inspired;
Hired a big brass band.

Chorus
When that big brass band began to play
Pretty music so gay, hats were then thrown away.
Thought them foolish people their necks would break,
When they quit their laughing and talking and went to walking
For a big chocolate cake. *(All bow in line.)*
Segue to "Put On Your Red Dress Baby"
Put on your red dress, baby,
Cause we're goin out tonight
Put on your red dress, baby,
Cause we're goin out tonight.
But you better bring your razor
Case some nigger might want to fight.

Put on your high-heeled sneakers,
And you wig-hat on your head,
Put on your high-heeled sneakers,
And you wig-hat on your head.
Cause I'm pretty sure, baby
Pretty sure we're gon knock 'em dead.
MINSTRELS *break character and make this a rock number;* INTERLOCUTOR
rushes on to restore order.
INTER: Gentleman—be seated. And now ladies and gentleman, another
    great Stephen Foster melody—"Uncle Ned." *(He sits with back to audi-
    ence, leads group in barbershop singing "Uncle Ned.")*
    Dere was an ol nigger dey call'd him Uncle Ned,
    He's dead long ago, long ago;
    He had no wool on da top ob his head,
    De place where de wool ought to grow.
    Chorus
    Den lay down de shubble and de hoe,
    Hang up de fiddle and de bow;
    For dere's no more work for poor Ol Ned,
    He's gone where de good Niggers go.
SOLO: 2. His fingers were long like de cane in de brake,
    He had no eyes for to see;
    He had no teeth for to eat de corn-cake
    So he had to let de corn-cake be.
    Chorus
SOLO: 3. When Ol Ned die Massa took it mighty hard,
    De tears run down like rain;
    Ol Miss Sue turn pale, and she gets bery sad,

Cause she nebber see Ol Ned again.

Chorus

MINSTRELS *drop out one by one and sit in audience, so that finally* BONES *is singing alone. At finish they applaud him sardonically.*

INTER: Where have you been these last three months, Mr. Bones?

BONES: Oh, I ben visitin my cousins.

INTER: You have cousins out of town?

BONES: Oh yeah, dey lives just east of here in de Congo.

INTER: In the Congo? In the African Congo?

BONES: Yeah, das de one.

INTER: Why, don't you know that's dangerous? You could have been killed.

BONES: Oh, I didn't have no problem when I was over dere. It was comin back here where I came upon some contusion.

INTER: You mean some confusion.

BONES: Dem irrigation fellas didn't want to let me come back.

INTER: That's ridiculous. You're a natural-born citizen, aren't you?

BONES: Das what dey asked.

INTER: Well, you are a natural-born citizen, aren't you?

BONES: Well, no. I came through a caesarean.

ALL: Yeah!!

KLINKER: *(Runs up on stage.)* Mista Interlocutor, I was in Africa too, I was.

INTER: Where in Africa were you?

KLINKER: Ethopa.

INTER: What were you doing there?

KLINKER: I was a stoojun ob de modern dance.

INTER: I didn't know they had modern dance in Ethiopia.

KLINKER: Oh yeah, very modern. Dey got one dey call derumba, named after de great leader.

INTER: The Rhumba happens to be a Cuban dance. It wasn't named after any African leader.

KLINKER: Oh, you wrong. Dis one heah named after Patrice Derumba and it a very satisfying dance. Everyone get in a big circle, and dey pass de bottle while de big pot stewin on de fire.

INTER: That doesn't sound like a dance, nor does it sound very modern.

KLINKER: Oh, it modern, all right. Dey not cookin no missionary in dat pot, but dey got a couple young girls from de pieces corps and dey goes real well wid a hot link.

ALL: Yeah!!

INTER: But, where does the dancing come in?

KLINKER: Well, you can't dance when you eatin. Dat give you a bellyache, so derumba don't come till a hour later.

INTER: Then what happens?

KLINKER: De drummer he drum, and de bass man he debases, and everyone get friendly, jump around a little and shout, "Derumba on man, choose your weapon!"

ALL: Yeah!!

GIMME: *(Runs up on stage.)* We had one ob dem rumbas right here in dis country a little while ago, in Watts.

HOKUS: What?

GIMME: Watts.

HOKUS: Watts?

GIMME: Watts. And Rochester.

INKSPOT: *(From audience.)* Rochester. Ain't dat a friend of Benny's?

ALL: Yeah!!

GIMME: Now I knows de real story on dat dere rumba dey had in New York a while back. In fact I's got it all worked out here to lets you watch it. *(KLINKER and INKSPOT join him.)* Me and Inkspot, here, am gonna be two 17-year-old kids in New York City. We standin on de corner ob 127th and Lenox and it's 11 o'clock at night. Now when you got two 17-year-old kids in New York City, 11 o'clock at night, 127th and Lenox, it adds up to one thing.

KLINKER: Riot.

GIMME: No.

KLINKER: Oh yeah, a violation of curfew.

GIMME: Now look here—seein as you so much on the ball, your muscles all wangin and twanin, I'm gonna give you a good part! I'm gonna give you de bes part! I'm gonna give you de fine part—Klinker, I wants you to be—a cop. *(KLINKER cracks up.)*

KLINKER: No! You ain gonna place dat burden on me!

GIMME: Now wait a minute, wait a minute, Klinker—you know ol Gimme better dan dat—now I wouldn't ask you to be no common, ordinary low life cop—boy, I wants you to better dan dat. I wants you to be—a white cop! *(KLINKER cracks up.)*

KLINKER: No! You ain gonna place dat white burden on me neither!

GIMME: Now, really cool down. Now would you do dis for me—if I was to tell you that I was gon let you play a genuine, authenticated, A.K.C. registered, Irish cop?

KLINKER: Oh, well—dat's different! Why diden you say dat in de firs place? Irish ain neither black nor white!

GIMME: Well now, long as you recognizin dat, jes step on off de stage and come like a cop.

INKSPOT: *(Slow.)* Hey Klinker—how do a cop come?

KLINKER: On the beat!

ALL: Yeah! *(With kick front.)*

GIMME: Hey awright now, we's ready. *(They take off jackets; become two kids; jive and play harmonica until)*

INKSPOT: Wait a minute, man. I read about some trouble las summer. Dey had a 15-year-old kid out dere dat killed somebody and de cops came and kill him.

GIMME: Aaah—now wait a minute—I know what you talkin about, man, dat kid didn't kill nobody, man.

INKSPOT: Now wait a minute, man—dey kill de kid; he musta killed somebody or somethin, I know dat.

GIMME: Git dis, man—wait a minute, now look. I got it right fum de hosses mouth.

INKSPOT: You tryin to tell me dey didn't kill de kid?

GIMME: No man—yeah, dey kill de kid but de kid didn't kill nobody.

INKSPOT: Yeah?

GIMME: All he did was borrow somebody's automobile for a weekend cruise.

INKSPOT: What? Wait a minute—wait a minute deacon. You mean to tell me de kid boosted a short, and dey wasted him?

GIMME: Precisely.

INKSPOT: God damn. How much is a car worth?

GIMME: Must be worth more dan a nigger. *(They crack up.)*

INKSPOT: Yeah, we'll git dat kid's mother some roller skates.

GIMME: Ah'm hip TO it, man—but dig it—you know what, man? Willy was right dere—he saw dat shit, you know?

INKSPOT: Well I know dat dude didn't take it lyin down—

GIMME: Ain't you hip TO it, baby!

INKSPOT: YEAH.

GIMME: Will got to stompin.

INKSPOT: Cuttin, baby.

GIMME: Stabbin.

INKSPOT: Stealin.

GIMME: Robbin.

INKSPOT: Rapin.

GIMME: God damn dey give some groovy parties out in California.

INKSPOT: I seen dose cats, man, out on de TV, pickin up mohair suits, and TV's—yo man didn't cut us in on shit, Jack.

GIMME: Now wait a minute, wait a minute. Befo you rank Willy, you oughta git clued in of what's been goin down.

INKSPOT: I'm clued dat dis is year ol suit, man.

GIMME: Now wait a minute, wait a minute. Dere's mo dan dem rags in de world—you know? Willy tryin to turn us ON, man—he tryin to turn us on to respect fo ourselves.

INKSPOT: Respect.

GIMME: Yeah shiiiit.

INKSPOT: Come on baby, you sound like Martin Luther King.

GIMME: Wait a minute, wait a minute—ain no Martin Luther King gig, Jack. Cause Willy, he don go dat way.

INKSPOT: Oh yeah?

GIMME: Dig? Willy done already tol me how you make dem uh—*(whisper)* Molotov cocktails.

INKSPOT: Shit! I didn't know Russians were in on it, man—later.

GIMME: Hey—no, no, now—ain no Russains in on dis here—dis jes a little domestic self-help program.

INKSPOT: Oh, well, solid—dat's cool.

GIMME: Yeah.

INKSPOT: Well lay it on me, man.

GIMME: Well, dig it man—tell me, is you hip to bottles?

INKSPOT: Oh yeah, dat's like a glass can.

GIMME: Yeah, dat's right. Now dig, dig. You take yourself a bottle.

INKSPOT: Um um.

GIMME: You git some gasoline.

INKSPOT: Yeah.

GIMME: Pour it into de bottle.

INKSPOT: Uh huh.

GIMME: Stuff a rag down dere.

INKSPOT: Yeah.

GIMME: Leave some hanging out.

INKSPOT: Uh huh.

GIMME: You lights it up; throw it up against your local police department and B LOO—OO—M. Instant peace.

INKSPOT: *(Awed whisper.)* Solid!

GIMME: Yeah, man.

INKSPOT: Dig it, man. You got to get hip. Learn somethin from the crackers dat run dis country, man. If you fight a war, you don fight it in your own country, right? Well now, if you live in Watts, and you want to hassle, you don burn down you own neighborhood. You fuck up Beverly Hills!

GIMME: Cooo—I can see it, man! We all march up there

INKSPOT: We get all the brothers together

GIMME: Wo—day got knives

INKSPOT: Day got RAZORS

GIMME: Chains

INKSPOT: Pistols

GIMME: Is dat de national guard over dere?

INKSPOT: Yeah—here come de police—*(cop voice)* Where you 60,000 niggers think you going?

GIMME: Oh baby—we jus goin ovah to Sammy Davis Junior's for fish fried matzo—*(They crack up. KLINKER appears wearing sign on hat: "White Cop.")*

INKSPOT: Hey man—cool it, man.

COP: *(After a silence; Irish accent.)* All right. Move along.

GIMME: Hah, hah, yes suh, officer, anything you say, baby—it's your world. *(COP passes.)* Shit, man.

INKSPOT: God damn, man, is dat a tiny motherfucker of a policeman? Hey, you know—you remember dem other ones? Dem imported ones, man?

GIMME: Oh you mean de ones dey brought from Oakland?

INKSPOT: I'm hip—de big with the BIG.

GIMME: 38-inch necks.

INKSPOT: Yeah, and the 44 inch pistols, man.

GIMME: I'm hip to it.

INKSPOT: Oo-oo.

GIMME: Jes as MEAN.

INKSPOT: Yeah, but you saw how SWEET dis cat come on.

GIMME: Aw of course, man—

INKSPOT: "Move along, kids."

GIMME: "Move along kids." Yeah, don wan any of dose—

INKSPOT: I know why, cause we showed em some resPECT.

GIMME: Dat's right, Jack—dem cats KNOWS we don take dat no more.

INKSPOT: We showed de mothers.

GIMME: Watts!

INKSPOT: Harlem!

GIMME: Mmm—Philadephia.

INKSPOT: San Francisco, man.

GIMME: Ain't you hip to it?

INKSPOT: They got resPECT for us, baby.

GIMME: Mm-hm.

COP: *(Offstage. Shouts.)* All right you black bastards, move that car!— Please!

GIMME: Well—

INKSPOT: Now well—

GIMME: A little bit of respect.

INKSPOT: Yeah, a little, baby. Another week dem ofay mothers be shinin my shoes.

GIMME: Ain't you hip to it, baby?

INKSPOT: I say, shine it, boy! Snap de rag, baby.

GIMME: God damn combin mah mohair, baby.

INKSPOT: Yeah.

GIMME: Shi-i-i-t.

INKSPOT: Yeah.

GIMME: I'm gon be so god damn bold, I think I—

INKSPOT: Aw, you bold man—I'm gon—*(cop enters.)* uh, oh.

GIMME: Uh, oh.

INKSPOT: Well, yeah *(louder)* take it easy, baby.

GIMME: Yeah, later man.

COP: I told ya both to move on!

INKSPOT: Well, man, I jus gotta take my aunt to de hospital. She's out in the car gettin sick now. Later!

COP: All right come here! Against the wall—both of ya.

BOTH: Wait a minute, man, wait a minute.

COP: Get against the wall before I bash ya both!

GIMME: Now wait a minute—what's de matter wit you? *(They stand backs to audience, arms raised, as if against the wall.)*

COP: No wise stuff, either. *(He frisks them.)*

INKSPOT: Want a little of dat, baby? *(Leering.)* God damn!

GIMME: Easy, man—don press de mohair!

COP: ALL RIGHT, WHAT'S YOUR NAME HERE?

INKSPOT: My name is Harry.

COP: Harry what?

INKSPOT: Finkelstein! Hah, hah *(They crack up.)*

GIMME: What you got against Jews, baby?

COP: NOTHIN AGAINST JEWS, I GOT A WHOLE LOT AGAINST ROTTEN NIGGERS. NOW WHERE'S YOUR ID CARD?

GIMME: Hey man—don you know I can't fit no ID in dese tight pants? *(Cracks up.)*

COP: *(phones.)* Flanagan! SEND ME A WAGON UP TO 127TH AND LENOX. GOT A COUPLE OF WISE NIGGERS UP HERE.

INKSPOT: *(Pleading and changing places.)* Hey, man.

GIMME: Dig de cat man.

INKSPOT: Wait a minute, wait a minute, baby—ain't no need to call de wagon, dig?

GIMME: We just jivin wit you, man.

INKSPOT: Come on.

COP: We'll all go. And I'll walk you down there.

GIMME: Hey, wait a minute now, man. Is this necessary? I mean I—

INKSPOT: My mother wants to see me.

COP: Well, I got someone who wants to see ya too.

GIMME: Ah shit—dis cat's too uptight, man.

INKSPOT: We ain't doin you nothin, man.

GIMME: You can't talk to his kind. What dis cat needs is soul, man. *(More jive; COP scared.)*

INKSPOT: Man—you need yourself a soul injection. *(Pulls harmonica from pocket like knife, then plays. COP shoots him. SECOND KID crosses to him. COP grabs harmonica and pockets it. Long freeze, then MINSTRELS come back onstage.)*

SNOWBALL: Das what I calls actin. Dat's de first time I seen a nigger hit de dust like a good nigger.

KLINKER: Man, you ain't dead?

INKSPOT: *(Rising.)* No, I isn't. I's just showin de folks the sociological man-ifustations of de chillin and de white Irish cops. *(Crossfire.)*

INTER: *(Entering.)* Why are all the cops Irish?

SNOWBALL: Cause dey's got to have a accent.

INTER: An accent?

SNOWBALL: Sho. Dey's got to speak with authority and vigor, like *(in Irish dialect)* "What the Hell's goin on here?"

INTER: Why do they have to do that?

HOKUS: If'n a cop came along and said, "Ah right, man, shuffle on," nobody would listen to him.

ALL: Yeah!

GIMME: Did you understand dat scene? Dat was a American scene.

HOKUS: American? Nah, dat was in de Noff.

GIMME: No matter, dat was American.

HOKUS: How you know?

GIMME: Well, did you hear dat red-faced man in dat blue uniform speak all dat white trash?

ALL: Yeah!

INKSPOT: Listen here. Why ain't dere no Chinese cops?

GIMME: Because dey don't know white from wong.

ALL: Yeah!

INTER: How is it that those two young kids were out in the street at 11 o'clock at night?

HOKUS: How come?

INTER: That is my question. How come those two young—

INKSPOT: We heard it de fust time.

HOKUS: How come?

INKSPOT: Well, dat's simple. If you was number 19 in a family of 18 you sho would be standin' on a corner.

HOKUS: How come?

INKSPOT: You couldn't do it inside.

ALL: Yeah!

KLINKER: De point is dat dese hyer kids wasn't suppose to be outside *(faster)* playin around and foolin in de middle ob de night, wastin dere time on useless talk, gamblin, joke crackin, singin, loiterin, resistin arrest, harrasin de police, talkin sass, pulaverin, and a whole list of other illegal violations.

INKSPOT: Wid dat kind ob analysis, dey would have to be dead to be good enough for you.

GIMME: One ob dem is already.

ALL: Yeah!

GIMME: What dem kids need is some rehabilitation—dey needs some urban renewal.

HOKUS: Oh, yeah. Dey gets dat. Urban renewal am called nego removal.

GIMME: Man, you need more den dat to remove de nego. You can't even do it wid Mr. Clean.

ALL: Yeah!

INTER: Gentlemen, how come that officer of the law saw fit to shoot that innocent little child?

HOKUS: How come?

BONES: Didn't you say dat before?

HOKUS: Uh-huh.

BONES: Ain't dis a different question?

HOKUS: Uh-huh.

BONES: Ain't you got no other answer?

HOKUS: Yeah!

KLINKER: De reason dat cop killed dat kid was because de cop knows dat kid had a knife.

BONES: Dat kid didn't have no knife.

KLINKER: No different if'n he didn't have one. *(Faster.)* He did, he would have he should have, he useta have one, his pappy had one, his brother had one, dey all has em, all God's chillin gots em.

INKSPOT: *(Jumping in.)* De problem wid dat scene is dat it weren't realistic.

KLINKER: Yes.

INKSPOT: It weren't de way it oughta be played.

KLINKER: Dat's right. None ob dem kids stands like dat anymore, no sir. Dey don't keep no hands in de pockets, dey leans like dis. An de cop he don't come walkin like dat, no sir.

INKSPOT: Dat's right. De other kid he leans like dis, dey waits . . .

KLINKER: I'll show you de real way to play dat scene. Hey, you. *(Picks out HOKUS to play COP.)* You come like a cop, none ob dat shufflin, brazen-like, with de head up. *(To INKSPOT.)* And you and me is standin here on de corner like de real kids.

COP: *(Enters, sauntering boldly.)* Aw right, you kinds, shuffle on!

KIDS: Yes, sir, officer. *(As* COP *passes first kid, both stab him. He falls, twisting to reveal sign saying "black cop." He freezes till next line.)*

GIMME: Dat was a very interestin story, but dey don't do things like dat no mo.

BONES: Dat's right, you don't spect us to believe dat story. Why nowadays when you find some coons stirrin up trouble dey don call no cops. Dey calls in de mercenaries.

SNOWBALL: Mercenaries? What am mercenaries?

GIMME: Oh, dem is a white soldier, from another country, who can't do it in his own place, doin it in yours.

SNOWBALL: Is mercenaries good guys or bad guys?

GIMME: Dat all depends on what color rebels dey's killin.

BONES: How come dey don't send dem mercenaries to kill some ob dem white Mississippi rebels?

GIMME: Why dat's downright inhuman, settin brother against brother!

HOKUS: *(Rising.)* I tell you what we needs in imipissi-pissamippi-mippa-sissi—one ob dem strong men wid de funny name like Mobutu, Abdoulu, Kasavubu—Campinella, somethin like dat.

KLINKER: You bet, dat's de only way we gets U.S. aid. We finds a strong man and asks for help to keep his muscles flexing. Den dey sends us some airi-planes wid dem Kooban Pilots and dey fly hoomanitarian rescue *(MINSTRELS into airplane positions)* missions and dey kin bomb de provincial capital of Natchez, while we has a holdin action at de central capital ob Jackson. Meantime we calls dem white man some rebel name like Simba *(ALL:* Simba!) or Cracker *(ALL:* Cracker!) and charges dem wid heenos crimes like eatin too many colored nuns, and den we calls upon de U.S. whilst we smuggles de guns in from Mexico.

HOKUS: Man, you talkin like one ob dem underdeveloped countries!

INKSPOT: Underdeveloped? You mean all dem countries is just stunted chillin?

HOKUS: No. I refers to de cultural state ob dere civilization.

INKSPOT: You mean dey ain learned yet dat we is better at killin colored rebels dan dey is at eatin white nuns.

GIMME: Missionaries, mercenaries—dey all sounds alike to me. And what do we get out ob it anyhow?

BONES: Ain't you got no national pride? Why you has helped save freedom in de Congo.

GIMME: I has?

BONES: Well, you ain foughten for de other side, has you?

GIMME: No.

BONES: Well, you showin yo true colors!

GIMME: How come you always talkin bout missionaries, mercenaries? What do you know about what's goin on right here in de ol U.S. of A.?

INKSPOT: Aw right, what is goin on right here?

GIMME: Well, I'll tell you. You takes me. I works in dis restaurant washin dishes an dere are two kinds of people in dat world. De ones dat works in de kitchen, like de lowly dog, and de ones dat comes in and eats de lowly slop.

INKSPOT: But surely you must meet a nice integrated clientele?

GIMME: Why, sure I meets em. For your edification, I'm goin to sho you how we meets. Let's say dis area here am de men's room.

BONES: *(Laughing.)* He thinks he's LeRoi Jones.

GIMME: I said de men's room, not de boy's room. Now looka here. Inkspot, I want you to play de white man.

KLINKER: Let's see how you do this time, Inkspot.

INKSPOT: Oh, dat's aw right. I takes any character part.

BONES: And what about me, what am I gonna play?

GIMME: Well, Bones, I saved you de big part *(BONES ad libs interest and then excitement here)* de strongest part, de biggest part. You can see it now, your name in blazin lights, in three feet high letters, up on Broadway— MIDDLE CLASS NEGRO!

BONES: And what you are you goin to play?

GIMME: I shall merely *(English accent)* endeavor to play truthfully and sincerely my own natural self.

INKSPOT: Come on, nigger.

All three exit, come on with signs: "Nigger" apron and "White" and "Negro" vests. Two MINSTRELS set up door and one is a flushing toilet. Negro and white approach the bathroom door.

WHITE: After you.

NEGRO: No, after you.

WHITE: Oh, go ahead, I can wait.

NEGRO: No, you were here first, I insist—

WHITE: No—*(more ad libbing by both.)*

NIGGER: *(Enters, listens to debate, anxious to get inside, pushes through.)* After me. Shit, you goin to stand there and debate who is goin to take de first piss?

NEGRO: *(Enters bathroom.)* Where's your manners? You're the kind that gives our race a bad image.

NIGGER: In dat case, I moves on over since you have to go so bad. Dere's room enough for two.

NEGRO: That's not what I meant.

NIGGER: Oh, who gives a damn what you meant. *(Flushes toilet, pantomimes combing hair.)*

WHITE: Maybe I should leave and that way it would be less crowded.

NIGGER: Wait a minute, boss, you mean you didn't even have to go? What de hell you come in here for and cause all dis trouble? You one of dem peeverts?

NEGRO: *(To WHITE.)* Pay no attention, sir. He's probably drunk.

NIGGER: Fuck you. Why you got to kiss de white man's ass?

NEGRO: Watch your language. Remember where you are.

NIGGER: I know where I am. I'm in de pissin room and I come in here to take one. I don't know what you come in here for, but it sure weren't for pissin.

NEGRO: If you were any kind of civilized human being, you would move aside and let the customers use the facilities first. I'm going to report you to the manager.

NIGGER: If you like de manager so much you can go ahead and piss in his room.

WHITE: I can see what you're up against. It's very difficult to deal with an uneducated person.

NEGRO: I agree.

NIGGER: *(To WHITE.)* Shit, man—you need an education to learn to piss more than one in a commode. And you *(To NEGRO)*—you need an education, you white ass kisser.

NEGRO: I resent that, you street nigger! *(Goes to punch him. WHITE MAN intervenes.)*

WHITE: Now wait a minute, let's be reasonable about this. Use some reason.

NIGGER: *(Pulls out razor.)* Here's my reason. I'm gonna settle somethin with Mr. Ass Kisser. You chicken shit Mr. Ass Kisser, you ain't no nigger no more. Don even carry a blade to defend yourself. Mighty educated.

NEGRO: Cool it, baby—we're brothers! Dere's de white man!

WHITE: Don't kill me, I didn't say anything. Honest.

NIGGER: Yeah, no one says nothin to me except clean dis and do dat. Well, now I'm sayin something. One of you is going to get it, maybe both. All I gotta do is figure out which one of you I hates the most. *(Freeze.)*

INTER: *(After 15–25 seconds.)* Well, we can't wait all night for you to decide. Remember, this is a Minstrel Show!

ALL: *(Action.)* Oh, yeah!

INTER: Let's "Jump Jim Crow!"

A MINSTREL: *(The following verse from "Jump Jim Crow" is sung once solo and then repeated by all the MINSTRELS.)*

Come, listen all you gals and boys, I'se just from Tuckyho;

I'm going to sing a little song, my name's Jim Crow.

Wheel about and turn about and do jus so,

Every time I wheel about, I Jump Jim Crow.

Banjos segue into "O, Dem Golden Slippers" while INTERLOCUTOR *recites and* MINSTRELS *dance.*

INTER: Oh, the Minstrel Show it's comin to a close, so we're gonna dance on our heels and toes, with tambourines and tappin shoes we're gonna have a ball. Now Bones does the shuffle while Gimme claps, and Inkspot wobbles and Klinker claps, and the whole troupe sings and romps about, dancing till de morning.

Chorus.

O, dem Golden Slippers! O, dem Golden Slippers!

Golden Slippers I's gwine to wear, because dey look so neat.

O, dem Golden Slippers! O, dem Golden Slippers!

Golden Slippers I's gwine to wear, to walk de golden street.

O, my Golden Slippers am a'laid away,

Cause I don't spect to wear em till my weddin day,

And my longtailed coat, dat I loved so well,

I will wear up in de chariot in de morn.

And my long white robe—dat I bought last June,

I'm gwine to get changed cause it fits too soon,

An de ol gray hoss dat I used to drive,

I will hitch him to de chariot in de morn.

Chorus

O, dem Golden Slippers! O, dem Golden Slippers!

Golden Slippers I's gwine to wear, because dey look so neat.

O, dem Golden Slippers! O, dem Golden Slippers!

Golden Slippers I's gwine to wear, to walk de golden street.

All bow.

The End

Olive Pits

1966, 1967

Script by Peter Berg and Peter Cohon (Coyote)

Introduction

Olive Pits is an adaptation of Lope de Rueda's sixteenth-century farce, *El paso de las olivas.* The original is a short skit about a husband and wife who begin counting the profits from their olives the day they plant the olive tree. Berg and Cohon added the character Scaramouche, who exploits both Pantalone and his family and their gullible neighbor Borracho with his promise of future wealth from the olives. They updated the play with references to the Vietnam War, the troupe's inability to get financial support from the city of San Francisco, and especially the economic squeeze on farmworkers. *Olive Pits* toured with *L'Amant Militaire* and *Eagle Fuck* during fall and winter 1967–68. The New York performances earned the troupe their first Obie (the off-Broadway awards presented by the *Village Voice*) for "uniting theatre and revolution and grooving in the park."

Olive Pits was banned at California State College at Fullerton. The Jack London Society had invited the troupe to perform it on their campus in February 1968. However, after learning from administrators about the troupe's use of obscene language in *A Minstrel Show,* the Faculty Council voted to forbid the performance. Four hundred students and faculty attended an anticensorship rally on campus, then walked off campus to an orange grove where the show was performed.

Commentary

Sandra Archer

Peter Berg and Peter Cohon (Coyote) took a Lope de Rueda play, tossed it at Mime Troupe actors, and, directed by R. G. Davis—voila! A one-act commedia was born. *Olive Pits* is a "slight" play, forty-five minutes, offered out-of-doors to lunch bag workers in downtown San Francisco, afternoon county fairs, and as a midday enticement at colleges and universities for the evening indoor performance of *L'Amant Militaire*. Get rich quick . . . still a timely temptation. Who are the Scaramouches today? Beware. Beware. (Telephone interview by Susan Vaneta Mason, 28 June 2002)

William C. Glackin

The comedy, like commedia, deals with the things about people which do not seem to change much over the years—cupidity, cunning, hostility, selfishness and sex—and certain aspects of society which derive from these qualities, such as, that the rich get richer and the poor get poorer. ("San Francisco Mime Troupe Shows Sly, Intricate Comic Style at Fair," *Sacramento Bee*, 28 May 1967)

Peter Coyote

Olive Pits . . . scripted by Peter Berg and me in one frenetic afternoon; we retired to separate rooms, each wrote a version, and then we returned to the rehearsal hall, where we cut and spliced the two scripts into a show that won the troupe a special Obie . . . later that year. (*Sleeping Where I Fall* [Washington, D.C.: Counterpoint, 1998], 57–58)

The Production

Olive Pits opened on 5 June 1966. The second version, which is given here, opened on 16 June 1967 in Delano, California, with the following cast:

Pantalone	*Arthur Holden*
Agueda	*Sandra Archer*
Menciguela	*Ellen Ernest*
Borracho	*Darryl Henriques*
Scaramouche	*Peter Cohon*

Directed by R. G. Davis and Sandra Archer. Set design by Jerome Marcel. Costumes by Ellen Zola. Masks and puppet: Francesca Green, Ann Willock. Technical director: Michael Oberndorf. Stage manager: Michael London. Publicity: Emma Grogan.

Characters (in order of appearance)

Pantalone, a farmer
Agueda, his wife
Menciguela, their daughter
Borracho, their neighbor
Scaramouche, a hustler

Olive Pits

Enter PANTALONE.

PANTALONE: Eh, Hombre, am I tired. Pantalone, why should a man as charming, as bright, and as able as you are have to work so hard? Why should you have to till the fields and sweat the way you do? Why God, why? *(Falls to knees.)*

MENCIGUELA, AGUEDA, BORRACHO, AND SCARAMOUCHE: *(Offstage.)* Because you're poor!

PANTALONE: Shaddup. Dat's my wife, Agueda, and my daughter, Menciguela. And I ask you. Do you know why I work so hard, sweating and putting every penny aside? It is for my daughter's dowry. So that she can stand a chance of marrying a nice young man from a nice rich home . . . and support me. Agueda, Menciguela, I want my supper!

They enter.

AGUEDA: Well, well, well, just look at our lord and master in another one of his nasty moods. What a wretched bunch of faggots you got loaded on your back.

PANTALONE: It took two of us to lift this wood from the earth. Take it away and make me some food.

AGUEDA: Take it away and make him some food.

PANTALONE drops wood on the floor.

MENCIGUELA: Take it away. *(Kicks wood offstage.)*

PANTALONE: What's in the house for supper?

AGUEDA AND MENCIGUELA: Well, let's see. In the house are: a barrel of red wine, a crate of figs, two jars of olives.

PANTALONE: . . . quick bring it here I'm starving.

AGUEDA: Not one pimiento! That and the money we've scrimped is for our poor dear Menciguela's dowry. So that she can marry a nice young man from a good family.

PANTALONE: Fine. She'll marry a man, not a stomach. Bring some food.

AGUEDA: You'll get what we normally eat. You'll not touch our daughter's dowry. Oh, that husband of mine, your Papa, always trying to fill his belly, ready to eat up the dowry. He doesn't realize that if we suffer a little now, eat less now, maybe for five or ten years, we will have saved a wonderful dowry for some husband for you, Menciguela.

MENCIGUELA: Yes, Mama, but haven't we saved enough by now? I myself am getting a little overripe.

AGUEDA: What? You are going to marry a good man, from a wealthy family. We are going to raise our position. Your, our little treasure box, will be our ticket to the shady side of the corrida.

PANTALONE: Come here, Menciguela.

MENCIGUELA: Yes, Papa.

PANTALONE: Ah, booby sweetie baby. Doesn't yous Papa work so hard?

MENCIGUELA: Yes, Papa.

PANTALONE: Who is it dat tills the fields all day for his sweet daughter?

MENCIGUELA: You, Papa.

PANTALONE: Who is it dat takes half of his money and gives it to little sweet booby for her dowry to marry a nice young fellow . . . a doctor?

MENCIGUELA: You, Papa.

PANTALONE: *(Hitting her.)* Me, eh? Go get me some food. I'm starving.

MENCIGUELA: I'm sorry, Papa, but you know that the dowry is for our future, not mine alone. It represents, among other things, a little nest egg for a rainy day; a little piece of security that should make you rest easier . . .

PANTALONE: In my grave! I ask for food, she gives me a passion play. Get out of here and fix me some food. Never mind. I'll fix my own food. *(He exits.)*

AGUEDA: On dat husband of mine. Not only are we never going to get anywhere because he don't do any work, but he has no sense of investments. He doesn't realize that if we suffer a little now, say for the first twenty or thirty years of our life, if we make ourselves miserable for the sake of our children, they will repay us a thousand-fold and we can live out the rest of our lives in comfort. Menciguela will marry a fine young man from a good home who will take care of us.

BORRACHO: *(From offstage.)* Graaanaaadaaa!

AGUEDA: It's dat drunken bum Borracho. Pantalone, quick!

PANTALONE *enters as* BORRACHO *comes in.*

BORRACHO: Pantalone?

PANTALONE *and family do a little song: "I am Rancho Grande."*

BORRACHO: Oh, Pantalone, what a happy family you have here. Singing and dancing, not like mine with my Serafina, fighting all the time.

AGUEDA: Why shouldn't she fight, you dolt? I'd fight too if I had a wineskin for a husband.

PANTALONE: Agueda, we should be hospitable to those less fortunate than ourselves.

AGUEDA: Okay, hospit, on them. Haach—*(She spits.)*

PANTALONE: Tooh! Hello, Borracho! My old friend!

BORRACHO: I knew that you wouldn't forget me, Pantalone. You remember when we were boys together? Dreaming of being great rancheros with herds of cattle and lots of pretty girls to comb our hair?

AGUEDA: Girls? What girls?

PANTALONE: Curls, Agueda! To comb our hair.

AGUEDA: What happened to your dreams, pissant?

BORRACHO: I'm proud to be a pissant. My people have been pissants for years, tilling the soil with honest, back-breaking labor. You are nouveau poor. Poverty has been in my family for generations.

MENCIGUELA: You do your best to maintain them old traditions, I see. But we have a dowry, and we have great dreams, and we are going to break the traditions of the poor.

PANTALONE: Yes, what about your dreams?

BORRACHO: The tradition of poverty is no small thing. It is carefully nurtured by the season, the soil, the climate, the rich. Ten years ago I tried to go against our Spanish tradition when a man came from Valencia with a scheme to make me millions from one olive shoot!

PANTALONE: Go on.

BORRACHO: He said that if I planted one shoot, then another, then another, that soon I would have trees on my land like grapes on the vine.

AGUEDA: Lucky you can't get juiced on olives.

BORRACHO: We talked about thousands of olives. I would raise them and he would market them, take the wagons, set up shop, pay off the inspectors. It was a good idea, no?

PANTALONE: But I've never seen olives on your land. You never grew them.

BORRACHO: We made a deal. I gave him all my money, ten Castilian reals . . . a fortune. He was to do it all. I never saw him no more. I couldn't pay my rent, I lost the house, the land. I was ruined. *(He weeps.)*

MENCIGUELA: You didn't have a contract?

BORRACHO: I never thought of it.

ALL: No contract! *(They laugh and then cry.)*

AGUEDA: Cretin!

MENCIGUELA: Fool!

PANTALONE: A contract! Dat's it you didn't have a contract.

BORRACHO: Oh! Pantalone. You were always so smart. Why didn't I know that you can't beat the system?

PANTALONE: You can't beat the system, dummy. Play with it. It's there to make people rich.

BORRACHO: No comprendo, amigo.

PANTALONE: Think a minute. Would anyone invent a system that didn't work? Would anyone labor for a system that didn't profit people? Would succeeding generations hold onto something dat didn't work?

BORRACHO: I don't know. Maybe.

PANTALONE: *(Hits him.)* Don't be a fool. All you have to do is know how to play. You didn't have a contract, that's all. You were dumb. This system was, after all, invented by the rich—by those people who had the benefit of education, of time to study, of food. Dey wouldn't make something that didn't work.

BORRACHO: What about the poor?

PANTALONE: They're stupid.

BORRACHO: Oh, Pantalone, this makes my throat dry. How about a little wine for old times sake—say a gallon?

PANTALONE: I'd be glad to help you out. *(PANTALONE hustles him off stage.)* Granaadaa!

DUMB SHOW: *The family shoots BORRACHO. He falls, they get him up, kick him out.*

PANTALONE: If only an opportunity would present itself, I would not make the same mistake as El Drinko, my neighbor.

SCARAMOUCHE: *(Enters between MENCIGUELA looking one way and AGUEDA looking the other. He pinches MENCIGUELA on the ass; she shrieks. AGUEDA looks around and winds up in SCARAMOUCHE's arms.)* Hey, Pantalone, what a fine family you got here!

PANTALONE: Ah, Scaramouche—the donkey thief.

SCARAMOUCHE: Those were the old days. I was a young boy . . .

PANTALONE: Then you went to stealing hubcaps . . .

SCARAMOUCHE: I was a wild youth, a crazy kid . . .

PANTALONE: Then it was selling holy water and bits of the cross . . .

SCARAMOUCHE: I was a foolish stripling.

PANTALONE: And last year, pimping in the Fillmore . . .

SCARAMOUCHE: Well, live and let live. You look marvelous, Pantalone. What a fine figure of a daughter you have. And your wife, I see is also alive.

MENCIGUELA: Is this the famous Señor Scaramouche? Where did you get those lovely clothes?

SCARAMOUCHE: You like them, my lovely?

MENCIGUELA: They're beautiful. Only last year you were so shabby, and now you look like . . .

SCARAMOUCHE: How about J. Paul Getty?

AGUEDA: How about an explanation?

SCARAMOUCHE: I struck it rich.

ALL: Rich?

SCARAMOUCHE: Rich!

PANTALONE: Rich like in money?

SCARAMOUCHE: Rich like in olives.

ALL: Olives?

SCARAMOUCHE: That's right. Olives. The finest olives in all of Spain. Cordovan olives: thick, sweet, and juicy. The kind that make children drool, women sweat, and men rich.

ALL: Rich?

MENCIGUELA: Sweat?

PANTALONE: Scaramouche, old friend, tell me about your prosperity.

SCARAMOUCHE: Well, Pantalone, that's exactly why I'm here. A minor trivial economic setback has forced me to find some aid—a partner if you will—and I immediately thought about my old friend.

ALL: You did?

SCARAMOUCHE: Of course. My stock of olive shoots has run low, and I find myself in need of minor amounts of capital to continue my prosperity. The returns, of course, are enormous: three or four hundred percent profit at the least.

PANTALONE: Three or four hundred percent? My God, we could be rich! Tell us what happens.

SCARAMOUCHE: Well, you start with one shoot and then another and another, and pretty soon you have a whole grove of olive trees, spreading their graceful branches across your acreage. They bear olives that will grace the tables of the finest homes; their oils will flavor the finest foods, their pits will clog the best toilets and drains . . .

PANTALONE: Okay, okay, but come to the point.

SCARAMOUCHE: The point, pinhead, is wealth. Gold, dineros, pesetas, shekels, gelt.

AGUEDA: Money. I know that Jewish syndrome.

SCARAMOUCHE: That's right, flowering lotus of Spain. Wealthy beyond your wildest dreams. Money. Clothes, food, good wines, blessings of the church, spices from the Indies, brukkas from the rabbi . . .

PANTALONE: All right—the business, the business, gimmee the business.

SCARAMOUCHE: I am here to give you the business. I am here to make you rich.

AGUEDA: He's here to make us rich. Blessed be the virgin. *(She goes down on her knees and kisses* SCARAMOUCHE'S *leg. He repeats line, she repeats.)*

PANTALONE: That's why we never get city support!

AGUEDA: Wait a minute, spittle-brain. What happens then?

SCARAMOUCHE: You will grow the olives; I will buy them. Simple as that.

AGUEDA: Ah, simple as that. Simple as that. We grow them. You buy them—and you sell them. Right?

SCARAMOUCHE: Right.

AGUEDA: How much you going to sell our olives for?

SCARAMOUCHE: I will sell your olives for fifteen dineros a half-peck.

PANTALONE: Fifteen dineros. Who would pay that much for a lousy olive?

SCARAMOUCHE: A lousy olive? A lousy olive? Pantalone, I'm ashamed of yourself. These are no ordinary wormy olives. These are Pantalone Premium Cordovan Gold. These will be the finest olives in all of Spain. Can you see your name up there on the banners over Córdoba and then Barcelona and Madrid? Pantalone Olives sold here. We will make the name Pantalone as big as baloney, Halvah, date-nut bread, even Coca-Cola . . .

AGUEDA AND MENCIGUELA *(Dance and sing.)* Coca-Cola grande, le da mucho mas.

SCARAMOUCHE: You will be famous. A power in Spain.

AGUEDA: Just a minute, goat droppings. You will sell them for fifteen dineros a half-peck. How much do we get for them?

SCARAMOUCHE: Well, let's see. It will cost eight dineros to market them, two to set up the stalls, two for Premises work, and I must make one dinero at least, so I could give you two dineros a half-peck. No, for friends I will cut out my profit completely so that I give you three dineros a half-peck.

AGUEDA: Three dineros!

SCARAMOUCHE: Calm yourself, my quivering silkworm of Spain. It doesn't sound like much, I know. After all, you say to yourself, "Self . . ."

AGUEDA: What can three dineros buy?

SCARAMOUCHE: You can't get into a pay toilet for that. But I would remind you that we are not discussing some crummy dirt farmer here. We are discussing Pantalone.

MENCIGUELA: There's a difference?

SCARAMOUCHE: We are discussing a man with thousands of trees at his disposal. We are talking about millions of olives. No?

MENCIGUELA: No.

PANTALONE: What do you mean, no?

MENCIGUELA: Yes?

SCARAMOUCHE: Of course, yes. Think big. Think olives. Olive loaf, olive jam . . .

PANTALONE: Olive drab, olive butter, Palmolive . . .

SCARAMOUCHE: Shall we call it a deal?

PANTALONE: Of course it's a deal. Do you think a genius would pass up a chance like this?

AGUEDA: Not so fast, bat guano. Remember your rummy friend.

PANTALONE: My father?

AGUEDA: No, Borracho. Come here? *(The family gets together.)* We need a contract!

PANTALONE: All right, Scaramouche. You thought you had us for a minute, there, but we have you now. The fox has outfoxed himself, and Pantalone the wife steps in where he stepped out. It's a deal with—and only with—a contract.

SCARAMOUCHE: A contract? Between friends? Between partners? Between brothers of business? A contract between you and me?

PANTALONE: A contract!

SCARAMOUCHE: *(Produces contract and feather pen.)* All right. Sign here.

PANTALONE: I can't read. *(Gives it to AGUEDA.)*

AGUEDA: I can't write. *(Gives it to MENCIGUELA.)*

MENCIGUELA: It says here that in one year he will return and we must produce twelve pecks of olives or the comparable price for them in money. If we don't, he owns the house and land.

PANTALONE: Why not my underwear?

MENCIGUELA: That's here, too.

PANTALONE: Is that all?

MENCIGUELA: No. There's another section here that says, "Fine Print."

AGUEDA: *(Fixing a beady eye on SCARAMOUCHE.)* Read it.

MENCIGUELA: It says: "Pursuant to capital expansion and maximal exploitation of resources, party of the first part finds it necessary to expropriate diverse monies from party of the second part and such monies will amount to a sum of not less than two hundred dineros."

PANTALONE: What the hell does that mean?

AGUEDA: We're dead.

SCARAMOUCHE: Not at all. A minor formality, I assure you. What, after all, are twelve pecks of olives to an olive millionaire dealing in thousands of pecks?

PANTALONE: What kind of peckhead would pass up a chance like that?

SCARAMOUCHE: Six pecks? Nothing. Don't founder your operation at the start with nickel-dime thinking, Pantalone.

AGUEDA: Nickel-dime is American money. We're Spanish. What about two hundred dineros which we ain't got?

SCARAMOUCHE: What about wealth, which you ain't got either? Think of your daughter. What will become of her? What about fine clothes, body lotions?

MENCIGUELA: Body lotions . . .

AGUEDA: We ain't got two hundred dineros, buddy. Forget it.

MENCIGUELA: Momma . . .

AGUEDA: What?

MENCIGUELA: What about the dowry?

AGUEDA: The dowry!

MENCIGUELA: The dowry.

AGUEDA: Pantalone. Did you hear that? The dowry.

PANTALONE: The dowry. You said the dowry? *(Hits her.)*

AGUEDA: Yes, the dowry we've put aside so that Menciguela can marry a rich young man to support us.

MENCIGUELA: Momma, I learned in school all about investments. The teacher invests, the principal invests. They all invest money to make money.

PANTALONE: What do you mean invest? How do you spell dat?

MENCIGUELA: R-I-S-K. "Invest." You take a risk and cause you do that, you make money or lose it.

AGUEDA: Yeah. What happens if you lose it?

MENCIGUELA: You invest someone else's.

SCARAMOUCHE: Listen, Pantalone. Invest the dowry. In a year you'll be a rich man and you can put it back. Anyway, by that time I'll be rich again, too, and I'll put it into the contract that I will marry Menciguela—with or without a dowry.

AGUEDA: You will marry Menciguela. Blessed be the Virgin. *(Repeat knee routine.)* Pantalone, our troubles will be over. Menciguela will be married and we'll be rich.

MENCIGUELA: Aha! I'll be married and they'll be rich . . . wait a minute . . .

SCARAMOUCHE: Sign the contract.

PANTALONE AND AGUEDA: Of course. *(La la-ing to the tune of "Rancho Grande" and doing a bamba, they sign one by one.)*

SCARAMOUCHE: All right, children. The money. *(All scurry.)*

PANTALONE: Here it is, Scaramouche. We give you this money because as Marx said, "You got a contract in de pocket, you got money in de bank."

AGUEDA: Dat wasn't Marx. Dat was Eisenhower.

SCARAMOUCHE: Pantalone, Agueda, Menciguela: hasta luego; hasta mañana. I'll see you in one year. And remember: Maledictum rottenum bonum pimentum MacNamarum est. *(Exits.)*

PANTALONE: What'd he say?

MENCIGUELA: Don't sell no olives to the Viet Cong.

AGUEDA: Hey, Pantalone, maybe we don't even need him. I could gather the olives, you could cart them off to town on your little ass, and our Menciguela could sell them. And Menciguela, be sure you don't sell nothing else.

MENCIGUELA: Yes, Momma.

AGUEDA: And don't you dare sell our olives for less than fifteen dineros a half-peck.

PANTALONE: Fifteen dineros! Good gracious, woman, what are you talking about? Such a price would give us nightmares. My conscience would quiver and, besides, the market inspector would never allow it.

AGUEDA: Seventeen?

PANTALONE: No. Nine or ten at the most.

AGUEDA: Posh, Pantalone. You're forgetting that our olives are the finest in all of Spain.

PANTALONE: Despite the fact that our olives are the finest in all of Spain, my price is right.

AGUEDA: Pantalone, up your prices. Menciguela, don't you dare sell our olives for less than fifteen dineros a half-peck.

MENCIGUELA: Yes, Momma.

PANTALONE: What do you mean, "Yes, Momma?" Menciguela, how much are you gonna ask?

MENCIGUELA: Whatever you say, Poppa.

PANTALONE: Uhh . . . nine or ten dineros.

MENCIGUELA: So be it, Poppa.

AGUEDA: What do you mean, "So be it, Poppa?" Menciguela, how much are you going to ask?

MENCIGUELA: Whatever you say, Momma.

AGUEDA: Fifteen dineros.

PANTALONE: What do you mean, fifteen dineros? I'll give you fifteen punches in the mouth if you disobey me. How much are you going to ask?

MENCIGUELA: Whatever you say, Poppa.

PANTALONE: Nine or ten dineros!

MENCIGUELA: So be it, Poppa.

AGUEDA: Whattaya mean, "So be it, Poppa?" You take this "so be it" and that "so be it" and this, and that . . .

PANTALONE: Don't brutalize the child. Well, what do you think of your Poppa now, children? Pantalone, the planter. From such tiny beginnings, one olive shoot, you could build a kingdom, a dynasty . . .

AGUEDA: A cosmic olive.

PANTALONE: Dat's right. Den we got to have the packing boxes, the pitting machines, the pimientos, and the small pointy-fingered Italians to fill the olive jars.

MENCIGUELA: We need books for the bookkeeping, a press for the pressing . . .

AGUEDA: Dat's smart, kid! Olive oil!

PANTALONE: Dat's right. Just what you look like.

MENCIGUELA: And trucks for the trucking, labels for labeling, workers for working, labor unions, scabs . . .

AGUEDA: Now there's only one way to take care of all this stuff. I propose we start a regular business.

PANTALONE: A corporazione.

AGUEDA: And I'm President of the Board.

PANTALONE: Whattaya mean? It was my idea. I'm President.

AGUEDA: Could I be Vice President? Please, Pantalone, a little vice presidency? For your Agueda? Your turtle dove for thirty years: always loyal, washing your shirts . . .

PANTALONE: Why not? All right. At least I can trust someone in the family . . .

AGUEDA: With power of veto, co-signee, and power of attorney! Thank you, Pantalone, father of our little Menciguela. To think that all this can come from one deal. I feel like breaking into song. *(Family dances around singing: "My mother was a capitalista, just like my fatha and my sistah . . . Oh, boy, oh, boy, oh boy.")* All this from one olive shoot. One tiny shoot. How sweet it is. Let me see it once. *(No one moves.)* Let me see the sweet and lovely little olive branch, the symbol of our prosperity. *(Nothing.)* C'mon, let me see it.

PANTALONE: I thought you had it.

MENCIGUELA: Me? No. I thought you had it.

AGUEDA: Where is it?

PANTALONE: Death. *(He falls down.)* Come quickly from the skies and kill me. Kill me before I am dishonored.

AGUEDA: Dishonored? What about disemboweled, you simpleton? You forgot the shoot. How could you?

PANTALONE: Maybe it wilted. Where's the contract?

AGUEDA: Screw the contract. We must get a shoot tomorrow. Right away. We plant one tomorrow and one the next day and we have a nice grove of olives in about . . . twenty-five years . . . *(Faints.)*

PANTALONE: Did she say twenty-five years? She couldn't have.

MENCIGUELA: She did.

PANTALONE: No!

AGUEDA: Yes.

PANTALONE: Yes! *(All start weeping. MENCIGUELA runs off, comes back with a twig.)* What's dat?

MENCIGUELA: An avocado shoot. Maybe he won't notice.

PANTALONE: *(Hits her.)* Shut up, dummy. Let your father think. *(MENCIGUELA drops on one knee. PANTALONE sits on the other and assumes pose of The Thinker. AGUEDA walks offstage and comes back with a sign: "Six Months Pass." She circles off and comes back with a sign that says "Eleven and 9/10 Months Pass." As she passes by, PANTALONE snaps to life.)* I'll be back soon. Don't despair. Pantalone will take care of everything.

AGUEDA: You've already taken care of everything, you dummy. What more harm can you do? We stand to lose the house and land. We've lost the dowry. Not only are we poor, but it looks like we have an old maid to support unless she marries that pimp. I wonder what your father will do this time, child . . .

SCARAMOUCHE: *(Enters.)* Well, well, well, if it isn't the twin sisters of high finance. How are you dumplings? I can almost smell the olives in the air.

AGUEDA: That's not olives. What do you want, Shylock?

SCARAMOUCHE: Want? Nothing. I came to see how our fortunes were coming, and thought I might pick up the lives or—heh heh—the money. And I thought that if, perhaps, only perhaps, you didn't have either the money or the olives, perhaps we could make some other kind of deal. *(Leers at MENCIGUELA.)*

MENCIGUELA: *(Blushes and curtsies, giggles like a schoolgirl, bows to SCARA-MOUCHE and shows him her tits.)* Meal ticket.

AGUEDA: Menciguela, you have no pride.

MENCIGUELA: I do, but it's not as big as my appetite.

PANTALONE: *(Rushing in.)* Hold it. Hold it! Stop everything! Stand back, you moldy dog. Pantalone is here to save the day. Don't worry, dear wife, you will not be poor. Don't worry, daughter, you will have your dowry. Here you are, Scaramouche. The money we owe you. Now, be off! *(Hands SCARAMOUCHE a wad of bills.)*

AGUEDA: How beautiful.

MENCIGUELA: A movie finish. It breaks my heart. We've saved the corporation.

SCARAMOUCHE: Fine, Pantalone. Fine. I'm glad to see you came through. Of course, I knew that you would, which is why I approached you in the first place. There is no need to panic. This is, after all, a deal among friends.

PANTALONE: Quite right. You see, there was nothing to fear.

AGUEDA: Where did you get all the money?

PANTALONE: Aha! I consolidated all my debts into one easy monthly payment. I borrowed from the Money Angel Corporation. So easy. No fuss or embarrassment. They saved the day with cash.

MENCIGUELA: Oh, Poppa! I'm so proud of you. I'm so happy! *(Family dances around in joy while SCARAMOUCHE pulls a paper from his pocket.)*

PANTALONE: Still here, eh? Well, Scaramouche, you can go now. You've gotten your money and we're free of you. All that's left now are my easy monthly payments to the Money Angel. A tough lesson, but one well-learned.

SCARAMOUCHE: *(Hands him the paper.)* I'm sorry to bother you in this moment of joy, Pantalone, but one minute more won't affect your rejoicing. Give me just a moment.

PANTALONE: Of course.

SCARAMOUCHE: If you will read here you will see that the Money Angel is a subsidiary of another company called SFC.

PANTALONE: SFC? What's dat?

SCARAMOUCHE: A little loan company called Scaramouche Finance Corporation. If you'll read the paper you'll see that the payments are not monthly, as you thought, but hourly—and the first installment is due right now. *(Holds out hand.)*

PANTALONE: Wait a minute! You're not the fellow I borrowed the money from. He didn't say anything to me about you. He had nothing to do with you. *(Turns to family.)* He was a gentleman with a big moustache! *(Turns to see* SCARAMOUCHE *wearing Dottore mask with moustache.)*

SCARAMOUCHE: Well, Pantalone, we're both gentlemen and, believe me, it's the last thing from my mind to press the point. I'm sure that between us we can come to some kind of amicable settlement. Here we have on the one hand you: impoverished, house and land gone, nothing to your credit except one mature, fully-ripened daughter; and, on the other hand, me with a pure and clean heart in my loins and your funds and property in my pocket.

MENCIGUELA: Aha! I see your plan, Scaramouche, and it will never work. We may be poor but we are honorable. Never let it be said that Pantalone, for want of food, funds, or housing, would sell his one and only daughter into the clutches of a fiendish Shylock. You do us wrong, sir. Tell him, Poppa. *(*PANTALONE *and* AGUEDA *have been adding up the deal.)* Poppa? Poppa!

PANTALONE: Shut, you ungrateful wench. After all, pah! you get what you deserve. Let that be a lesson to the ingrate. Just remember: we all get what we deserve. Let's go pack her bags. *(*PANTALONE *and* AGUEDA *exit.)*

SCARAMOUCHE: *(Grabs* MENCIGUELA *in a Valentino clutch.)* The moral of this small romance, where the poor play at high finance, should be immediately accessible to you ken, if you've ever played the game of borrow-lend. We that control the system, take your values and then we twist them. So it makes no difference what you do, we get richer and you get screwed!

The End

Telephone

1970

Script by Steve Friedman

Introduction

Telephone, originally published in *Ramparts* (August 1970), makes use of a form of guerrilla theater: gutter puppets. It is also a Mime Troupe *lehrstücke*. Just as the man sets up the operator, Babs, to catch her teaching customers how to cheat the phone company, the play is a set up to inform spectators how to charge long-distance phone calls to corporations. The judge puppet at the end is the ultimate fall guy, naively bringing up other scams while trying to ascertain Babs's crime. Meanwhile the information about how to charge long-distance calls to corporations is repeated three times.

Commentary

R. G. Davis

Gutter puppets arose out of a general cooperative thinking process. The box might have come from Peter Schumann's Bread and Puppet work. We used a gutter puppet in *L'Amant Militaire*. The puppet box was outside the show frame, and he would critically attack the content, from a more militant view. For example, the puppet suggested blowing up an induction center (it was a puppet, remember!) Another puppet show was put together by myself, Eric Bern, and Charlie Degelman for Friends of the Library. For this I wrote *Bookworm* and Bern wrote *Little Black Panther*. The park lunchtime shows, another venue, had a constant audience, since we obtained permits to play where office workers ate their lunch. *Meter Maid* and *Telephone* were designed for them. The idea for tab tops in parking meters and credit card calls, we learned from hippies and others who had discovered these scams. Breaking the law via these penny ante efforts was less dangerous if everyone did it; quantity could turn into quality. In this affluent country, pilfering, petty thievery, shoplifting, is an American sport—we didn't believe that this would lead to any revolution, only a way to survive daily sniveling annoyances. It was a kind of jolly practice for other, larger, "crimes against the state." (Interview by Susan Vaneta Mason, 10 May 2002)

David Kolodney

Public opinion polls indicate that the general popularity of the phone company is somewhat less than that of the parking meter industry. The new Mime Troupe entertainment, thus assured a good, hostile audience, is essentially educational. It describes a method for making up do-it-yourself telephone credit cards for use on station-to-station calls from phone booths. ("San Francisco Mime Troupe: Ripping Off Ma Bell," *Ramparts*, August 1970, 26)

The Production

Telephone was first performed in 1970 with the following cast:

Operator	*Sharon Lockwood*
Man	*Jael Weisman*
Judge Puppet	*Steve Friedman*

Characters (in order of appearance)

Babs, an operator
A Man
Judge Puppet

Telephone
MAN *dials* OPERATOR.

OPERATOR: May I help you?
MAN: Yes, operator, I'd like to place a long distance call to Zap, North Dakota, station to station.
OPERATOR: Please deposit three dollars and 95 cents.
MAN: Three dollars and 95 cents?

OPERATOR: Yes, sir, for the first three minutes.

MAN: But operator, I'm calling my Guru!

OPERATOR: Your Guru, sir?

MAN: Yes, operator, he's very sick. And I don't have that kind of change.

OPERATOR: Perhaps you could place the call from your home phone, sir.

MAN: I don't have a "home phone sir."

OPERATOR: Would you care to reverse the charges?

MAN: That might kill him!

OPERATOR: Oh, sir, don't you have a credit card?

MAN: A—credit card?

OPERATOR: Yes, sir. With a credit card you could place the call at your employer's expense.

MAN: I could?

OPERATOR: Yes, sir. Suppose for example you worked for the Bank of America here in San Francisco. When the operator came on the line you would simply say, "Operator, I wish to make a credit card call. My credit card number is S-756–0400–158." And the call would go through without any further ado.

MAN: What was that code again, operator?

OPERATOR: S as in Sabotage, 756–0400–158.

MAN: Thank you, and you are out of service.

OPERATOR: This is a recording?

MAN: It's no use, Babs, we gotcha.

OPERATOR: But how? . . . How?

MAN: We've had our eye on you for a long time, Babs—first it was just a bit of grass in the ladies' room on your breaks—now it's the big time, isn't it, Babs? The old story. Yeah, yeah, yeah.

OPERATOR: All right, I don't care, I hate Pacific Telephone! Why do they get away with being a monopoly? Why don't they lower their rates instead of printing all those glossy brochures to send out with the phone bills? Who for God's sake needs a Princess Phone?

MAN: *(Pulls a gun on her.)* You're going to the Big House, Babs, for a long, long stretch.

OPERATOR: *(Gives Man a karate chop and runs into audience.)* OK, everybody, the phone code goes like this: The credit cards are renewed annually and S is the code for 1970. The second part can be any number in the San Francisco phone book. I just picked Bank of America because they're such a big company—they'll never notice a little extra padding on their phone bill. Did you know that 10,000 false credit card calls were charged last year to the Dow Chemical Company alone?

MAN: All right, Babs, one more word and I'll blow your goddam head off.

OPERATOR: The last part, 158, is the city code of San Francisco. So the code is really S—any number in the San Francisco phone book—158. Always call from a pay phone—and always call station-to-station.

MAN: All right, Babs, take that *(Fires gun at her.)* These goddam M-16s.

OPERATOR: Because that way, even if they do catch you, there's nothing they can do—if the person you call is cool and just denies receiving the call. It's a bug in the system—and brothers and sisters, they can afford it.

MAN: OK, Babs, it's all over. There's only one problem with your little scheme. Why take it out on the innocent public-spirited companies like Dow, United Fruit, Levi Strauss?

OPERATOR: Because they're imperialist lackey running dogs and we should screw them whenever we get the chance!

MAN: Hey, wait a minute, you're not gonna claim to be one of those political prisoners, are you?

OPERATOR: Sure, why not? In Cuba the phones are free. All of them!

MAN: OK, Babs, seeing as how you have all these weird opinions and all, we're going to have to throw the book at you. *(Takes out a small book and throws it at her.)* It'll be a swift and speedy trial, so let's pay a little call on the JUDGE-O-MAT.

OPERATOR: The what?

MAN: THE JUDGE-O-MAT—instant justice! The latest device in the war against crime and overcrowded courtrooms. Let's take a little mosey. *(OPERATOR and MAN cross to puppet box.)*

JUDGE: Order in the court! Charge, please!

MAN: Misdemeanor, your honor-mat.

JUDGE: Offense, please.

MAN: Telephones, your honor-mat.

JUDGE: Oh, you must mean the old stamp dodge.

MAN: The old stamp dodge, what's that?

OPERATOR: The old stamp dodge—you know—not putting a six cent stamp on your phone bill, so the phone company has to pay the postage.

MAN: Oh no, it's worse than that sir.

JUDGE: Then you mean the old spindle swindle.

MAN: The old spindle swindle?

OPERATOR: The old spindle swindle—that's punching an extra hole in your phone bill so the computers freak out.

MAN: No, your honor-mat, this is credit cards.

JUDGE: Oh—you mean the old S—any number in the SF phone book—dodge.

OPERATOR: Hey—you're hip to the phone code—you musta been talking to some of my friends.

JUDGE: Felony! Felony!

MAN: No, no, it's a misdemeanor, your honor-mat.

JUDGE: Talking is conspiracy; conspiracy to commit a misdemeanor is a felony. Please deposit an additional ten cents. *(MAN does so.)* Sentence! Six months suspended, three weeks Santa Rita, one semester *(name school)*. Lock her up.

OPERATOR: Fascist scum, your days are numbered!

OPERATOR OF JUDGE PUPPET: *(Emerging barefaced.)* Come on, lady, I'm just trying to do my job!

OPERATOR: *(To the tune of "Yellow Submarine," dancing.)* Call your friends, it's just a dime / from California / on company time / say my cre-e-e-dit card is S / any nu-umber 158.

MAN: *(In rhythm.)* You're under arrest.

BOTH: *(Dancing together chorus line fashion.)* Call your friends on the People's Telephone, People's Telephone, Call your friends *(Etc. Dance off.)*

The End

2. The 1970s: All Art Is Political

During the 1970s the San Francisco Mime Troupe struggled to reinvent itself. Besides learning how to operate as a collective, they adapted their membership and outreach to reflect a multicultural society. They created over twenty original productions in addition to Brecht's *The Mother* and Dario Fo's *We Can't Pay, We Won't Pay*, were awarded their second Obie, and made their first European tour. They bought a studio in the Mission District, still their home, and began an eight-year battle against the construction of an elite Performing Arts Center. Although the company started the decade at the top of its form with two back-to-back successes, later in the decade, during the Carter administration, the work was less successful. Nevertheless, Stewart McBride praised them in the *Christian Science Monitor* in 1980, saying they had lowered their "elephant gun on everything from urban renewal to inflation, male chauvinism to big business, nuclear power to rough toiletpaper."[1]

Although domestic issues dominated the troupe's focus during the decade, their biggest, most successful productions focused on American policies abroad. Public protests against the war in Vietnam escalated as the United States invaded Laos and Cambodia and Lt. William Calley was sentenced to life for his role in the massacre at My Lai. The war did not end until 1975, and by then fifty thousand American soldiers had been killed in Southeast Asia. Watergate and the resignation of President Nixon in 1974 completed the collapse of public trust in the government. This loss of faith in traditional institutions prompted the emergence of identity politics on both the right and the left: Christian fundamentalists, feminists, environmentalists, American Indian activists, the farmworkers movement. President Carter's greatest victory and defeat occurred in quick succession late in the decade: the Camp David accord that brought Egypt and Israel together in 1978 was followed by the Iran hostage crisis. The decade ended with a near-disaster at Three Mile Island reminding the public of the potential devastation in the conflict between business and the natural world.

The Company

The San Francisco Mime Troupe's transition into a collective at the end of 1969 was, in Joan Holden's view, inevitable.[2] As the group's political ideology evolved during the 1960s and the plays increasingly advocated social change, the organizational structure had to change as well. During the first decade the company had employed various degrees of collaboration in the creation of productions (*The Dowry* and *A Minstrel Show* in particular were collaborative efforts), and had attempted systems of shared artistic governance twice, in 1968 and 1969. However, once the troupe chose to become a collective, that structure informed everything they did: administrative operation, the creation of productions, relationships with the public, and, as an expression of politics, the subject matter of plays.

The idea of reorganizing as a collective had been planted in 1969 while the troupe worked on the production of Brecht's *Congress of Whitewashers* by studying Marx's theory of common ownership of the means of production. Robert Scheer notes the irony in Davis's helping "the company to take seriously the ideas of Marx and the Chinese Revolution, while still seeking to maintain his individual prerogatives. It could not hold."[3] However, when Davis left, the troupe first reverted to traditional structures. According to Joan Holden, "Sandy Archer, who was second in command to Davis—this was typical of how we weren't moving collectively—automatically became the director. But she wasn't ready to assume the burden of being 'the genius' of the company. . . . when she left [with Saul Landau in 1971], we had to face the idea that we were going on without 'geniuses.'"[4]

A great mystique seems to have grown around Davis's departure, and much has been written about it, but Arthur Holden described the process simply: "The break was pretty much of an ideological one, having to do with how you organize a group of people for artistic enterprises. . . . Obviously Ronnie having been the boss, he was on that side; and all of the others of us were the workers. It was pretty straightforward."[5] In the documentary *Troupers* (1985), Joan Holden says "There were three years of fighting between the company and Ronny, and they were really about authority and control. . . . Most of us didn't want Ronny to go, but we just wanted to have more to say."[6]

Like Davis's departure, the troupe's transition into a collective has generated a great deal of commentary, and comparisons between the two eras abound, from both troupe members and outsiders.[7] It may be useful to consider the structural reorganization as one of a series of changes, albeit the most sweeping one, and to consider what stayed the same despite the changes. The troupe's political ideology continued to develop but did not shift radically between the two decades. Many aspects of Davis's practical methods and aesthetic values were also retained: weekly meetings, a weekly schedule of work, rehearsals, and performances, the reading of political theory, the park setup procedure, passing the hat and college tours to generate income, the performance style, training in specific acting skills, and the mission of social change. The company's reputation was retained as well. Furthermore, as former trouper Denny Partridge noted, "Art was always the uniting factor in both the 60s and the 70s."[8]

In spite of political theories, the troupe had to find its way into collective organization. Steve Friedman, who wrote or cowrote about eight of the troupe's plays, recalled "a surge of creativity after Davis left, because people were very frightened by the idea of working without a director. We just didn't know of any precedents for a theatre group that didn't have a person in charge."[9]

During the first phase, roughly 1970–74, all members at one time or another participated in all aspects of putting on productions. Their creative output was enormous and varied. The first structure that emerged equalized responsibility: all members assumed an administrative, a household, and a creative job. In his doctoral dissertation, Lance Jencks describes the minutes from troupe meetings in the 1960s as "neatly typed in outline form, with reports offered department by department." Minutes after 1970 "are usually hand-written, and record rambling, unorganized discussions among Troupe members."[10] However, members found a kind of freedom in adopting unfamiliar roles, and everyone who stayed was committed to the viability of the organization. In 1977 Holden noted the difficulties and benefits of collectivity: "It's hard to create anything collectively, it's hard to run anything collectively, but in the end, it's the only way to form a cohesive group."[11] Later, in 1983, she attributed the company's endurance to their collective organization: "the company has survived because of the investment we've all put into it. It's 20 times the energy we would have put in if we had felt we were working for one person."[12]

In 1970, the troupe created a "three point program" that defined their goals and expressed a clear ideology: (1) All art is political. (2) Serve the people. (3) Smash individualism.[13] All three focused the troupe's revolutionary mission established in the 1960s.

The company had already embraced the political role of art in the 1960s when their mission was to "direct society toward change." However, their political ideas about social change and, consequently, the political content of the plays became clearer in the 1970s.[14] All their plays, Holden noted, shared a common message directed to working-class spectators: "There is a class system in this country that is not run in your interest. It is run in the interest of rich people and they fool you about your interest."[15]

The charge of serving the people translated into addressing and representing the concerns of working-class people from diverse cultures in their plays and expanding the demographics of their audience. To accomplish both, the company had to become multiracial. Although *A Minstrel Show* included black actors in the cast and the creation of the text, and Luis Valdez had spent a season with the troupe, in 1970 the company was, according to Friedman, essentially "white middle-class college dropouts or disgruntled college graduates" playing to a middle-class white audience.[16] Mindful of the moral and ethical issues raised by white cultural colonialism, in 1974 the collective voted to put a hiring freeze on white actors. "The group was still discussing how best to implement the affirmative action policy, when African American actor Lonnie Ford walked in and announced he was joining the company. Deb'bora Gilyard, Esteban Oropeza, and Maria Acosta soon followed."[17] By the end of the decade the troupe had achieved cultural diversity with white, black, and Latino members. The growing Asian population in California would change the company's demographics again in the 1980s. After 1974, all the troupe's plays became multiracial.

In an attempt to reach more diverse spectators, especially from the working class, they tried to shift their emphasis away from performing on college campuses to performing for union organizations and various community action groups. College tours continued, but the troupe also did benefits for the United Farm Workers, supported striking longshoremen, and aided the organizing efforts of taxi drivers. They performed in the county jail once a year.

Smashing individualism was achieved through their collective company structure and the collective creation of their plays. However, in her article describing their collective process, Holden was quick to point out that the troupe never abolished the writer, director, or designer, but rather gave members the opportunity to try different areas.[18] They did, however, discontinue individual attribution on their programs. Many shows in the 1970s were identified as authored by the company, and individual cast members were not identified with specific roles. Writers and composers were listed only if they were not members of the collective. In *By Popular Demand*, consisting of scripts and songs from the 1970s, credits for the plays are listed with a statement describing the company's collective practices:

> All plays in this book were collective productions in the sense that their content was developed by the company as a whole. The scripts were written in different ways: by one writer, by two or several, by a writer working with performers, by a writer working with a committee. Suggestions and criticism from informed outsiders were always solicited, and often

incorporated. Each piece was more or less heavily revised in the course of rehearsal and performance, so the scripts as they appear here bear the mark of the performers and directors as well as the writers. In the same fashion, technicians and musicians contributed to the designs they executed and the music they played. With this disclaimer, credits are given, although they have not appeared in the company's programs.[19]

Davis had begun the practice of soliciting suggestions and criticism from outsiders. He had, for example, invited members from the civil rights organizations CORE (Congress of Racial Equality) and SNCC (Student Nonviolent Coordinating Committee) to attend *A Minstrel Show* previews and give feedback. The troupe continued this practice in later shows. In 1970, the committee defending Los Siete (seven Latinos in the Mission District accused of killing an undercover policeman) was invited to rehearsals of *Los Siete,* and feminist organizations previewing *The Independent Female* caused Holden to make significant changes in the script.[20]

Other aspects of their collective practice were to be found in daily organization and salaries. Each of the eighteen company members had "a creative function, a paper-work assignment, and a housekeeping job" in their six-room studio in a warehouse at 450 Alabama Street. "We serve lunch for twenty-five cents. Once a week, on Mondays, when there's an evening meeting, dinner is served for fifty cents."[21] One room in the studio was the library, where required political reading was available. Company members worked eight to ten hours a day, six days a week. In 1970 company members earned thirty dollars a week. With these poverty wages, many members lived together in three or four different houses.

Touring college campuses continued to be the primary means of support for the company throughout the decade. The fall tour generally ran from late October to early December, and a spring tour usually followed. Contributions at summer shows supplemented tour proceeds. The fee for touring productions was $750 in 1970, and increased to $1,500 in 1973.

In 1974 the company's budget grew to $84,000, and members were earning $40 a week. By the end of the decade the budget had grown to $130,000 and salaries to $100 a week. A good park day in the late 1970s yielded $1,600 in donations.

The troupe continued the policy established in the 1960s of not applying for government grants. They did, however, apply for local funding. In San Francisco a hotel tax is collected for a Publicity and Advertising Fund allocated to individuals and organizations that promote tourism in the city. The troupe had been awarded $1,000 from the P & A Fund in 1964 and again in 1965. However, the latter allocation was rescinded after Davis's arrest. They continued to apply and were denied funding every year from 1966 to 1977.

The lion's share of the P & A funding went to elite organizations (the opera, the symphony, ACT) with allocations of under $10,000 awarded to a variety of smaller groups. After yet another rejection from P & A in 1973, the San Francisco Mime Troupe and Mission Media Arts filed a complaint in Superior Court against Chief Administrative Officer Thomas Mellon and city officials for dispersing hotel tax funds illegally. Mission Media Arts had received funds in 1971 and 1972, but after joining a grassroots organization protesting the building of a downtown Performing Arts Center, funding was denied. The Mime Troupe had been outspoken in their opposition to the Performing Arts Center as well, especially in their 1972 production, *San Fran Scandals.*

In September 1974, Judge Ira Brown ruled that the city had to change the way funds were distributed. The troupe still received nothing from P & A. A few months later Herb Caen decried this oversight in his column in the *San Francisco Chronicle*: "The SF Mime Troupe, performing Brecht in New York [*The Mother*, 1973], has been getting great spreads in the *New York Times* but still not a cent from the San Francisco Hotel Tax Fund, and that's ridiculous."[22] Finally, in 1977, after Mellon, who had distributing the funds since 1964, was replaced, the troupe was awarded $10,000 from the Hotel Tax fund, their first grant since 1965. The company has received funds from P & A, now Grants for the Arts, ever since, an acknowledgment of its cultural value to the city.

In 1976 and 1977 the company also received grants of $22,000 from the California Arts Council to subsidize tours. Two of Governor Jerry Brown's appointees to the CAC were former Mime Troupe members, Peter Coyote and Luis Valdez, who recognized the integrity and importance of the troupe's work as well as their very real financial need.

The back-to-back successes of *The Independent Female* and *The Dragon Lady's Revenge* at the beginning of the decade ensured the company's financial success and gave them the funds to buy a permanent home: "Proceeds from *Dragon Lady*, and help from a friend, Evelyn Silver, supplied the down payment on a vacant warehouse in the Mission District at 855 Treat Avenue in 1973."[23] The warehouse, once a recording studio for Fantasy Records, has office space and a kitchen upstairs, with a rehearsal room, shop, and storage downstairs.

Turnover in company membership was high as a direct result of their financial struggle. In the mid-1970s Holden, like Davis a decade earlier, commented on the burnout of actors "with these struggling groups that don't have any money."[24] In 1971 the collective included Dan Chumley, Steve Friedman, Joan Holden, Sharon Lockwood, Joan Mankin, Larry Pisoni, Peggy Snider, Andrea Snow, Denny Partridge Stevens, Patricia Silver, and Jael Weisman. By 1976, only five of the original collective remained (Chumley, Holden, Lockwood, Silver, and Snow). Arthur Holden had rejoined, and new members included Maria Acosta, Bruce Barthol, Lonnie Ford, Deb'bora Gilyard, Ed Levey, and Esteban Oropeza.

The Productions

In order to develop a more diverse audience, the troupe began looking for an American equivalent of commedia. In a 1971 interview about troupe practices, Friedman explained that commedia was an indirect, metaphoric way of making political commentary and that the company was "saying things much more directly now."[25] Although commedia had remained the principal style in the 1960s, the troupe had investigated other styles in *A Minstrel Show, The Exception and the Rule,* and *Congress of Whitewashers,* among others. Although commedia characters were dropped in 1970, elements of commedia, such as exaggerated acting, touring, and performing outside, have remained fundamental to the Mime Troupe's style for their entire history, and commedia character work is still part of their actor training. They still use masks on occasions, often when portraying world leaders.

Their experimentation with American forms of popular entertainment in the 1970s included melodrama, comics, movies, circus techniques, and musical theater. Melodrama in particular became a major genre for the company and one to which they have returned often. Musical theater emerged as their established style by the mid-1970s. In addition, they continued working with epic techniques Davis had employed in *The Exception and the Rule* and *The Congress of Whitewashers.*

Melodrama was not only the most popular American theatrical style in the nineteenth century, it remains the dominant style of movies and television dramas. The plot of melodrama, according to Holden, is simply "an underdog fights an overlord and wins." She suggests that the strength of the genre is its moral simplicity: "We know who the big polluters are; why the country is in debt; what 'freedom fighters' are doing in Third World nations and who puts them up to it. We know that the country, plus as much of the world as it can reach, is coming to be ruled by a secret government of spies and right-wing billionaires. These things come down to matters of right and wrong."[26] Davis, on the other hand, criticized the troupe's use of melodrama for failing to challenge leftist attitudes: "the form complements the left's assumption of right-ness at the precise moment of its greatest confusion."[27] This distinction highlights some basic differences between the troupe in the 1960s and 1970s and an ongoing debate within what Robert Scheer calls the "fratricidal left" about how best to do leftist work.[28] Davis's target audience was leftist intellectuals, and he championed an overtly intellectual, analytical approach; the collective sought a broader class base and thus drew from diverse forms of popular entertainment, especially melodrama with its clear-cut right and wrong.

Holden's belief in the political potential of melodrama is shared by Peter Brooks, who has written about the origins of the genre in the French Revolution and its underlying democratic nature: "Among the repressions broken through by melodramatic rhetoric is that of class domination, suggesting that a poor persecuted girl can confront her powerful oppressor with the truth about their moral conditions."[29] That confrontation between oppressed and oppressor, found in numerous troupe shows since 1970, is perhaps clearest in such landlord eviction plots as *San Fran Scandals* (1972) and *Hotel Universe* (1977). However, the most direct use of melodrama was in Holden's first original play, *The Independent Female, or A Man Has His Pride* (1970).

Although *Independent Female,* Holden's feminist melodrama, first parodied the form, she discovered the power of its moral dimension and in revisions played it straight, with ironic character and plot inversions and more comic relief than a classic melodrama. The story involves Gloria Pennybank, caught between her betrothed, John Heartright, and her liberated coworker Sarah. John wants Gloria to give up her job and be a homemaker once they are married; Sarah wants Gloria to stay at work and organize the women to strike for equal pay for equal work. John eventually kills Sarah, and Gloria, rather than assuming the traditional gender role John has in mind, carries on Sarah's work. In a traditional Victorian melodrama, John would be the hero, Gloria the heroine, and Sarah the villain. Played within the context of the feminist movement of the 1970s, John and the patriarchy he represents are revealed to be the villain and Sarah is the hero, rescuing Gloria from an unrealized life. The happy ending is not the marriage of John and Gloria, but Gloria's independence. The production was a big success.

With *The Dragon Lady's Revenge* (1971), writers Joan Holden, Patricia Silver, Andrea Snow, and Jael Weisman, combined a *Terry and the Pirates* comic style with Josef von Sternberg's Shanghai spy thrillers. Inspired by a *Ramparts* story on the CIA's involvement with drug traffic in Southeast Asia, the play reveals the economics underlying the war in Southeast Asia while implicating the United States in the drug addiction of many of our own soldiers.[30] The production was a huge success with the public and the press and earned the company its second Obie.

The troupe returned to epic staging with Brecht's *The Mother* (1973) and *False Promises/Nos Engañaron* (1976). For *The Mother* the troupe used half masks, signs, some cross-gender casting, and Hanns Eisler's music, to which they added songs about Ho Chi Min and *huelga* (strike) of the United Farm Workers, and songs from the Spanish Civil War. In addition to Brecht's scene titles, they added statements from American history, such as "'Communism is evil because it denies God and defies Man,' Richard Nixon, 1952," and "'Our march has begun. We will not go back,' Cheyenne Warrior, 1878."[31]

False Promises/Nos Engañaron ("we've been had"), created for the U.S. bicentennial, combined the style of an American western with epic staging. The play examines American imperialism at the time of the Spanish-American War in three interrelated stories showing policymakers in Washington, D.C., and the working class affected by their decisions. Ted Shank, who documented the collective creation of the play, describes how the seventeen-member collective progressed from committees promoting several potential subjects to a final vote between two, and the ensuing development of the production. According to Shank, the competition between the two final scenarios was particularly heated because the one that was eventually rejected was created by two Chicano company members and focused on issues of race. Furthermore, Holden, who wrote the competing scenario, had already written or cowritten eight plays since 1970, and the collective was committed to sharing artistic roles.[32] Struggles involving ethnicity and authority continued to challenge the troupe's commitment to collectivity up to the end of the twentieth century.

With the exception of *The Mother* and Dario Fo's *We Can't Pay, We Won't Pay* at the end of the decade, all the plays in the 1970s were original. Writers, whether one or more, began creating roles for specific actors, and a new set of stock characters began to develop in the company, based partly on commedia, partly on melodrama, and partly on the individual qualities of the performers. Holden summarized some of these characters: "Joan Mankin (Gloria in *The Independent Female*) played the ingénue bursting with initially repressed passion; Melody James played beauties of every age." Sharon Lockwood (Sarah Bullit in *The Independent Female*), who would remain with the company until the mid-1990s, emerged as both "a character actress and leading lady, playing comic men and the sharp-tongued, take-no-crap working-class heroine." Eventually, as Holden emerged as the principal playwright, Lockwood played Holden's recurring alter ego, "the idealistic but angst-ridden and overstressed public servant: a role also sometimes played by Andrea Snow." Snow, also the troupe's principal composer and lyricist for much of the decade, created "the company's one femme fatale, the title role in *The Dragon Lady's Revenge*." The collective's first African American actors, Lonnie Ford and Deb'bora Gilyard, both "had the gravitas for working-class heros, dramatic or comic, his young, hers middle-aged." Dan Chumley played "the white worker who through error betrays his class: often the love interest." Ed Levey, who excelled at physical comedy, "played a wide range of clown roles and also a dramatic character: the tragically failing revolutionary." Steve Friedman played "a tortured, intelligent everyman and also the cold-blooded capitalist villain." With his departure, the troupe lost its bad guy. Arthur Holden inherited the villain roles for a time, but "his stage presence proved too sympathetic. His true role emerged in the 1980s: the fall guy."[33]

Actors' singing abilities influenced the songs written for them, and music played an increasingly important role in the troupe's shows. In the early 1970s, musicians wore clown makeup and raggedy costumes; juggling, clown tricks, acrobatics, and music preceded and followed shows. With *The Dragon Lady's Revenge,* songs were part of the action, making it the troupe's first musical theater production. Music was used extensively in *The Mother* (1973), and the principal characters in *San Fran Scandals* (1972) are a song-and-dance team.

From 1968 to 1976 the Gorilla Marching Band, usually including Barry Levitan, Andrea Snow, Ted Sobel, and Jack Wickert, accompanied productions. In 1976 it evolved into the Mime Troupe Band about the time Bruce Barthol, formerly the bass player for Country Joe and the Fish, joined the collective. Composer Eduardo Robledo joined the following year, adding a Latino sound. By the late 1970s music was more dramatically integrated into the plays, and musicians were sometimes characters. The troupe even created a fictional punk rock band, Mark Antony and the Nileists (aka Nihilists, Nile-ists), that appeared as a character in five productions.

According to critic Robert Hurwitt, who had been a member of the troupe in the mid-1960s, the shows in the 1970s became fairly predictable and "lost something of their daring." However, he singled out *False Promises* and Dario Fo's *We Can't Pay, We Won't Pay* (1979) as exceptions.[34] Later, when *Hotel Universe* was revived in 1986, he praised it for withstanding the test of time and judged "We Won't Move" as one of the best songs Barthol had written for the troupe.[35] Toward the end of the decade, during the Carter administration, the plays dealt primarily with domestic issues such as inflation, the gas shortage, and factory working conditions. Joan Holden acknowledged that those were not their best shows: "We lost our direction somewhat during the Carter years."[36]

Some of the company's productions in the 1970s grew out of community activism. Of these mobilizations the largest began in 1973 when the Mime Troupe joined with several other arts organizations (the Julian Theatre, Casa Hispana, the Neighborhood Arts Coalition, Project Artaud, San Francisco Progress, Mission Coalition, Mission Mediarts, and Project II) as the Community Coalition for the Arts to oppose Mayor Joseph Alioto's proposed Performing Arts Center at the Civic Center. The *Berkeley Barb* referred to the PAC as "a civic tombstone estimated at between 18 and 40 million dollars" and quoted a Citizen's Analysis that compared the proposed edifice to New York's Lincoln Center, "the mausoleum of the Old Culture elite."[37] The Community Coalition for the Arts, much like its anarchist predecessor, the Artist Liberation Front, proposed alternatives to the PAC including a network of neighborhood facilities.

On 3 April 1973 four troupe members (Andrea Snow, Joan Mankin, Steve Friedman, and Dan Chumley) brought an unannounced skit to a public supervisors' meeting to draw attention to their opposition to the PAC. Friedman, clad in a tuxedo, stood and spoke of the need for the center for the muses and the needy rich. Chumley approached him juggling. A conflict over popular and elite art ensued. Snow, in an evening gown, began singing opera until Mankin told her to shut up and shoved a pie in her face, splashing shaving cream. Diane Feinstein, then president of the board of supervisors, stopped everything, sputtering, "Clean this up."[38] A lively debate in the press followed. A troupe letter to the *San Francisco Chronicle* on 20 April noted that their little play "dealt with the fact that a basically white elite cultural facility is proposed for a site where 400 poor families now live and a black cultural arts facility now thrives at 330 Grove Street."[39]

In another letter to the editor on 6 August, the troupe went after one of the major supporters of the center: "Mr. Zellerbach [of the Crown Zellerbach Corporation and the Arts Commission] recently let it be known, through the little theatre grapevine, that groups which continue to attack the Performing Arts Center should cease to look for support from the Zellerbach Family Fund." The following month the troupe opened the play *San Fran Scandals,* in which millionaire Harold Smellybucks destroys a neighborhood to build a cultural shrine.

The troupe provided distractions at the groundbreaking for the PAC on 24 February 1978. Then, when the center finally opened on 16 September 1980, the troupe protested with signs reading "No Music Teachers, No Art Teachers in Our Schools," "Millions for Marble, but. . . ," and "Art for Whom?" *San Francisco Examiner* music critic Michael Walsh referred to the troupe's "bogus charge of elitism."[40] The troupe fired off another letter to the editor on 30 September: "We merely pointed out that when the library can't afford books and the schools can't afford teachers and the plants are dying in Golden Gate Park, building a shiny new symphony hall is just too much like saying, 'let them eat cake.'"[41]

The Mime Troupe's activism frequently involved work with some of the most radical groups in the United States. Their FBI dossier in the 1970s includes Students for a Democratic Society, The Guardian, the American Labor Party, the Progressive Labor Party, U.S. Vietnam Day Committee, Young Socialist Alliance, Student National Coordinating Committee, the Black Panther Party, and the Fair Play for Cuba Committee. Composer Bruce Barthol reports that troupe members speak of this file with pride.[42]

In 1971 the troupe created a play on the shah of Iran with the International Confederation of Iranian Students and a skit, *Paper Tiger*, celebrating the founding of the People's Republic of China. *Chile Acto* (1973) was a response to the U.S.-supported military coup against Allende. *Los Siete, Soledad,* and *Seize the Time* (all 1970 and 1971) were created to serve specific individuals and groups in the United States. The latter, about the trial of Black Panther Bobby Seale, toured in the east, with Tom Hayden speaking after performances.

In 1979 the troupe joined with several San Francisco community-based, socially concerned theater companies as the People's Theatre Coalition, for "like-minded groups to share technical equipment, publicity tasks, creative ideas."[43]

The political agenda of the Mime Troupe's work kept them an anomaly in the United States, but created interest and a large following abroad, and in the 1970s they became increasingly international. They traveled to Mexico City in 1974 to perform *The Mother* at a radical theater festival, and their first European tour in 1977 took *False Promises* and *Frijoles, or Beans to You* (1975) to West Germany, Italy, and France. The ten-week tour netted over twenty thousand dollars, and the company played to packed houses in most German sites. The Italian and French visits were less stellar, but the troupe learned to integrate their host's language into shows. *Hotel Universe* was created in La Rochelle, France, during this trip as a demonstration of their collective practices.[44] The company would make four return visits to West Germany in the next decade, becoming extremely popular with the German public and scholars.

An important but unheralded change in the company in the 1970s was the advent of the red star logo that still identifies the Mime Troupe. Barry Levitan, a musician with the company through much of the 1970s, reports that he first put the star on T-shirts in 1975 as a symbol of the revolution. The genesis of the star is the Gorilla Band drum. Levitan was a drummer, and in photographs of the band from about 1968 into the 1970s, the words "Gorilla" and "Band" on the drum are divided by a small star.[45] The red star, a vestige of the Mime Troupe's guerrilla past and radical politics, announces the troupe on T-shirts, programs, flyers, letters, truck, and studio on Treat Avenue.

Notes

1. Stewart McBride, "Laughter with a Sting," *Christian Science* Monitor, 20 February 1980.

2. Glenn Silber and Claudia Vianello, *Troupers,* Catalyst Media, 1985, videocassette.

3. Robert Scheer, introduction to Davis, *First Ten Years,* 11.

4. Joan Holden, "Collective Playmaking: The Why and the How," *Theatre Quarterly* 5 (June–August 1975): 34.

5. Nancy Scott, "Celebrating the Presence of Mime," *San Francisco Examiner,* 5 July 1992.

6. Silber and Vianello, *Troupers.*

7. The most recent addition to the discussion of the formation of the collective is Laurence Michael Dilday, "Experiment in Collectivity: Revolution and Evolution in the San Francisco Mime Troupe," Ph.D. diss., University of California, Davis, 2000.

8. Denny Partridge, email to Susan Vaneta Mason, 6 May 2002.

9. William Harris, "The San Francisco Mime Troupe: Nineteen Years Old and Still Pure," *Soho Weekly News,* 23 November 1978.

10. Lance Haro Jencks, "The San Francisco Mime Troupe in Its Social Context," Ph.D. diss., University of California, Davis, 1978, 117.

11. Ibid., 118.

12. Dan Sullivan, "Mime Troupe Still Has the Message," *Los Angeles Times,* 22 May 1983.

13. J. Dennis Rich, "An Interview with the San Francisco Mime Troupe," *Players* 46 (December–January 1971): 55.

14. Holden, "Collective Playmaking," 34.

15. Theodore Shank, *American Alternative Theatre* (New York: Grove Press, 1982), 73.

16. Rich, "Interview with Mime Troupe," 58–59.

17. "San Francisco Mime Troupe: The First Forty Years," Fortieth Anniversary program, n.p.

18. Holden, "Collective Playmaking," 32.

19. San Francisco Mime Troupe, *By Popular Demand* (San Francisco: San Francisco Mime Troupe, 1980), 296.

20. Holden, "Collective Playmaking," 28.

21. Barbara Falconer, "Revolution or Tomatoes?" *San Francisco Examiner and Chronicle,* 11 October 1970.

22. Herb Caen, *San Francisco Chronicle,* 9 December 1974.

23. "San Francisco Mime Troupe: The First Forty Years," n.p.

24. Holden, "Collective Playmaking," 36.

25. Rich, "Interview with Mime Troupe," 55.

26. Joan Holden, "In Praise of Melodrama," in *Reimaging America,* ed. Mark O'Brien and Craig Little (Santa Cruz, Calif.: New Society, 1990), 280–81.

27. R. G. Davis, "Politics, Art, and the San Francisco Mime Troupe," *Theatre Quarterly* 8 (June–August 1975): 26.

28. Davis, *First Ten Years,* 11.

29. Peter Brooks, *The Melodramatic Imagination: Balzac, Henry James, Melodrama, and the Mode of Excess* (New Haven: Yale University Press, 1976), 44.

30. Frank Browning and Banning Garrett, "The New Opium War," *Ramparts,* May 1971, 32–39.

31. Mel Gordon, "San Francisco Mime Troupe's *The Mother,*" *Tulane Drama Review* 19 (June 1975): 94–101.

32. Theodore Shank, "The San Francisco Mime Troupe's Production of *False Promises,*" *Theatre Quarterly* 7 (fall 1977): 43.

33. Joan Holden, email to Susan Vaneta Mason, 7 June 2002. During an inter-

view on 9 May 2002 Holden gave me notes on actors in the 1970s. On that basis, I wrote descriptions of the actors, which Holden edited.

34. Robert Hurwitt, "Fo Sure," *East Bay Express*, 21 March 1980.

35. Robert Hurwitt, "Back to the Future," *East Bay Express*, 22 August 1986.

36. Sullivan, "Troupe Still Has Message."

37. "Art for Nabes or Knaves on the Burner," *Berkeley Barb*, 9 February 1973.

38. Andrea Snow, telephone interview by Susan Vaneta Mason, 7 August 2002.

39. San Francisco Mime Troupe, letter to Robert Commonday, 20 April 1973, SFMT files.

40. Michael Walsh, "The Charge of Elitism," *San Francisco Examiner*, 28 September 1980.

41. San Francisco Mime Troupe, letter to editor, 30 September 1980, SFMT files.

42. Bruce Barthol, interview by Susan Vaneta Mason, 19 July 2000.

43. Barbara Isenberg, ed., *California Theatre Annual, 1981* (Beverly Hills: Performing Arts Network, 1981), 217.

44. William Kleb, "*Hotel Universe:* Playwriting and the San Francisco Mime Troupe," *Theater* 9 (spring 1979): 15–20.

45. Barry Levitan, telephone interview by Susan Vaneta Mason, 2 August 2002.

The Dragon Lady's Revenge

1971

Script by Joan Holden, Patricia Silver, Andrea Snow, and Jael Weisman with Sharon Lockwood

Introduction

The play was inspired by an article in *Ramparts,* "The New Opium War" (May 1971), breaking the story of the CIA involvement in Indochina opium trade. It combines the style of the *Terry and the Pirates* comic strip with spy movies from the 1940s such as *Shanghai Gesture.* The troupe billed it as "An International Spy Thriller Mystery Love Comedy Hoax." The complex plot involves the son of the U.S. ambassador to Long Pinh, a bar called the White Monkey run by the Dragon Lady, a bar girl named Blossom, a puppet president supported by the United States, a drug murder, and the exposé of Mr. Big, in charge of drug traffic. The show received excellent reviews at home and on tour and won the company its second Obie Award. *Dragon Lady* was also the company's most successful early attempt at collective writing. The troupe successfully revived it in 1987 during the Iran-Contra hearings that implicated the U.S. government in cocaine trade in Central America.

Commentary

Joan Holden

Five of us made up a story, stealing a lot from the movies, and three of us took turns writing scenes. ("Collective Playmaking: The Why and the How," *Theatre Quarterly* 5 [June–August 1975]: 30)

Ed Levey

I was doing Shakespeare at Berkeley Rep when I saw *Dragon Lady* in the park. I had known something was missing in my work, and I realized its relevance to today. They were replacing the actor playing Clyde. I auditioned, got the part, and stayed with the troupe through 1978. I had to learn a new acting style, a new group of people, and it was a crash course in politics. Being in the Troupe has made me picky about theater ever since. (Telephone interview by Susan Vaneta Mason, 18 July 2002)

Andrea Snow

When major moments hinge on the use of a crucial prop, as they do in *The Dragon Lady's Revenge,* it's easy to imagine the shock of the actor who realizes that he forgot to bring his prop on stage. In that instant of discovery, when he reaches into his costume and finds nothing, the actor has no choice but to press on and commit to whatever pops into his (or her) skull. This happened many times during the run of the play, not least of all with me. Once as the Dragon Lady I danced this seductive tango with the Lieutenant, and as we sank to the floor, I was *supposed* to produce a syringe from the folds of my gown. When I realized I'd forgotten the needle, I reached for a hair ornament (an old Christmas tree decoration that was sewn into my wig and looked like an inverted spider), leaned my head over the Lieutenant's arm and jabbed him with one of the spidery "legs." Thanks to Michael Christensen (the Lieutenant), who immediately swooned as if drugged, the bizarre attack of the hair ornament made perfect sense. (Letter to Susan Vaneta Mason, 23 July 2002)

Frank Browning and Banning Garrett

Adding glamour to the labyrinthine intrigue of Vietnam's opium trade throughout the late 1950s and early '60s was the famous Madame Nhu, the Dragon Lady of Saigon. ("The New Opium War," *Ramparts,* May 1971, 37)

Wilma Bonet

The Mime Troupe was one of the first theatres that I saw when I came out here from New York. I saw *The Dragon Lady's Revenge* at a park in Berkeley and said, "Yes! That's what theatre is about." (Quoted in "Forty Years with the San Francisco Mime Troupe," *Callboard,* December 1999, 22)

Jack Kroll

A savagely partisan show in its depiction of nefarious American politicos and military men and South Vietnamese officials, it also transcends partisanship in its skewering assault on archetypal greed and villainy. (*Newsweek,* 22 January 1973, 65)

Robert Hurwitt

The play is a broadly satirical, hilarious, but deeply disturbing, tale of covert operations, casual corruption, military adventurism, and deniability. (*East Bay Express,* 17 July 1987)

The Production

The Dragon Lady's Revenge opened on August 1971 in Washington Square Park, San Francisco, with the following cast:

Harold	*Larry Pisoni*
Clyde	*Michael Christensen*
Drooley	*Jael Weisman*
Tran Dog	*Randall Craig*
Ambassador	*Jason Harris*
Rong Q	*Joan Mankin*
Blossom	*Sharon Lockwood*
Dragon Lady	*Andrea Snow*

Directed by Denny Partridge Stevens and Jael Weisman with Dan Chumley. Designed and executed by Peggy Snider, Peter Snider, Trina Johnson, Patricia Silver, Dan Chumley, and Denny Partridge Stevens. Stage managers: Peter Snider, Trina Johnson, Denny Stevens, Patricia Silver, Joan Holden, Merle Goldstone. Music by Randall Craig, Barry Glick, Andrea Snow, Theodore Sobel, and Jack Wickert. Lyrics by Randall Craig, Barry Glick, and Joel Weisman. Musicians: Jack Dowding, Harvey Robb, Theodore Sobel, Jack Wickert, Larry Pisoni, Ed Levey, Michael Christensen.

Characters (in order of appearance)

Harold Saunders, the Private
Clyde Dillsworth Junker III, the Lieutenant
A mysterious priest
Tran Dog, the Servant
Clyde Dillsworth Junker II, the U.S. Ambassador
General Rong Q, the Head of State
Blossom, the B-girl
A mysterious Fakir
The Dragon Lady
Reverend Tim Drooley, the Counter-Insurgency Agent
A mysterious fencing student
A mysterious fencing instructor
A mysterious nun
Mr. Big

tion into foreign languages, are strictly reserved. All inquiries should be addressed to San Francisco Mime Troupe, 855 Treat Avenue, San Francisco, CA 94110.

The Dragon Lady's Revenge

Place: Long Pinh, capital of Cochin, a small country in S.E. Asia
Time: Near the middle of the twentieth century

Prologue: A Street in Long Pinh

HAROLD enters, sick. CLYDE enters, with camera—discovers HAROLD.

CLYDE: My God—Saunders! Is it really you? What's happened, man? You look awful?

HAROLD: This is no place for you, Lieutenant. You'd better go back to the base and leave me alone.

CHORUS: Say, is that any way to talk to an old buddy? Look—I know this great little place where we could go for some tea—the atmosphere is really authentic!

HAROLD: Just get out of here, Clyde—I'm meeting someone and I don't want you around.

CLYDE: Knock it off, Harry. God, if you're worried about being AWOL, forget it—I have influence.

HAROLD: Open your eyes, Clyde. Look at me—what I'd like right now is a fix! I'm here to cop and my pusher is late. Man, if he sees you, he's not going to come near me!

CLYDE: I won't leave you like this, Harry—you've got to come back with me and see a doctor!

HAROLD: I can't go back—the drug's only part of the reason. The rest you don't even have a glimmer of. But it's big, Clyde—really big, and I know too much to go back with you.

CLYDE: What are you talking about?

HAROLD: Oh, shit —I'm going to be sick—bring me that garbage can.

Points, CLYDE moves, HAROLD dashes off.

CLYDE: What garb—there are no garbage cans in Asia! Harry!

Follows. DROOLEY enters disguised as priest, through trap door marked "sewer." HAROLD enters.

HAROLD: You got the stuff?

DROOLEY: I got it. (*Pulls out heroin addict's outfit; his crucifix is the syringe. They prepare the fix. CLYDE enters; HAROLD kneels; DROOLEY makes the sign of the cross.*) In nomine padium filii—(*Holy music.*)

CLYDE: How moving. Harry's taken the first step toward rehabilitation. Amen. (*HAROLD shoots up. DROOLEY exits. HAROLD staggers to his feet, smiling.*) God is indeed—(*HAROLD falls.*)—Harry!

HAROLD: O.D . . . double . . . cross—got to stop . . . White Monkey . . . C . . . I . . . a-a-a. *(Dies.)*

CLYDE: Harold—murdered! What did he say? O.D—odd! Got to stop—odd white monkey! Harry—I swear, over your dead body, that I shall not rest until I have found your murderer! *(Carries body off.)*

Music—Overture

INTRODUCTION (*Spoken by* TRAN DOG.)

In a time not so distant from our own, the western empire set out to conquer the east. The armies of the west were the most powerful the world had ever seen. Some easterners, who thought the invaders would surely win, joined them. Others waited for the outcome. Many more were determined to resist. Each year, the west sent more soldiers. Each year, the eastern soil put forth more defenders. But the west was proud, and determined to conquer—until its army was stricken by a terrible sickness. The affliction spread through the ranks, until the army was greatly weakened; then crossed the sea and struck the empire in its very heart—its children. No one could understand this misfortune. Kind ladies, honorable gentlemen, comrades, the San Francisco Mime Troupe proudly presents *The Dragon Lady's Revenge*!

Act One

Scene 1: The American Embassy

AMBASSADOR enters. TRAN DOG *dusts.*

AMBASSADOR: Ah—Tran Dog! They told me about you. How long have you worked here at the Embassy?

TRAN DOG: Since French leave.

AMBASSADOR: And before that?

TRAN DOG: I work for Japanese.

AMBASSADOR: And in all that time, you've never been tempted to run away and join the nationalists—the revolutionaries?

TRAN DOG: I take my bowl to man who serve rice. *(Holds hand out.)*

AMBASSADOR: Ah, Tran Dog—if more people were like you, we'd have an easier time in this world. *(Gives him money.)* Here—buy yourself something to smoke. I'm expecting your President, General Rong Q. What kind of man is he? What do the people say about him?

TRAN DOG: Very smart man. Very big pockets.

AMBASSADOR: Big pockets, eh? Just what they told me at the briefing. *(Bell rings.)* Show him in.

RONG Q enters.

TRAN DOG: General Rong Q, Mister C. Dillsworth Junker—new American Ambassador. *(Exit.)*

AMBASSADOR: Good afternoon. Do you speak English?

RONG Q: I received my B.A. degree from Michigan State University.

AMBASSADOR: The Spartans! *(They shake hands.)*

RONG Q: I need many things. The situation is not so good. We want to
fight—we are very warlike—but we cannot fight with old weapons. I plan
to march to the North. For this I need planes. I need helicopters. I need
bombs. I think the time may be ripe for—Secret Weapon X 90!

AMBASSADOR: General! I am not here to talk about classified weapons. My
President dispatched me to deal with your health crisis.

RONG Q: I do not understand.

AMBASSADOR: ADDICTIVE DRUGS.

RONG Q: No.

AMBASSADOR: ILLICIT NARCOTICS.

RONG Q: No.

AMBASSADOR: SMACK?

RONG Q: I understand.

AMBASSADOR: We're shipping home thousands of addicted G.I.'s. In the
President's own words: "Drug addiction is spreading with pandemic
virulence." Once, it lurked in the ghettoes—OK—but now it's reaching
our suburbs, and the American people and my government will not
stand for it!

RONG Q: Very serious problem. I think maybe it is a Communist plot, calling for extreme solution—X 90!

AMBASSADOR: Out of the question! If the drug trade is a Communist plot, a
surprising number of your people are growing rich on it. Look, Rong
Q—Long Pinh is well known as the capital of the drug trade. Beginning
immediately, you must clean up the city. There are also rumors of drug
profits flowing to surprisingly high levels of your government. We need
solid assurances that these rumors are false. I see you are angry.

RONG Q: Have I not always been a faithful friend of the U.S.? In or out of
office, have I not always served your government? Have I not fought the
Communists for 20 years? And now I am rewarded with insults and dis-
trust!

AMBASSADOR: Oh, come now, General—

RONG Q: Perhaps I have made a mistake. Perhaps those who say the war is
not really in our interest are right. Perhaps, if you no longer have
confidence in us, we could reach an agreement with the other side.

AMBASSADOR: Perhaps. But there are many ambitious generals in your
country, and my President has asked me to advise him as to which one
merits our confidence. If you get behind our clean-up campaign, I am
prepared to offer you the presidency here for life.

RONG Q: How can this be arranged?

AMBASSADOR: Through free and democratic elections.

RONG Q: To sterilize Long Pinh will not be easy, Ambassador.

AMBASSADOR: Who is the number one drug supplier in the area?

RONG Q: Some say it is a female, known as the Dragon Lady, who operates out of a nightclub called the White Monkey Bar—very popular with your G.I.'s.

AMBASSADOR: Start there. I want her closed down.

RONG Q: The Dragon Lady is a very powerful woman.

AMBASSADOR: But fortunately, only a woman.

RONG Q: Not exactly. Behind her, there is said to be a mysterious Mr. Big.

AMBASSADOR: You deal with the Dragon Lady. The American government will take care of this Mr. Big.

RONG Q: It would be easier if the American government supplied Secret Weapon X 90.

AMBASSADOR: The American government has learned to be cautious about military solutions to political problems.

Exeunt.

Scene 2: White Monkey Bar

CLYDE enters, searching.

CLYDE: I've been to the White Monkey laundry, the White Monkey Fortune Cookie Factory, the White Monkey Teahouse . . . (BLOSSOM *enters behind.*) . . . and now I've come to the White Monkey Bar. *(Music. BLOS-SOM dances.)* This must be the place. Uh . . . do you . . . speak . . . English?

BLOSSOM: Yes, sir. Americans have been in my country ever since I was born. So—this is your first visit to the White Monkey Bar?

CLYDE: Yes, well—I usually go to the officer's Club.

BLOSSOM: Ah! You are officer? You must have a lot of men in your command.

CLYDE: Oh, not too many—150 or so—armored infantry division.

BLOSSOM: *(Writing.)* That's a lot! I bet you got a lot of big weapons too.

CLYDE: Nothing special: a half dozen tanks, a few APC's . . .

BLOSSOM: *(Writing.)* Rockets? 60's?

CLYDE: Rockets, 60's, 90's, fragmentation bombs, anti-tank guns, what not.

BLOSSOM: *(Writing.)* What's a whatnot?

CLYDE: Army jargon . . . I'm looking for a priest.

BLOSSOM: At the White Monkey Bar?

CLYDE: That's just it! Do you know one?

BLOSSOM: Anything can be arranged, sir.

CLYDE: Say—what kind of a place is this?

BLOSSOM: I think you are beginning to understand.

CLYDE: Poor Harold!

BLOSSOM: Harold?

CLYDE: Don't deny it, baby—you know who he was.

BLOSSOM: Not I, sir—I cannot tell one American from another.

CLYDE: Drop the act. Harold was murdered by enemy agents who hooked him in the first place—Commie agents who stoop so low they disguise themselves as priests! (DROOLEY *enters disguised as a fakir, with suitcase marked "Air America."*)

DROOLEY: The kid!

CLYDE: The more I think about it, the more it disgusts me! This place is probably a Commie front! Sometimes it seems like everyone in this darn country's the enemy.

BLOSSOM: Why don't you go home then?

CLYDE: (*Sees* DROOLEY.) All right—(*pulls gun*)—don't move. (*To* BLOS-SOM.) Who's that?

BLOSSOM: He's what you might call a faker.

DROOLEY: FAKIR.

BLOSSOM: He does business here.

CLYDE: What's in the suitcase, fakir?

DROOLEY: Nothing in suitcase—just some junk, that's all.

CLYDE: Well, get your junk together and get out of here.

BLOSSOM: Put that gun away, you crazy.

CLYDE: I could never shoot a woman anyway. (*Puts it away.*) I've got to find out where that priest is! (*Hands emerge from back curtain, take suitcase from* DROOLEY.)

BLOSSOM: It's not the priest you should be after.

CLYDE: I've got to get to the bottom of this.

BLOSSOM: Why not get to the top?

CLYDE: So you do know something.

BLOSSOM: Just as a stream is to the sea, so is that priest to Mr. Big.

DROOLEY: Did you say Mr. Big?

CLYDE: As the sea is to the river, so is the stream to Mr. Bigfoot—

BLOSSOM: No.

CLYDE: Who is this Mr. Big?

DROOLEY: Mr. Big again.

CLYDE: Is the priest connected to Mr. Big? (BLOSSOM *nods.*)

DROOLEY: That's one question too many! (*Attacks* CLYDE.)

CLYDE: Wait! (*To* BLOSSOM.) Looks like there's going to be a little rough stuff here, Miss. You'd better step aside. (DROOLEY *knocks him off stage. He climbs back.*) All right! (DROOLEY *sprays him with Mace, he falls.*) My eyes!

BLOSSOM: Could you hold this for a minute? (*Hands* DROOLEY *her nail file—wastes him with two karate chops and kicks him off stage.*)

CLYDE: Wow! Where did you learn to fight like that?

BLOSSOM: In the mountains. *(Helps him up.)*

Gongs sound. DRAGON LADY *enters.*

DRAGON LADY: What is all this commotion?

CLYDE: Who's that?

BLOSSOM: That's the Dragon Lady. Everything is in order now, madam. *(Exits on signal from* DRAGON LADY.*)*

DRAGON LADY: Tell me, Lieutenant—is this rowdiness the customary behavior of officers visiting the native quarter?

CLYDE: I—well—you ought to know, toots.

DRAGON LADY: My, how ardent. You'd better run along now back to your barracks. I'm sure you and your fellow officers can amuse yourselves— run along now, Lieutenant, before it's too late.

CLYDE: But I have to speak with you—it's very important!

DRAGON LADY: I'm sure it is, Lieutenant, but it's well past bed-time, so if you'll excuse me—

CLYDE: Harold Saunders! Did you know him?

DRAGON LADY: Saunders? *(Smiles.)*

CLYDE: I think he was murdered!

DRAGON LADY: You are no doubt correct, Lieutenant, but if you are smart, you'll take my advice and leave the dead alone.

CLYDE: It's my duty to find his murderer.

DRAGON LADY: Very noble, my dear Boy Scout. You know you're not dealing anymore with the U.S. Army, Lieutenant.

CLYDE: You can't frighten me.

DRAGON LADY: As you wish. Tell me—does not my humble establishment interest you? Every evil known you can find here, my friend: gambling, whiskey, special massage . . . or is it something else that might interest? There is a plant grown in the highlands of my country, known as the flower of Nepenthe—as you may know, this is the house specialty.

CLYDE: I know—all about that filthy poison you people are killing our soldiers with—Harry! Get away from me, murderess!

DRAGON LADY: Did you know, Lieutenant, that this poison was spread throughout Asia, in the last century, by the British and French colonialists? Very profitable—and very soothing to the population. Do you know who Nepenthe was, Lieutenant?

CLYDE: Why—she was the goddess of sleep and dreams!

DRAGON LADY: I see you are not a high school dropout, Lieutenant. *(Sings "Song of the Nepenthe Flower.")*

Look on the ruin and the wrack

Of generations that have gone before:

First the Japanese, then the French—

And now, they tell me, the American war.
Is it the fool going where the angel fears to tread?
Take the sleep of Nepenthe—give in
Dream the dream of Nepenthe,
And float forever to the sea. *(They dance.)*

So take a look at the river
As it floats from Long Pinh to the sea—
Can you swim against that strong current?

CLYDE: Yes!

DRAGON LADY: Never! Think it over, I'm sure you'll agree.
So take the sleep of Nepenthe—give in.
Dream the dream of Nepenthe
And float forever to the sea.

They sink to the floor. DRAGON LADY *caresses* CLYDE's *arm, then plunges a giant syringe into his vein.*

DRAGON LADY: Blossom! *(BLOSSOM enters.)* I think we have a new Client.

BLOSSOM: Yes . . .

RONG Q: *(Staggers through curtain, drunk and dishevelled.)* Dragon Lady! I have something to discuss with you.

DRAGON LADY: Welcome to the White Monkey Bar, Lieutenant. *(Argues with* RONG Q *upstage.)*

CLYDE: *(Rising languorously.)* All right! *(Gets sick.)* I don't feel so well—can you get me home?

BLOSSOM: Where is your home?

CLYDE: The American Embassy. *(Gong.)*

DRAGON LADY: How can you betray me like this?

RONG Q: Oh, shut up, you sniveling bitch! *(Exeunt.)*

CLYDE: Can you get me home all right?

BLOSSOM: You're in safe hands, my friend. *(Exeunt.)*

Act Two

Scene 1: The Embassy, the Next Morning

TRAN DOG *enters dusting;* CLYDE *enters distracted, jostling* TRAN DOG.

CLYDE: Go on—get out of here. *(TRAN DOG gives him a long look before departing.)* Just as the river is to the priest—that's not it! Just as—

AMBASSADOR: *(Enters.)* Good morning, son!

CLYDE: Good morning, Dad.

AMBASSADOR: It's swell to be together again. Although the servants tell me you were a bit under the weather when you came in last night.

CLYDE: A bit.

AMBASSADOR: A lot of temptations out here for an American boy—I remember Singapore when I was your age . . . We'd just licked the Japs, and the entire Pacific basin lay spread out before us . . . I remember the scent of jasmine, and a Eurasian beauty so eager to please . . . But it's best to take these things in moderation, Clyde. You don't want to let Asia get under your skin.

CLYDE: Dad—why are we here?

AMBASSADOR: Where?

CLYDE: Here—in Asia—fighting this war!

AMBASSADOR: You ask questions now, like all the restless, inquiring young folk in your generation. And THAT's why I'm here, to answer your questions. What was the question?

CLYDE: Why are we here?

AMBASSADOR: Oil is part of the answer, but only part. Basically, we are here because we desperately want to get out.

CLYDE: I don't get it.

AMBASSADOR: The President has promised that he will wind down the ugly and unpopular war. And we are, as you know, implementing orderly withdrawals of our troops to neighboring countries. But, realistically, we cannot get out of this war until we can trust the people here to go on with it.

CLYDE: That's the part I don't understand.

AMBASSADOR: It's our only hope, Clyde. In the words of Harry S. Truman: "The American system can only survive if it becomes the world system." And that's how it is, my boy: a struggle to the death between capitalism—what we call democracy—and communism. And we can't just let this struggle work itself out in the marketplace, because communism has an unfair advantage.

CLYDE: What's that?

AMBASSADOR: People like it. That's why the most peace-loving nation in the world has been at war with the world since the World War. But what's got you worried, son?

CLYDE: It's—sometimes I get the feeling the people here just don't like us.

AMBASSADOR: That's a feeling you'll learn to live with Clyde—I did. And it isn't that bad: I'm going to show you that the average Asian basically appreciates what you can do for him. *(Calls.)* Tran Dog! *(To* CLYDE.*)* I'm going to introduce you to a real character.

TRAN DOG enters.

TRAN DOG: You call, sir?

AMBASSADOR: Tran Dog, my son the lieutenant here feels that your people don't like the American soldiers. What do you say to that, Tran Dog?

TRAN DOG: My people very ignorant—very poor people. Sometimes they think American have too many dollar. (*Puts hand out.* AMBASSADOR *gives* CLYDE *money to give to* TRAN DOG. TRAN DOG *smiles.*) You see? Everybody rich, everybody like everybody. Hee, hee hee.

AMBASSADOR: (*Joined by* CLYDE.) Ha, ha, ha.

TRAN DOG: You likee Long Pinh, Lieutenant?

CLYDE: Er—yes, it's a very interesting city.

TRAN DOG: Got gambling, whiskey, girls—very good for American. But one thing very bad—Nepenthe flower. You stay away!

AMBASSADOR: Very good advice, Tran Dog, though I doubt my boy— what's the matter son?

CLYDE: It's dope, dad! Dope! That's what's on my mind!

AMBASSADOR: Oh, no!

CLYDE: No, not me, dad—not me! It killed one of my men—he died in my arms. Harold!

AMBASSADOR: That's tough, son.

CLYDE: And it's everywhere. They say fifteen percent of our soldiers are hooked—that's hundreds of thousands of addicts created by this war! And it's all a huge sea of corruption. Harold didn't just die—he was murdered! Murdered because he knew too much!

AMBASSADOR: Did he tell you what he knew?

CLYDE: He gave me one clue. I followed it out and discovered there's a Dragon Lady in it—and a Mr. Big.

TRAN DOG: Mr. Big! (AMBASSADOR *and* CLYDE *stare at* TRAN DOG). Everybody hear of him—nobody know him!

AMBASSADOR: Clyde—you haven't asked your dad why he's here.

CLYDE: Why are you here, dad?

AMBASSADOR: On special assignment—to clean up the dope trade.

CLYDE: Dad—that's great!

AMBASSADOR: And, I don't mind telling you, I've made considerable headway.

TRAN DOG: HEAD way? (*Exits.*)

CLYDE: Boy, we really need you here, dad—and I think I can help!

AMBASSADOR: You can help all right, son—by staying as far away from this thing as possible.

CLYDE: But, dad—

AMBASSADOR: No buts. If these drug people found out who you were, they might try to harm you to get back at me. (*Doorbell.*) I'm expecting one of the key people in our strategy. (DROOLEY *enters disguised as a Jesus Freak.*)

DROOLEY: Bom Maharishi! Haftarah shanti shanti Jesus loves you!

AMBASSADOR: This is the Reverend Tim Drooley. Tim—my son, Lieutenant C. Dillsworth Junker III.

DROOLEY: *(Aside.)* The kid!

CLYDE: How do you do?

DROOLEY: What's happening? *(Checks CLYDE's arm.)* Yeah! My friends call me Spike.

AMBASSADOR: You might not know it to look at him, but Spike here is a medically trained missionary, and he's setting up our methadone program for us. We feel that he's the right kind of person to deal with our drug-dependent G.I.'s.

DROOLEY: God plus methadone equals Hope.

CLYDE: What's methadone, Spike?

DROOLEY: Methadone is the only sure cure for junk. It's the cool drug—you don't get sick, you don't get high: you just stay on it.

CLYDE: How come?

DROOLEY: Because it's ten times as addictive—yeah—and the government gives it away for free. And it's a clean drug, lieutenant; it comes in a nice clean white Dixie cup. Like which would you choose, lieutenant—this? *(Shows cup.)* Or this? *(Shows needle.)* I didn't mean to freak you out, Lieutenant.

CLYDE: *(Aside.)* My god—the priest!

AMBASSADOR: That's a very effective demonstration, Spike. We'll remember your technique when we set up our next methadone center.

DROOLEY: Isn't one enough?

AMBASSADOR: I intend to clean up this city. I'm going to start at the bottom and go straight to the top!

DROOLEY: You're going to take on Mr. Big?

AMBASSADOR: Just how much of this drug traffic does Mr. Big really control?

DROOLEY: He's the Superstar—the big cheese—and he eats too much meat. You're a heavy cat yourself, Ambassador—a very heavy cat. A crusader against junk . . . but this is the twentieth century, and crusaders have got to be careful. Dig it?

AMBASSADOR: Thanks for the advice, Tim. I'll try to get some press boys down there to do a story for the American public.

DROOLEY: That's where it's at, Ambassador. Now I got to split. I got to see a man. Later, Lieutenant, and remember, "The meek shall inherit the earth"—but "Woe to him who seeketh after knowledge, for he shall know no peace." Peace! *(Gives V sign, exits.)*

AMBASSADOR: I'd have thought you'd get a positive hit off of Tim.

CLYDE: *(To audience.)* Oh my God—what'll I do? I can't tell him.

AMBASSADOR: What's the matter, son?

CLYDE: I've—got to see a man, too. Goodbye, Dad. Be careful! *(Exits.)*

TRAN DOG enters with glass on tray.

TRAN DOG: Very big hurry.

AMBASSADOR: *(Drinks.)* I wonder what's gotten into that boy. *(Exeunt.)*

Scene 2: A Street in Long Pinh

DROOLEY enters through sewer, disguised as a fencing student. CLYDE *enters running.* DROOLEY, *as if by accident, stops him with foil.*

DROOLEY: Excusez-moi.

CLYDE: Did you see a goofy-looking guy in a platinum wig and dark glasses come by here?

DROOLEY: *(With French accent.).* Goofy-looking. . . ? I do not believe so. Why are you looking for him?

CLYDE: I saw him kill my best friend, Harold Saunders!

DROOLEY: So . . . you are an eyewitness to a murder.

CLYDE: The only one, too.

DROOLEY: How interesting to meet you all alone on this deserted street.

CLYDE: Doesn't it just make you want to puke? The hypocrisy in this world!

DROOLEY: You don't know the half of it.

CLYDE: He was disguised as a priest. He had the hat, he had the robe, he had the rosary; he even had the cruci—*(Recognizes* DROOLEY's *hypo-cross.)*

BOTH: Fix!

CLYDE gets it in the vein.

DROOLEY: Okay, dough-boy—who else have you told about this priest?

CLYDE: Blossom . . .

DROOLEY: *(Dumps* CLYDE *down sewer, sings "CIA Song.")*
I am the prototype of an agent of intelligence
I graduated Yale, I have mixed with men of affluence
I give guns here, junk there—I inspire confidence
From Michoacan to Katmandu to counterbalance insurgence

CHORUS: *(Sung by* MUSICIANS.*)*
   To counterbalance insurgence

DROOLEY: Of the Bay of Pigs the press was moderately critical
With the Gulf of Tonkin, citizens grew skeptical
Thus embarrassed, Washington conceded points political
But the budget's growing yearly

CHORUS: Yearly, yearly, yearly.

DROOLEY: For my service indispensable.

CHORUS: His service indispensable.

DROOLEY: You've heard about the Halls of Montezuma—Shores of Tripoli but blood and guts has been replaced with an updated policy: Infiltration, co-optation.

CHORUS: Murder!

DROOLEY: For democracy—after all
   What ship of state could stay afloat
CHORUS: Glug, glug, glug, glug.
DROOLEY: Without its counter-insurgent agency?
CHORUS: Its counter-insurgent agency.
DROOLEY exits.

Scene 3: A Fencing Salon

BLOSSOM enters disguised as a fencing master, hangs sign, "Fencing Salon,"
exits. RONG Q enters, in fencing gear.
RONG Q: At last I can tell that second-rate James Bond exactly what I think
   of him. I am going to lay it right on the line. "Tim, you rotten, hairy son
   of a bitch . . ." *(DROOLEY enters.)*
DROOLEY: Yes, Q?
RONG Q: Tim!
DROOLEY: Q! New development to discuss with you.
RONG Q: No, new development to discuss with YOU.
BLOSSOM enters as a fencing master.
BLOSSOM: Messieurs. La classe commence. *(DROOLEY and RONG Q take posi-*
   tions.) Un, deux, trois, quatre, cinq, six! En garde, messieurs. *(DROOLEY*
   and RONG Q fence; BLOSSOM stands observing.)
RONG Q: Now get this. The chicken has decided to fly the coop.
DROOLEY: WHAT?
RONG Q: The sheep has found greener pastures.
DROOLEY: Have you gone batshit?
RONG Q: The kiwi has found new boots to polish.
DROOLEY: What are you trying to say, Q?
RONG Q: I'm getting out of the trade, pinhead!
DROOLEY: You can't get out.
RONG Q: Oh, yes, I can.
DROOLEY: You need us, Q.
RONG Q: No, I don't—Tim.
DROOLEY: Yes, you do!
RONG Q: *(Swinging sword.)* No—I—don't!
DROOLEY: You can't get out—you're essential to the operation!
RONG Q: Perhaps—but I no longer NEED an operation. *(Puts up sword.)* You
   see, if I get out, the Ambassador has offered me the Presidency for life.
DROOLEY: *(Aside.)* Oof. It takes us ten years to set up a perfect network, and
   Washington sends us an amateur who tears it down in one day!
RONG Q: So, if you'll excuse me, I'll go take a shower and work on my elec-
   tion speech.

DROOLEY: Too bad we can't discuss—X 90!

RONG Q: X 90?

BLOSSOM: X 90? *(They stare at her.)* Ahem—what is this X 90?

RONG Q: Something like H_2O. I am very thirsty. Go and get me a glass of water.

BLOSSOM: Mais, monsieur—

RONG Q: Go!

BLOSSOM: Continuez la classe! *(They resume. She exits.)*

RONG Q: X 90? You can't get it for me.

DROOLEY: Listen, Q. Who set you up in business?

RONG Q: You did, Tim.

DROOLEY: Who stuffed the ballot boxes and got you elected?

RONG Q: You did. And who sent troops swarming all over my country and made a mess out of everything?

DROOLEY: That was the Pentagon, not the CIA!

RONG Q: Bullshit!

DROOLEY: And when those troops are gone, you're going to be all alone, Q.

RONG Q: Alone?

DROOLEY: Surrounded by Commie hordes! They'll be coming at you, Q— from all directions. Their mouths foaming with red saliva—

RONG Q: We've got to stop them!

DROOLEY: And now we CAN stop them—with this miracle weapon. It's new, it's revolutionary, it destroys the enemy without touching the ecology— X 90.

RONG Q: But the Ambassador told me it was out of the question.

BLOSSOM *enters.*

DROOLEY: Then we must eliminate the Ambassador. *(Discovers BLOSSOM.)*

BLOSSOM: Your drink, monsieur.

RONG Q: *(Drinks, splits.)* This—is—water!

BLOSSOM: But you asked for water!

RONG Q: I never drink water. Go and get me a cheeseburger.

BLOSSOM: Continuez! *(She exits.)*

RONG Q: You . . . would have me . . . kill the Ambassador?

DROOLEY: That's right, Rong.

RONG Q: How?

DROOLEY: This is a perfect assignment for the Dragon Lady.

RONG Q: But I've already told her I have to shut her down!

DROOLEY: She has reason to do away with the Ambassador—more reason than she suspects. *(Shows RONG Q a photograph. BLOSSOM enters.)*

BLOSSOM: No cheeseburger. Golden Arches closed. *(Signals them to resume. They fence.)*

DROOLEY: The Ambassador's son was seen last night at the White Monkey Bar. I have gained intelligence from him that a certain Blossom might be wise to our activities.

RONG Q: Blossom!

BLOSSOM: Recommencez, messieurs! *(They do.)*

DROOLEY: I'll take care of the kid. I leave Blossom to your imagination.

RONG Q: But I have no imagination!

DROOLEY: *(To BLOSSOM.)* Je suis fini.

RONG Q: Et moi aussi.

BLOSSOM: Je suis fini. Les classes sont finis. *(She exits, but eavesdrops on what follows.)*

RONG Q: Tim, about X 90—what exactly is it?

DROOLEY: X 90 is a fatal viral disease, developed in our Presidio laboratories, that preys on the chromosomal characteristics of Orientals.

RONG Q: What does this mean?

DROOLEY: A disease that attaches itself only to yellow skin.

RONG Q: Only to yellow skin? It's perfect—you see, all my enemies—all the communists—they all have . . . yellow skin. *(Sees own hand, screams.)* Tim! What about me?

DROOLEY: Don't worry, old man. With you, it's only skin deep.

Exeunt. BLOSSOM enters, removes mask.

BLOSSOM: So, the disease that attaches itself only to yellow skin—is that what they will send in place of bombs? I know they will stop at nothing, but how far that goes still surprises me. Now—how do I stop those dogs from getting a free hand? *(CLYDE enters in pursuit, drugged.)*

CLYDE: Fencing . . . Fencing Salon. *(Sees BLOSSOM, pulls gun.)* Hold it right there.

BLOSSOM: Lieutenant. What happened? *(Sees his arm.)* Not again?

CLYDE: Doesn't matter—I know who killed Harold. It was . . . the Reverend Tim Drooley.

BLOSSOM: Drooley! I have just learned that he is the U.S. counter-insurgency agent who is working with General Rong Q.

CLYDE: That's impossible. That murderer doesn't work for my government. No.

BLOSSOM: They're planning to kill your father.

CLYDE: Dad? But why?

BLOSSOM: Because your father wants to clean up the dope trade—and he is the only obstacle to Secret Weapon X 90.

CLYDE: So the Reverend and the General are really Commie agents . . .

BLOSSOM: No, they are really anti-Commie agents, and the dope trade holds their mercenary forces together. Junk is the mainline of Tim Drooley's policy. But never mind that now—you've got to hurry! Go warn your father of the plot against his life! And remember—you're in danger! Don't stop for anyone you may meet. Remember your mission.

BOTH *start off in opposite directions.*

CLYDE: Blossom—aren't you going to come with me?

BLOSSOM: I have to get back to the White Monkey Bar. I must reach the Dragon Lady before Rong Q does. *(Going.)*

CLYDE: Blossom?

BLOSSOM: Yes, lieutenant?

CLYDE: Blossom . . . ?

BLOSSOM: Yes, lieutenant?

CLYDE: Gee, Blossom, you're swell!

Exeunt

Scene 4: A Street

DROOLEY *enters through sewer, disguised as a nun.* CLYDE *enters running.*

CLYDE: I've almost completed my mission!

DROOLEY: *(Hobbling. Shrieks.)* Oh, pain! Distress!

CLYDE: I must not stop for anyone I may meet. *(Starts off.)*

DROOLEY: Oh, agonizing pain!

CLYDE *hesitates.*

VOICES: Remember your mission!

DROOLEY: Pain, pain, pain!

CLYDE: Can I help you?

DROOLEY: Yes. *(Jumps into his arms.)*

CLYDE: Jesus Christ. You're heavy.

DROOLEY: Oh, soldier! Please don't take our Lord's name—in vein! *(Shoots CLYDE with hypo-cross, dumps him down sewer. Takes a bow and follows.)*

(IF INTERMISSION IS DESIRED . . . THIS IS THE PLACE FOR IT.)

Scene 5: The White Monkey Bar

DRAGON LADY *enters, upset.*

DRAGON LADY: Blossom! Bring me my tranquilizers! *(BLOSSOM enters, hands DRAGON LADY money, which DRAGON LADY begins counting.)*

BLOSSOM: Madame! General Rong Q is about to shut us down.

DRAGON LADY: I know.

BLOSSOM: We've got to do something!

DRAGON LADY: Here, count this. I find it has a soothing effect.

BLOSSOM: If I were you, I would kill that viper before he killed me. I happen to know that the General is on his way here now, to say that he is your friend.

DRAGON LADY: How grotesque!

BLOSSOM: Will you be ready for him?

DRAGON LADY: *(Sings "Dragon Lady-Blossom Duet.")*

He won't be the first
I know his two-faced kind
He won't be the last
To die before his time.
I was born to fight
I fought right from the start.
Someone crosses me,
I tear the fool apart.
When I was young, I trusted a man.
He left me flat, didn't give a damn.
Since that day I've had my way.
Since that day I've made my way—alone!

BOTH:

There're always those who try
To make our lives their own
They'll get you if they can
They'll tear you to the bone.
We've always fed their needs,
The men who prey on us.
It's when we've learned their tricks
That things begin to change.
When you know the moves they make,
Then you know the move to take.

DRAGON LADY: I fight—alone!

BLOSSOM: We fight—together!

DRAGON LADY: *(Speaks.)* Blossom, for one so young, what do you know?

BLOSSOM: *(Sings.)*

I know what life can be:
Simple harmony.
We were of the land.
We shared our days together.
Working in green fields,
Mountain tops, morning mists.
Then I saw my village burning,
Saw my family dying.
When we saw the planes returning
We all left our homes.
Forced into the city,
How we fight to stay alive.
So I'm here to work for you—

Please soldier to survive.

BOTH:

There're always those who try

To make our lives their own.

They'll get you if they can . . .

DRAGON LADY: *(Speaks.)* I'll cut him down, I'll win!

BLOSSOM: *(Sings.)*

Killing the General is all very fine.

Why not see something bigger this time?

If you were fighting for more than YOURSELF

How much greater your victory would be—

TOGETHER!

DRAGON LADY: *(Cuts off music.)* Don't preach! I need no one—and I don't like to share. Here. *(Hands BLOSSOM money.)* Put this away and bring me my headache box.

BLOSSOM *exits with money, returns with jeweled box containing hypo.*

BLOSSOM: Pretty strong for a headache, don't you think? *(Doorbell chimes.)*

DRAGON LADY: Go and see if that's my headache coming on now. *(Hides needle in hair.)*

BLOSSOM *ushers in* RONG Q.

RONG Q: Surprised to see me, Frou-Frou?

BLOSSOM: The perpetual puppet—I mean President—at the White Monkey Bar!

RONG Q: *(Ignores BLOSSOM.)* I have good news!

DRAGON LADY: Have they offered you the throne?

BLOSSOM: Perhaps they are going to make him the first Asian Pope.

RONG Q: *(Stroking BLOSSOM's neck menacingly.)* What a charming young girl—always laughing and joking—what a pity! Dragon Lady, I wish to speak to you ALONE.

DRAGON LADY: Go and play with your dolls, Blossom. *(BLOSSOM exits through beaded curtain, but spies on following.)* So, toad—you've returned.

RONG Q: I could not stay away.

DRAGON LADY: You make me sick.

RONG Q: You hate me, don't you? Well, go ahead, hate me—I deserve it. *(Grovels.)*

DRAGON LADY: This is not a screen test, Q. What do you want?

RONG Q: I want the fire of your breath—the cold caress of your talons—the blinding gleam of your syringe. I want us to kill the Ambassador.

DRAGON LADY: So the worm has turned. Now you want the Ambassador dead? What's in it for you, Q?

RONG Q: A new weapon. X 90, the disease fatal to all Asians.

DRAGON LADY: Have you lost what little mind you had?

RONG Q: No, simply I am no longer Asian.

DRAGON LADY: Oh, come off it.

RONG Q: The agency assured me. With this weapon, I have total victory—as soon as we kill the Ambassador.

DRAGON LADY: What do you mean, WE, white man? *(Takes hypo from hairdo.)* I'm going to kill you, Q.

RONG Q: But what about my plan?

DRAGON LADY: I prefer mine. Say goodbye to rainbows, ice cream sodas, and the monsoon season you love so well—. *(Advances.)*

RONG Q: Wouldn't you rather kill—Dillsey?

DRAGON LADY: *(Stops dead.)* Dillsey?

RONG Q: Yes. DILLSEY.

DRAGON LADY: No! It can't be . . .

RONG Q: It is. Clyde Dillsworth Junker II—the new American Ambassador! *(Gongs crash.)*

DRAGON LADY: The only man who ever crossed me and lived. At last fate has brought us together . . . my revenge must be exquisite.

RONG Q: And that young officer you ENCHANTED last evening—

DRAGON LADY: The kid?

RONG Q: His name is Clyde Dillsworth Junker III.

DRAGON LADY: His son! It's perfect. Oh—come to me, my handsome devil. How could I resist the man who provides me with a perfect revenge!

They kiss. She whips him with her feather boa. He begs for more until his ecstasy is complete.

RONG Q: What are you going to do now, Frou-Frou?

DRAGON LADY: I think we'll invite His Excellency to a special celebration.

RONG Q: A party! I like it—I like it very much, only there is just one more little thing—*(Tiptoes to curtain, reaches in suddenly and pulls BLOSSOM out by the wrist.)* Blossom knows too much.

BLOSSOM turns to DRAGON LADY, who turns away. RONG Q brandishes needle.

BLOSSOM: *(To DRAGON LADY.)* You're making a bad mistake!

RONG Q: See you at the party, Frou-Frou. *(Exits with BLOSSOM. DRAGON LADY starts to exit. Gong, cymbals, drums. MR. BIG enters, masked and hooded, huge, in dazzling Chinese robes.)*

DRAGON LADY: You! *(Falls to knees.)* But I wasn't expecting you—

MR. BIG: *(Intones.)* Listen to me, Dragon Lady. Do not interrupt or question what I have to say. The time has come to close down our operation.

DRAGON LADY: What?

MR. BIG: SILENCE!! We seek new markets. Things have grown too complex here. We must leave Long Pinh immediately.

DRAGON LADY: But—

MR. BIG: You dare to Question MR. BIG?!!!!

DRAGON LADY: So—the White Monkey Bar is to be closed after all. I have been happy here.

MR. BIG: No sentiment, please.

DRAGON LADY: Forgive me, O faceless one. But I beg of you—give me until midnight. I must take care of one last detail.

MR. BIG: Till midnight, then. I Shall Return! *(He sweeps off.)*

DRAGON LADY: So little time—and so much to be done. My last and greatest soiree at the White Monkey Bar. *(Exits.)*

Act Three

Scene 1: The Embassy, That Night

TRAN DOG enters dusting; AMBASSADOR enters carrying letter.

AMBASSADOR: Your famous Dragon Lady breathes out more incense than fire. She has just sent me an extremely sweet-scented message. *(Reads.)* "When the eagle soars, all the beasts tremble, but the dragon's heart quivers with love." Then, she invites me for cocktails. What do you think? *(Sniffs letter.)*

TRAN DOG: I am reminded of ancient proverb, "When wind blows very hot, beware of snakes in the grass."

AMBASSADOR: Snakes in the grass, eh? Number one snake is that idiot, Rong Q. Despite the promise I got from him yesterday, the White Monkey Bar is still doing business. And Drooley—oh, I don't doubt he's competent, but sometimes I wonder if the Agency knows what it's up to.

TRAN DOG: Ambassador, you no get too deep in this White Monkey business. I think you better stay home, maybe?

AMBASSADOR: To stamp out the drug trade, I'm prepared to take a few risks. Here, take my acceptance to the Dragon Lady.

TRAN DOG: She-Dragon magnificent creature. But, very dangerous.

AMBASSADOR: Wait for me there. And if there's any trouble, don't hesitate to use this. *(Gives TRAN DOG gun. TRAN DOG fumbles with this strange object.)* Who knows? Perhaps she might even introduce me to Mr. Big. *(Exits.)*

TRAN DOG: Maybe not even Dragon Lady can do that, Ambassador. *(Twirls gun, does quick draw routine, laughs, exits.)*

Scene 2: A Dungeon beneath the White Monkey Bar

RONG Q throws BLOSSOM on, laughs nastily. BLOSSOM's hands are in chains.

RONG Q: So, my little Blossom. This will teach you not to meddle. *(Exits.)*

BLOSSOM: Where am I? *(Sign appears: "In the clutches of the CIA." CLYDE enters, drugged, moaning.)*

CLYDE: I must save . . . save . . . father . . .

BLOSSOM: Oh, no! Lieutenant! It's me, Blossom!

CLYDE: *(Tries to grab her.)* Blos . . . som . . . Baby . . .

BLOSSOM: No! Did you reach your father? Did you warn him?

CLYDE: Fa-ther. I must warn father . . . *(Passes out.)*

BLOSSOM: Oh, no! He's probably on his way to the White Monkey Bar right now. This is ridiculous; me trying to save the American Ambassador? Well—the enemy of my enemy is my ally, for now. Get up! *(CLYDE gets up, suddenly alert, then collapses on her again.)* Okay. We're going to go for a little walk. *(Walks CLYDE around stage, counting paces.)*

CLYDE: The clouds are parting. I can see clearly now.

BLOSSOM: Can you untie this?

DROOLEY enters in trench coat, knocks CLYDE aside.

DROOLEY: Cute couple. They out to make a movie about you, "G.I. Junkie Meets Commie B-Girl."

BLOSSOM: Very amusing. You could show it as a double feature with "Priest Gets Creased."

DROOLEY: Jesus loves you, Lieutenant. Booster time! *(Holds out hypo. CLYDE hesitates, licking lips.)*

BLOSSOM: No. Don't do it!

CLYDE: Just this once. *(Takes needle.)*

BLOSSOM: No!

CLYDE: Shut up! *(Shoots up.)*

DROOLEY: *(Holds BLOSSOM, forcing her to watch. Hooks her bound hands to curtain pole.)* Now, sonny ready to see daddy?

CLYDE: Da da.

BLOSSOM: Why do you waste so much time doing evil, when you know you're going to lose the war?

DROOLEY: So, you want to talk politics. *(He kisses her.)* What's your Red Book say about that? *(BLOSSOM spits in his face.)* Oh, a little spit-fire! Here's a trick I learned at Yale. *(Pulls back curtain, revealing torture machine. Turns switch, machine advances on BLOSSOM.)* Struggle, sister! *(Exits with CLYDE.)*

BLOSSOM struggles, machine bears down on her. TRAN DOG enters through sewer.

BLOSSOM: You . . . old man . . . up here! The switch! Get the switch! *(TRAN DOG turns it off just in time, releases BLOSSOM.)* But, who are you? *(TRAN DOG puts finger to lips, hands her a gun. Both exeunt through sewer.)*

Scene 3: The White Monkey Bar

DRAGON LADY enters with goblet on tray, followed by RONG Q, drinking. As he talks, she sets tray, produces poison vial, mixes cocktail.

RONG Q: Oh, Frou-Frou, you look terrific. Think of it—by this time tomorrow, I shall rule Long Pinh supreme and unchallenged. X 90, priceless potion. I wonder how it works? *(Reaches for goblet to drink.)* Mmmm, what is this?

DRAGON LADY: I wouldn't touch that if I were you. That is a special cocktail for the Ambassador. I think it will intoxicate him—permanently.

RONG Q: What a woman. Don't think, my dear, that I will ever forget the part you played in my rise to power.

DRAGON LADY: Will you continue to adore me, General, after X 90 has attached itself to my yellow skin?

RONG Q: *(Shrinks in disgust.)* Ugh! But maybe there's a cure.

DRAGON LADY: And, anyway, do you really think Drooley will give it to you?

RONG Q: He promised! *(Bell rings. DROOLEY enters with CLYDE.)*

DROOLEY: Where do you want the kid stashed?

CLYDE: Da da.

DRAGON LADY: The usual place. Now when I give the signal I want him to come out, crawling like a baby.

CLYDE: Da da.

DROOLEY stashes CLYDE.

RONG Q: You are such a character, Tim! Did you bring it, X 90?

DROOLEY: Sure thing, Q. Say, how about getting me a drink first?

RONG Q: Good idea, let's all get drunk. *(Exits.)*

DROOLEY: Jasmine—Jasmine! *(Kissing her.)*

DRAGON LADY: Please, Tim—not now.

DROOLEY: You always say that—and I always let you get away with it—why? Because I always put the operation before everything. Well, listen, I got some news for you: Q's cuckoo! He's a threat to the operation.

RONG Q returns with drink.

RONG Q: I want to see it now, Tim!

DROOLEY: Is this Scotch? *(Takes sip.)*

RONG Q: No. Japanese.

DROOLEY: Get me a Coke. *(RONG Q exits again.)* When you finish with the Ambassador, I'm taking care of Q.

DRAGON LADY: It's convenient, but what will you replace him with?

DROOLEY: Ever hear of General Big Dong?

DRAGON LADY: No, but he sounds all right.

DROOLEY: He's trustworthy, levelheaded, ruthless, cunning, corrupt—

DRAGON LADY: Who is he?

DROOLEY: Myself! From here on out the Agency takes no chances. *(RONG Q, tipsy, enters with coke.)*

RONG Q: Tim, they only had it in the can. *(Bell rings.)*

DRAGON LADY: At last—after 25 years!

AMBASSADOR *enters in full evening dress.*

AMBASSADOR: Permit me to introduce myself. My Excellency, C. Dillsworth Junker.

DRAGON LADY: Life has named me the Dragon Lady. (*The* AMBASSADOR *bows.*) I think you know General Q?

AMBASSADOR: Why, yes. We had a long talk only yesterday. But I'm afraid there was a failure of communication. (*Takes coke, as if* RONG Q *were a waiter.*)

RONG Q: Not really—merely a change in situation. (*Falls down drunk.*) Oh, excuse me.

DRAGON LADY: And of course you know Mr. Drooley.

DROOLEY: Hare rama, Ambassador.

AMBASSADOR: I think we can speak English now, Tim.

DROOLEY: (*To* AMBASSADOR.) I don't trust these people any farther than you can throw them.

AMBASSADOR: Admirable prudence.

RONG Q: Tim—let me look at it!

DRAGON LADY: Since you gentlemen are already acquainted, why don't you retire to the billiard parlor?

RONG Q: Good idea. Tim—let me see it.

DROOLEY: Don't touch me!

RONG Q: Don't hit me!

BOTH *exit fighting.*

DRAGON LADY: Well, Ambassador. My humble premises blush at the honor you do them.

AMBASSADOR: Yes, it's a magnificent setting.

DRAGON LADY: Why don't you come closer and admire the jewel?

AMBASSADOR: I can see it from here, thanks. It's a dazzling antique. Dragon Lady, I came here to talk to you man to man.

DRAGON LADY: (*Offers goblet.*) Have a drink then.

DROOLEY: (*Offstage.*) I said no, Q.

AMBASSADOR: Drooley's in it with you, isn't he? Well, don't expect any protection from him. I want you to close up shop and get out of town.

DRAGON LADY: You know—you amuse me, Ambassador. Why should a man of the world, like yourself, get so upset over a simple thing like my humble product?

AMBASSADOR: I don't expect you to understand. (*Sips coke.*) Here in Asia, a human being's just so much garbage. (*Tosses can offstage.*)

DRAGON LADY: So, you're not a newcomer to the East then, Ambassador?

AMBASSADOR: I spent the best years of my life here.

More argument backstage.

DRAGON LADY: You must have known many of our women.

AMBASSADOR: Pearls of the orient without number. There was one in particular—a common bar girl in Singapore. Funny, I couldn't remember her face if my life depended on it, but I'll never forget the smell of—(*sniffs*)—jasmine . . .

DRAGON LADY: (*Offers drink.*) Try my cocktail, Ambassador. It's guaranteed to bring back those old times.

AMBASSADOR *takes goblet, still in reverie. Still more argument backstage.*

AMBASSADOR: Look, Dragon Lady. The American government is prepared to make you an offer.

DRAGON LADY: What is it?

AMBASSADOR: A million dollars. To take your business elsewhere—anywhere we don't have an army.

DRAGON LADY: And where might that be, Ambassador?

AMBASSADOR: There must be some place.

DRAGON LADY: A million dollars. I wonder if you know what my business is worth.

AMBASSADOR: That's our offer. You can think about it and let me know. (*Tries to hand goblet back.*)

DRAGON LADY: Wait. It's not out of the question. I might accept . . . I accept!

AMBASSADOR: Swell!

DRAGON LADY: On one condition—that we drink to it.

DROOLEY: (*Offstage.*) I said no, Q!

RONG Q: (*Offstage.*) I said yes, Tim!

AMBASSADOR: Oh, did I forget to mention that I never drink alcohol? (*Hands back goblet.*) But I'll gladly shake on it. (*DRAGON LADY is agitated.*) Why, it's an old custom in . . .

DRAGON LADY: (*Pulls gun.*) So you still remember Singapore, eh Dillsey?

AMBASSADOR: Singapore—Dillsey—Jasmine—it's you! How awkward!

RONG Q *throws* DROOLEY *onstage and jumps on him, knocking* DRAGON LADY'S *gun out of her hand and offstage.*

RONG Q: White devil!

DROOLEY: Yellow dwarf!

RONG Q *and* DROOLEY *fight all over stage. General chase ensues.* AMBASSADOR *vanishes. Finally* DROOLEY *staggers on, quaffs goblet, falls off edge of stage and freezes, paralyzed, as on a cross.* DRAGON LADY *enters, doesn't see him.*

DRAGON LADY: Junker's gone! Idiots! Animals! I'll sauté your livers!

Twelve gongs. MR. BIG *enters.*

MISTER BIG: Have you completed your preparations?

DRAGON LADY: Oh, these idiots let the prize slip through my fingers!

MISTER BIG: But what have you done to Drooley?

DRAGON LADY: (*Sees* DROOLEY *for first time.*) The cocktail!

RONG Q groans backstage. DRAGON LADY *opens beaded curtain,* RONG Q *falls out dead, a giant hypo stuck in his back.*

MISTER BIG: Dragon Lady, you never cease to amaze me. The most sordid tasks accomplished with such flair. You leave me nothing to do—except this. *(Pulls gun.)*

DRAGON LADY: What?

MISTER BIG: You've received your last shipment.

DROOLEY: *(With great effort.)* No . . . no . . . no.

MISTER BIG: Farewell, Dragon Lady—and you too, Drooley. You have served me well. But I have no choice—it's the law of the market.

DRAGON LADY: You can't do this!

MISTER BIG: You can't stop me. *(Takes aim.)*

BLOSSOM *enters in black pajamas, with submachine gun.*

BLOSSOM: But I can. Reach for the moon, Mr. Big!

MISTER BIG: Who are you?

BLOSSOM: A soldier of the People's Liberation Forces. And who are you?

MISTER BIG: Commander of the capitalist legion. Would you like my card?

BLOSSOM: Very amusing. You stop at nothing! *(Pulls* CLYDE *onstage.)*

DRAGON LADY: What are you doing?

CLYDE: I know . . . who you are . . . you're Mr. Big, the real killer! *(Tries to attack him.)*

MISTER BIG: *(Overpowers him without effort.)* My God—Clyde! Who did this to you?

DRAGON LADY: "Clyde?"

BLOSSOM: You did—*(Pulls his mask off.)* AMBASSADOR!

DRAGON LADY: Dillsey!

CLYDE: Dad!

DROOLEY: No—no—no. *(Dies.)*

AMBASSADOR: Please, son, I know this looks bad—but don't judge me too quickly.

BLOSSOM: Is the American government behind the dope trade, or is the dope trade behind the American government?

AMBASSADOR: Can you understand me, son?

CLYDE: Go ahead, dad.

AMBASSADOR: The drug trade is exceedingly profitable. Our government, as you know, encourages profit.

CLYDE: But it's criminal!

AMBASSADOR: Can anything that makes billions REALLY be called criminal?

DRAGON LADY: So—your cleanup campaign was just a publicity stunt.

AMBASSADOR: With a solid basis in fact—we are rerouting the traffic to the mass market.

DRAGON LADY: Where?

BLOSSOM: The United States. They found it works better on their people than on ours.

AMBASSADOR: Picture them, Clyde: hundreds of unemployed discontented young people, many of them racially disgruntled—we've found an efficient, pharmacological way of keeping them happy.

CLYDE: I'm not happy.

AMBASSADOR: I'm sorry, son. That's what happens when a powerful weapon falls into the wrong hands.

BLOSSOM keeps AMBASSADOR back with gun.

DRAGON LADY: Are these the wrong hands, Ambassador? *(Caresses CLYDE.)*

AMBASSADOR: Get your filthy talons off him, you disgusting whore!

DRAGON LADY crosses to AMBASSADOR, fiddling with hairpiece. She attacks with hidden hypo. They struggle.

DRAGON LADY: Shoot, Blossom—shoot both of us! It would be worth it! (*AMBASSADOR stabs her with her own syringe.*) Blossom—your greater victory will be my revenge! *(Slowly falls, dies.)*

AMBASSADOR: Clyde—disarm the girl!

CLYDE: No, dad. You'd kill her.

AMBASSADOR: *(Calls.)* Tran Dog! *(TRAN DOG enters.)* Get her gun.

TRAN DOG: No, Mr. Junker. I do not work for you any more.

AMBASSADOR: What about your rice bowl?

TRAN DOG: Your rice was very bad. I got sick on it. (*BLOSSOM raises gun.*)

AMBASSADOR: Don't shoot—please! Look—I'm a powerful man. In my pocket, Clyde—traveller's checks. Take as much as you want! I'm a generous man—tell her, Clyde!

CLYDE: *(Standing between gun and father.)* He's—he's—he's exactly what you think he is! And I'm in the middle.

TRAN DOG: There is no middle—only two sides.

AMBASSADOR: I'm a human being. *(Cowers.)*

BLOSSOM: *(Lowers gun.)* If we kill you, they will only put another in your place. Our fight is with all of your kind, not just with one. The important thing is for your people to see who you are. Let's go.

CLYDE: Where are you taking him?

BLOSSOM: To show our peasants, whose villages he has destroyed, and your workers, whose sons he has taken, and the young people who are shooting his dope, to show them all who the real Mr. Big is!

AMBASSADOR: They'll never believe it: they're too stupid.

BLOSSOM: They get smarter every day. *(Starts to march him off.)*

CLYDE: Blossom. Can I come with you?

BLOSSOM: I hope so.

TRAN DOG: People in different countries are fighting one enemy. Some start early, others are slow to understand. But one day, all together, we will sweep him away.

Exeunt. Trumpet plays "Ballad of Ho Chi Minh."

The End

Hotel Universe

1977

Script by Joan Holden with Dan Chumley and the Cast

Introduction

Hotel Universe was created during a two-week residency at the Rencontres Internationales de l'Art Contemporains in La Rochelle, France, in July 1977. William Kleb describes the process in "*Hotel Universe:* Playwriting and the San Francisco Mime Troupe" (*Theater* 9 [spring 1978]: 15–20). The play is one of six troupe shows about urban redevelopment destroying low-income housing. It also employs a favorite troupe action: political awakening. The characters are pushed to a point where they unite and stand up to their oppressor. *Hotel Universe* is based on the true story of the tenants of the International Hotel in San Francisco who fought for seven years to save the hotel from demolition. When the play was first created in France, the ending was optimistic because it looked as though the tenants might win. By the time the play opened in San Francisco a month later, the tenants had been evicted, and the ending was changed.

Hotel Universe toured in the United States, Europe, Cuba, Canada, and Nicaragua and was revived in San Francisco in the summer of 1986. It is probably the most-performed show in the troupe's history because the plot and dialogue are simple. It can be understood by spectators who do not know English, although in Cuba spectators didn't understand the concept of a landlord. It can also be easily translated and was first performed in a combination of French and English. In Cuba and Nicaragua it was performed in Spanish and English.

Commentary
Bruce Barthol

There were two *Hotel Universes;* one was the show created in La Rochelle that became the basis for the show done in San Francisco and thereafter.

The International Hotel was the last remnant of Manilatown in San Francisco. The hotel tenants were mostly old Filipino and Chinese men who had never married due to the race laws when they came to California. The most distressing thing is that the site of the International Hotel is still a hole in the ground twenty-five years later. (Telephone interview by Susan Vaneta Mason, 16 July 2002)

William Kleb

Hotel Universe has the simplicity and acuity of a political cartoon: the characters are graphically outlined (what they say is less important than what they do), and the action, on the whole, moves quickly, logically and *visually* forward, animated throughout by a single, consistent idea. ("*Hotel Universe:* Playwriting and the San Francisco Mime Troupe," *Theater* 9 [spring 1979]: 20)

Barry Levitan

The irony is that the site of the International Hotel is still an empty lot. It's a terrible waste of a resource. It wasn't just housing; it was a home. And that policy continues. It's worse today. People don't pay attention to evictions anymore. Being in the Mime Troupe ruined me—since then I've expected so much more of people in life—that spirit of helping each other. (Telephone interview by Susan Vaneta Mason, 16 July 2002)

Sylvie Drake

The hotel is a painted curtain, the flames and ashes are chiffon strips of appropriate hue, and the spoofing is splendidly underscored by musical sound effects. Proof that a good imagination . . . is the only true essential in the theater. ("S.F. Mimes in *Hotel Universe*," *Los Angeles Times,* 9 November 1977)

Ed Levey

It was very simple and very physical. It's probably the only Mime Troupe show created through improvisation that I had a background in. It was a blast. We got to create the characters and put them in various situations roommates might find themselves in. It was fun. Other shows, like *False Promises,* were fun, too, but much more work. (Telephone interview by Susan Vaneta Mason, 18 July 2002)

Audrey Smith

When we did *Hotel Universe* in West Berlin, there was a squatter movement, and when I sang "We Won't Move" there was an emotional explosion in the audience—cheers, yelling, screams of support. The show is still powerful.

"We Won't Move" is a song that continues to live. (Telephone interview by Susan Vaneta Mason, 30 July 2002)

Nancy Scott

I loved it. I loved the content, which is about something happening to real people right now. ("Check into the Mimes *Hotel*," *San Francisco Examiner*, 16 December 1980)

The Production

Hotel Universe was first performed in La Rochelle, France, in July 1977, then opened on 12 August 1977 in San Francisco's Civic Center, with the following cast:

Sailor	*Ed Levey*
Landlord, Judge	*Barry Levitan*
Mayor	*Bruce Barthol*
Manuel, Lowrider	*Eduardo Robledo*
Gladys, Nurse	*Deb'bora Gilyard*
Myrna, Mrs. Gallo	*Sharon Lockwood*
Olga, Georgette	*Joan Mankin*
Reporter	*David Topham*

Directed by Dan Chumley. Music and lyrics by Bruce Barthol and Eduardo Robledo. Stage managers: Cyndy Turnage, Brian Freeman. Musicians: Bruce Barthol, Ed Levey, Barry Levitan, Eduardo Robledo, David Topham.

Characters (in order of appearance)
An old sailor
Residents of the Hotel Universe in days gone by
A landlord
The Mayor of San Francisco
Manuel, a longshoreman replaced by a machine
Gladys, a former hot-dog lady at Seals Stadium
Myrna, who ran the bumper cars at Playland at the Beach
Olga, once a prima ballerina
A reporter
Supporters of the Hotel Universe in the present
Citizens

ject to license and royalty. All rights including, without limitation, reproduction in whole or in any part by any process or method, professional use, amateur use, film, recitation, lecturing, public reading, recording, taping, radio and television broadcasting, and the rights of translation into foreign languages, are strictly reserved. All inquiries should be addressed to San Francisco Mime Troupe, 855 Treat Avenue, San Francisco, CA 94110.

Hotel Universe

Scene 1: In a Foreign Port

SAILOR: *(Kicked onstage, he yells back.)* Oh, yeah? Well, screw you! I wouldn't sign onto your goddamn ship if I was marooned on a melting iceberg! *(He sings "Sailor's Song.")*
I've been a sailor for these forty years or more,
Worked tankers down in Veracruz and junks in Singapore.
I've sailed every ocean, had a home in every port,
And now they say I'm getting old and must be put ashore.

It's hard to be at anchor after running with the wind.
How can one place be my home after every place I've been?
It's got to have a taste of every corner of the globe.
Guess it's time to hoist my sails and point my bow towards home—
Back to San Francisco.
(As music fades.) San Francisco. I know a great little spot there. *(Takes bottle from hip. Drinks.)* The Hotel Universe! *(Music starts.)* I can almost hear the music!
Dream sequence. A waiter dances on with glass on tray; SAILOR drinks; a couple enters and dances; SAILOR cuts in, dances with girl; her boyfriend calls SAILOR out, socks him, slaps her; blues singer enters, sings.
Oh, I love my baby, and I don't know why.
I love my baby, and I don't know why.
Because he whips me and beats me, and he makes me cry.
All are costumed as in late '40s. As SAILOR tries to embrace singer the vision fades. Music changes to "La Strada," which is the SAILOR and OLGA theme.
SAILOR: The Hotel Universe. That's the way it was. I got a date there. *(Shows photo of younger OLGA.)* She promised to wait for me. I'm a little late— *(Looks at bottle.)* Twenty-five years. I hope she's still there. *(Exits, gazing at photo and drinking.)*

Scene 2: Forty-fourth Floor of a San Francisco High-Rise

LANDLORD enters, sets signs. Music. MAYOR enters.
LANDLORD: Your honor, this is an honor. Come right on in.
MAYOR: I'll come right to the point. You've bought up more buildings downtown.

LANDLORD: Only small ones.

MAYOR: You're the worst thing to hit San Francisco since the earthquake! You've leveled whole neighborhoods—evicted thousands of people. It's sickening, it's inhuman, and I want it to stop—at least until after the election.

LANDLORD: Is it that time again? *(Reaches for checkbook.)*

MAYOR: You can't buy me, Ben—I belong to the people. Park your bulldozers.

LANDLORD: *(Aside.)* Election fever—but I've got the cure. *(Displays picture: "1955," showing old San Francisco skyline.)* Remember this?

MAYOR: I'd almost forgotten. My God, will you look at all those houses!

LANDLORD: And all that sky going to waste. Quaint, but unproductive—a lot like your rhetoric. Now we're looking at a different picture. *("1977," showing new San Francisco skyline.)*

MAYOR: We're looking at a billion-dollar rip-off.

LANDLORD: Mr. Mayor, do you know what they're saying about you?

MAYOR: Out of date? Me? Look at this suit!

LANDLORD: I am. *(Changes pictures to "1955," showing worker in overalls.)* Check out this profile of the average voter.

MAYOR: That's Joe Gonzales, from the Laborer's Union! How ya doin', Joe? He's the real thing—your old San Franciscan. Not many guys like him left.

LANDLORD: Exactly. Not many at all. *(Changes picture to "1977," showing executive with briefcase.)*

MAYOR: I'll tell you what's out of date—it's these robber baron . . . who's that?

LANDLORD: That's you, new San Franciscan.

MAYOR: Good morning—are you registered to vote?

LANDLORD: These people work in our office towers. They live in our high-rise apartments. They want condos and dildoes and parking lots—and yes, they vote—by the hundreds of thousands. *(MAYOR ponders.)* Now, I've just acquired a small piece of property. *(Changes picture back to "1977" skyline and points to the spot.)* The last empty space.

MAYOR: That's not empty—it's a hotel, full of old people.

LANDLORD: Old people, or new people?

MAYOR: Listen, where can I get some new clothes?

LANDLORD: *(Leading him out.)* I'm going to introduce you to my tailor. *(They exit.)*

Scene 3: Lobby of the Hotel Universe

MANUEL: *(Hobbles on with mandolin and TV.)* Well, it's Sunday afternoon—time for the big game. And those Giants are going to get their asses whipped again! *(Turns on TV, sits. Music: "Take Me Out to the Ball Game.")*

TV SPORTS ANNOUNCER: We got baseball on a Sunday. Los Angeles versus San Francisco.

MANUEL: All right!

TV: Now the Giants have lost—count them—two hundred and ninety-nine consecutive games. Will it be three hundred? Okay, here we go—the Dodger pitcher winds up and it's—low! Ball one!

MANUEL: He's still alive! Come on, Giants! *(GLADYS shuffles on with tambourine, heads for TV.)*

TV: He delivers. *(MANUEL motions GLADYS to get out of way.)* It's a hit! *(MANUEL nearly falls out of chair.)* It's going deep into right field! *(MANUEL falls out of chair. GLADYS reaches TV and changes the channel. Gospel music. MANUEL starts for TV.)* Amen! Thank you, Jesus!

GLADYS: Sunday afternoon, time for religion! Thank you, Jesus. *(MANUEL reaches TV and changes the channel.)*

TV: Did you see that play? *(GLADYS starts for TV.)*

MANUEL: No!

TV: Too bad! It's just unbelievable! Well, here we go—the Dodger pitcher winds up—it's another hit! Deep into right field! It's going, going— *(GLADYS changes the channel.)*—Amen, amen!

GLADYS: Hallelujah! *(Clapping and singing, backs toward chair, MANUEL takes chair with him as he goes to change channel.)*

TV: *(As a tug-of-war develops over the chair.)* He's safe! My God, what an incredible play! Oh—who just walked into the booth but a man who is a legend in his own mind, Coward Hosell! Coward? *(New voice.)* Thank you, Grimsby. Well, that was cer-tain-ly one of the MOST fan-tas-tic a-chieve-ments—

GLADYS: Gimme back my chair.

TV: —in the an-nals of base-ball. *(Etc., etc.)*

MYRNA: *(Bounces in with sign, singing "There's No Business Like Show Business," sees fight, blows whistle. MANUEL lets go of chair, MANUEL falls.)* I can't leave them alone for two minutes. *(Crosses to TV and turns it off, covers it with sign: "Coming Soon: Hotel Universe Seniors Amateur Talent Show.")* Come on kids—it's time to rehearse for the big talent show!

MANUEL: "Maniaca Myrna and Her Rickety Reject Revue." How many times I got to told you, I don't want to be in your talent show!

MYRNA: Fine, we'll go on without you. *(He starts off.)* You can go back to your room and count cockroaches—alone! *(He stops.)* Come on, Gladys.

GLADYS: I was in a show once.

MYRNA: Yes, we know. You already told us.

GLADYS: At the Divine Light of Holiness Church yearly outing. I had a robe like an angel. Sang like an angel. Sure raised the devil! *(Giggles.)*

MANUEL: What you gonna do with her?

MYRNA: I'll tell you, there's one tonic the both of you need—activity! There's just one way out of being down and out, and that's get up and get doing! All together now—one, two, three . . . *(They start to play, she starts to dance.)*

MANUEL: *(Sings.)* Yo fui soldado de Pancho Villa . . . *(MYRNA blows whistle.)* Ai, yi, yi.

MYRNA: This is a tap dance, it ain't no god damn rumba. Now let's take it from the top one more time. *(They play "No Business Like Show Business." MYRNA dances.)*

OLGA: *(Enters, cuts them off.)* What is all this commotion?

MYRNA: It's your cue, actually.

OLGA: I don't dance today. I'm too distressed.

MANUEL: Looks like heartburn.

OLGA: I, Olga Danskaya—once the greatest ballerina in all of Russia—I have led the tragic life. *(Music: "Sailor and Olga Theme." She shows picture of younger SAILOR. Mimes his departure, waves farewell.)* It is twenty-five years ago today that he was to meet me here. *(Dances a few steps of the dying swan.)* When my heart she break, my arch she fall. A great career ruined. Nyet, my friends—I don't dance today. I need a little space. *(Grand exit.)*

MANUEL: When her arch fell, her mind snapped.

MYRNA: Well now, kids, the show must go on. Let's take it from the top—one, two, three . . .

They start over. LANDLORD enters with scroll, hands one end to MYRNA. As she dances across stage, scroll unrolls to read: "Eviction."

MANUEL: Hold it, hold it. *(They stop.)* What is this?

MYRNA: Who are you?

LANDLORD: I am your landlord.

MYRA: Well, we're very pleased to meet—

LANDLORD: And I'm going to tear down this hotel.

TENANTS: Tear it down?!

LANDLORD: But there's no rush, folks—you have fifteen minutes.

MYRNA: If, if . . .

GLADYS: And, and . . .

MANUEL: But, but . . .

LANDLORD: No ifs, ands, or buts about it. Now you have ten minutes. Get out!

MANUEL: Viva Villa! *(Goes after LANDLORD with mandolin as club.)*

LANDLORD: No violence! No violence!

MANUEL: This no violin, it's a mandolin. *(LANDLORD escapes.)*

MYRNA: Oh, look, Manuel—there ain't nothing we can do. He owns this building.

MANUEL: Sure he owns it. I bought it for him, with the rent I paid for the last fifteen years, ese hijo de la chinalaria. Last time I got evicted, it took me fifteen minutes to pack. Ten minutes? I'm late already. *(Exits.)*

MYRNA: Well, Gladys, old girl—looks like it's back on the road again. *(Exits with sign. GLADYS crosses slowly to chair and sits. Music: "Sailor's Song.")*

SAILOR: *(Enters with bouquet. Shocked by decay of hotel.)* Twenty-five years . . . *(Sees GLADYS.)* Excuse me. I'm looking for my sweetheart. *(Shows photo. GLADYS just looks away.)* Nice talking to you. *(MYRNA enters with suitcase, muttering.)* Hey, you there! *(MYRNA elbows him aside.)* What's going on here? *(MANUEL enters with trunks, muttering.)* Hey Grandpa— you ever seen this lady? *(Shows photo.)*

MANUEL: This lady? ¿Van a tumbar este hotel, y tú con "this lady"?

SAILOR: They're going to tear this place down?

MANUEL: That what I said, didn't I?

SAILOR: I'll never see her again! *(Music: "Sailor and Olga Theme." SAILOR stabs himself with bouquet, drops it, take bottle from him, exits drunk.)*

OLGA: *(Enters.)* Was someone here? I thought I heard his voice.

MANUEL: You heard the landlord.

OLGA: We been evicted.

OLGA: Evicted? But how will he find me now?

MANUEL: Who cares?

OLGA: Yes, who cares? He will never come back no more, perhaps, maybe, never . . . *(Sees bouquet.)* Ah! *(Picks it up.)* Wild flowers—my favorite. *(Exits.)*

MYRNA: There's one space-case for you. Come on, Manuel—we gotta— *(Sees GLADYS asleep in her chair.)* Oh, will you look at her.

MANUEL: ¡Levántate, vieja!

MYRNA: Come on, Gladys—we gotta get out of here! *(Shakes her awake.)*

GLADYS: I'm—I'm staying right here. *(Music starts: "We Won't Move.")* I won't move!

MYRNA and MANUEL: You won't move?

GLADYS: I won't move!

MYRNA and MANUEL: She won't move!

GLADYS: *(Gets up and sings "We Won't Move.")*
I won't move—been moved before—
I won't move no more.
They'll have to carry me out the door.
I won't move.

My city was people, not concrete.
Parking lots and cars didn't make my street.
Lived there so long, had friends all around,
Then the man come and he tear it down.

And he leave me with nothing but a memory,
Of how my city used to be.
Built a lot of nothing that nobody needs.
Show me the reason, can you show me the rhyme?
Got nowhere to run, got nowhere to hide.
I won't move, I won't move this time.

GLADYS *sits.* MYRNA *thinks as music vamps.* MANUEL *heads for door with trunks.*

MYRNA: I won't move! (MYRNA *and* GLADYS *jump up, start barricading doors with suitcases.)*

MANUEL: "I won't move." ¡Están bien locas! The landlord's gonna come—they're gonna get in a big fight . . . fight? *(Likes idea.)* I won't move. *(Stacks trunks on barricade.)*

ALL SING:

We won't move! We won't move!
We won't move—been moved before.
They'll have to carry us out the door.
We won't move—no, we won't move!

LANDLORD: *(Enters, crashes into barricade.)* What's this?

TENANTS: *(Sing.)* We won't move! We won't move!

LANDLORD: Oh, you'll move, you'll move! I'll move your ass! *(Exits.)*

TENANTS *exit singing.*

Scene 4: Outside the Hotel, Sometime Later

SAILOR: *(Enters drunk, carrying lamppost. Bumps into hotel.)* It's the Hotel Universe! They didn't tear it down! *(Brightens, then remembers* OLGA *is gone. Cries.)*

LANDLORD: *(Enters in trench coat and dark glasses.)* P-s-s-t, sailor!

SAILOR: Hey, mister—have you ever been in love?

LANDLORD: No.

SAILOR: 'S worse'n being in jail.

LANDLORD: You want to make ten dollars? *(Holds out bill.* SAILOR *takes it, blows nose on it. Exasperated,* LANDLORD *takes Molotov cocktail and lighter from his coat, pantomimes lighting it and throwing it into hotel.)* Okay?

SAILOR: Okay. *(Takes it.)*

LANDLORD: Be quick about it. *(*SAILOR *drinks it.* LANDLORD *grabs it back.)* Why do I have to do everything myself?

SAILOR: Do it yourself. *(Collapses around lamppost.)*

LANDLORD *throws Molotov cocktail into hotel, scurries off. Hotel bursts into flame. Sirens, screams, music.*

MYRNA: *(Enters, blowing whistle.)* The hotel's on fire, the hotel's on fire! *(Rouses* SAILOR; *he gets bucket from offstage, spills water.* MYRNA *rushes around, blowing whistle.* SAILOR *fetches second bucket, sloshes confetti on audience, exits.* MANUEL *staggers on, coughing. He and* MYRNA *embrace.)*

GLADYS: *(Within.)* Help! Help!

MYRNA: Save her! *(*MANUEL *rushes into hotel, emerges with broken mandolin.)*

GLADYS: Save me! *(*MANUEL *and* MYRNA *rush into hotel, emerge with* GLADYS *just as* SAILOR *enters with third bucket, sloshes all three, exits.)*

OLGA: *(Above.)* Save me! Save me! *(Trio tries to save her but heat drives them back.* SAILOR *enters with fourth bucket; throws water, follows it in, emerges with* OLGA *draped around shoulders and dumps her on* MANUEL. *Fanfare. Fire dies, leaving hotel black.*)*

MYRNA: Mister, you were fantastic.

GLADYS: And you ain't no kid, neither.

SAILOR: Lady, I'm an able-bodied seaman.

MYRNA: We could use an able body around here.

SAILOR: Hey, an' I could use some people 'at wouldn't turn a good man down. They retired me, see, then my sweetheart up and left me—

OLGA: *(Reviving.)* O-o-o-h . . .

SAILOR: —Aah, the hell with her. I'll be back with my duffel bag. *(Exits.)*

OLGA: Whom must I thank for saving my life?

MYRNA, GLADYS, and MANUEL: Thank him.

OLGA: Whom?

MYRNA, GLADYS, and MANUEL: He's gone!

OLGA: Slovobolga! Where is it? My picture? I must find my picture!

MYRNA: You can't go in there!

OLGA: I must! *(Exits into hotel.)*

MANUEL: Let 'er go. *(*TENANTS *now see damage to hotel.)*

GLADYS: Burnt to a crisp! *(She crosses, sits, goes to sleep.)*

MYRNA: *(Blows whistle.)* Well, now—it's gonna take a lot of energy to fix this place up! A lotta energy, a lotta Geritol. Chin up, Gladys—you look depressed. Come on, Manuel—we can do it.

MANUEL: *(Holds broken mandolin.)* She was the only thing I brought with me from Mexico.

MYRNA: You can fix that as soon as we fix the hotel. Let's see now—we're gonna need hammers, nails . . .

MANUEL: Plumbers, electricians, building inspectors—maybe twenty years

*The fire is strips of colored silk attached to a stick which is shaken. The burn stains were black silk streamers dropped over the hotel.

ago we could do it. My dreams always went up in smoke. Why should I expect any different?

MYRNA: Come on, Gladys—Gladys! *(GLADYS is asleep.)*

OLGA: *(Enters.)* It's a miracle. There was no damage.

MYRNA and MANUEL: No damage!

OLGA: To my picture. All the rest—boi-zhe moi. And it's no wonder, when people around here have been getting so very *(Wakes GLADYS.)* careless. Which of you left this on the stairway? *(Holds out exploded Molotov cocktail. Doom music.)*

MANUEL: ¡A la ve!

GLADYS: Lord have mercy.

MYRNA: Arson!

Music: "Hail to the Chief." MAYOR enters with REPORTER. MAYOR wears button, "Vote Me."

MYRNA: It's the mayor! Mr. Mayor, someone set fire to the Hotel!

MANUEL: Someone wants this place bad enough to kill us for it.

GLADYS: What are you going to do about it?

MAYOR: *(As REPORTER takes notes.)* I fully sympathize with you victims of this devastating tragedy.

REPORTER: "Devastating tragedy." *(Kicks TENANTS into pose, shoots picture.)* Got it!

MAYOR: Though it does prove one thing: this building was a firetrap.

TENANTS: A firetrap?!

MAYOR: But your mayor would never let our senior citizens stay homeless on the street.

REPORTER: Say cheese.

MYRNA: Limburger.

GLADYS: "Vote Me!" . . .

MAYOR: Because I believe that housing is a right, not a privilege. So I am privileged to present the housing—*(gets picture from backstage)* that is right for you. *(Shows picture: "Public Housing.")*

MANUEL: Looks like a waffle. *(Gathers women.)* If I move, I move. But nobody's gonna push me.

MYRNA: *(Breaking huddle.)* Mr. Mayor, that is a turkey, and we're not biting.

GLADYS: We won't move!

MANUEL: We're going to stay right here and fix up the hotel.

OLGA: "We're going to stay right here and fix up the hotel."

MANUEL: Right.

OLGA: Wrong! You're going to stay and fix it up. Because as for me, after twenty-five long years, I am sick to death of living in a fleabitten flophouse. *(To MAYOR.)* Monsieur, j'accepte votre hospitalité.

MAYOR: Fix it up? Even if you could, they'd tear it down anyway. And I just want to say you old people are a real bringdown. I came all the way over here—in the dark. *(Exits with* OLGA *and* REPORTER.*)*

MYRNA: Yeah, well you can go home in the dark! You'll always be in the dark!

GLADYS: Olga, you're making a bad mistake!

MANUEL: "Fleabitten." ¡Más fleabitten tiene las nalgas!

MYRNA: Oh, forget about Olga! Did you hear what he said? They're going to tear it down anyway. You know what we need?

GLADYS: We need help.

SAILOR: *(Enters, singing.)* "Be it ever so humble, there's no place like—" Hiya, roommates! Anybody want a little drink?

MYRNA: Listen, shiphead—you better shape up. Somebody tried to burn us out! *(Shows Molotov cocktail.)*

SAILOR: I saw the whole thing! I saw the guy that threw it!

MYRNA: Would you recognize him?

SAILOR: Course I would. He had a very big nose.

MYRNA: That'll be your assignment. Find that nose!

SAILOR: Find that nose!

MYRNA: Now what we gotta do is—we gotta . . .

MANUEL: We got to do like the old days. We got to organize.

MYRNA: Right! We gotta get organized! We gotta get it together!

MANUEL: No, no. We got to get a lot of people together.

GLADYS: A lot of people . . .

MANUEL: Mr. Gallo has a printing press in the back of his store!

SAILOR: And I'll find the nose!

MANUEL: We need to set up a network or communications.

GLADYS: *(Off by herself.)* Now if I call Lula Mae . . . and Lula Mae called Sister Anne . . .

MYRNA: I can get a telephone put in the lobby!

SAILOR: And I'll find the nose!

MYRNA: You find the nose.

GLADYS: . . . and Sister Anne called Marybelle . . . and they all got their congregations . . .

MYRNA: If that turkey wants to stay mayor, he's gonna have to save the Hotel!

MANUEL: We got to contact the community organizations.

MYRNA: Gladys knows all the churches!

GLADYS: . . . My, that'd be a whole lot of people!

ALL: Yeah! *(Music.)* We won't move!

Dance number: "Seniors' Soft Shoe." SAILOR *follows the leader. Exit.*

Scene 5: A Street, Some Months Later

LANDLORD: *(Enters.)* Now you're all cheering for the poor tenants. If there one person, just one person in this vast crowd, willing to speak out for the poor landlord? You people believe—and I think you're sincere—that the tenants have a right to their home. Well, if you believe that, you can't believe in our system. Our laws don't give anyone the right to a home— but they give everyone the right to own property. If these people were real Americans, they'd own their own home. Our laws are fair.

SAILOR: *(Enters to music, drunk, with lamppost.)* "Find that nose."

LANDLORD: This wino—he owns that bottle. I can't take it away from him.

SAILOR: Get your god damn hands off my bottle.

LANDLORD: I own forty-six buildings and seventeen parking lots, and he can't take them away from me.

SAILOR: *(Sings.)* "I can't take them away from him." *(Picks up cigarette butt.)*

LANDLORD: Now you may say if I own so many buildings, I could afford to give one up.

SAILOR: Anything you say, bucko. Got a light?

LANDLORD: But if these tenants win here, other tenants in other buildings are going to get the same idea. Then you'll have a fire we'll never put out.

SAILOR: *(Recognizes the lighter. Doom music. Aside.)* It's him! *(Pantomimes Molotov cocktail business.)*

LANDLORD: I have an important appointment, friend, so get out of my way. *(Brushes past him.)*

SAILOR: "Find that nose." *(Picks up lamppost and follows.)*

Scene 6: Lobby of the Hotel Universe, the Same Day

Phone rings.

MYRNA: *(Enters with broken printing press and ringing phone.)* Just a minute! *(Sets press, answers.)* Yello? Yes. No. Maybe. *(Hangs up.)* Shit! *(Fusses over press.)*

GLADYS: *(Enters.)* Myrna? *(Phone rings.* GLADYS *makes no move to answer it.)*

MYRNA: Oh— *(Rushes to phone.)* Hello? *(Sound of heavy breathing at other end.)* No, Edgar. I can't go out tonight! *(Hangs up.)*

GLADYS: Myrna?

MYRNA: What?

GLADYS: The landlord has a very big nose. *(Phone rings.)*

MYRNA: *(Answers.)* Whattaya want, for Chrissakes? . . . uh, yes, Reverend. We'll be there.

GLADYS: Myrna?

MYRNA: Gladys, do you think you might pick up the phone someday?

GLADYS: Myrna, my hearing!

MYRNA: Pass out leaflets?

GLADYS: My knees.

MYRNA: Get the bills paid?

GLADYS: My eyesight.

MYRNA: Gladys, fix that machine . . .

GLADYS: Me?

MYRNA: If you don't, we won't print no leaflets. No leaflets to pass out tonight, nobody at the rally tomorrow. *(Crash, screams offstage.)* Oh, the painters! I'm coming! *(Exits.)*

GLADYS: Nobody at the rally! *(Laying hands on machine.)* Dear Jesus, please heal this poor, sick machine. *(After many false starts, GLADYS fixes the machine.)* Thank you, Jesus.

MANUEL: *(Enters.)* Is the machine working?

GLADYS: It's working just fine.

MANUEL: Well, I couldn't get nobody to write the leaflet.

GLADYS: *(Sighs.)* I'll call Myrna.

MANUEL: No! Wait! See—I wrote one myself.

GLADYS: My! *(Takes it.)* Let's try it. I will put it in . . .

MANUEL: I will roll it . . .

MYRNA: *(Enters.)* And I will take it out. *(They do this.)*

GLADYS: How do it look?

MANUEL: It's perfect. *(Music. He sings "Manuel's Song.")*

Yo fui soldado de Pancho Villa.
I rode with him en la revolución.
But when that causa, it was forsaken,
I had to come up to esta nación.

I started working on Embarcadero.
Con los longshoremen, hicimos la unión.
But when they sold out my job to a forklift,
It was my last cause en la revolución.

But they pushed me and pushed me, los ricos patrones,
My house isn't safe from those rich old ladrones.
Que viva la causa del Universe Hotel,
Y esos cabrones can all go to hell.

I worked en los campos, también en los shipyards.
I earned my right to a comfortable home.
Si un patroncito me quita mi casa,

I'll fight till I die and I won't be alone.

They can push me and push me, los ricos patrones,
I'll keep my house safe from those rich old ladrones.
Que viva la causa del Universe Hotel,
Y esos cabrones can all go to hell.

GLADYS: Is that the leaflet?

MANUEL: Sí.

MYRNA: But that's the story of your life!

MANUEL: Yes.

MYRNA: Well, that's—it's . . .

GLADYS: It's just right!

MYRNA: Yeah!

ALL: (*Sing.*)

They can push us and push us, los ricos patrones,
We'll keep our house safe from those rich old ladrones.
Que viva la causa del Universe Hotel,
Y esos cabrones can all go to hell.

Phone rings.

GEORGETTE: (*Enters in hard hat, carrying two-by-four.*) Hi, Myrna?

MYRNA: Excuse me, Georgette—I gotta get the phone. (*She answers. Other two print.*)

GEORGETTE: (*Turns, nearly braining MYRNA with two-by-four.*) Hi, Manuel. Hi, Gladys. Say, we got a whole crew of volunteer spacklers coming in tomorrow to finish off that drywall. Myrna, I got to talk to you for a minute. See, we're going to have to shut off the electricity tomorrow for about an hour, okay?

MYRNA: (*Still on phone.*) That'll be fine.

GLADYS: Georgette, could you give us a hand over here?

GEORGETTE: Sure! (*Goes to press, dropping two-by-four on MYRNA.*) Hey, a new leaflet! When you finish these, I'll take some with me to the union meeting; then I can pass them out later tonight. (*MYRNA is struggling with phone cord tangled with two-by-four. Hangs up.*) Oh, Myrna! Why don't you give that to me?

MYRNA: (*Brandishing it.*) I think I will! I was getting a little bored.

GLADYS: Board? (*Shoulders two-by-four.*) Oh! Well, guess I better get back to work! So long! (*Turns, nearly beheading all three. Exits.*)

MYRNA: She doesn't know her own strength.

MANUEL: We better hurry and get these things out. (*Back to work.*)

TRUMPETER: (*Enters, super-cool, with sign: "Trumpet Players United to Defend the Hotel Universe." Addresses the group.*) What it is?

MYRNA: I don't know—what is it?

TRUMPETER: Well, it's Trumpet Players United to Defend the Hotel Universe.

ALL: Yeah!

TRUMPETER: Dig! You people are what's happening! We're gonna get a thousand musicians down there tomorrow to support you at that demo. Lay your ears on me one time, I'll run down the riff we been working on. *(Blows . . . and blows. Tenants finger-pop, applaud, wait politely.)*

MANUEL: We gotta get back to work. *(All but TRUMPETER exit, with press, phone, etc.)*

TRUMPETER: *(Finishes his riff, looks around.)* Wow—I guess I blew 'em away. *(Exits.)*

Scene 7: A Street

GEORGETTE: *(Enters with fellow CARPENTER.)* You call that a union meeting? I wanted to put something on the agenda, and the president told me to sit down and shut up!

CARPENTER: Hell, girl—that's an old story. What do you think this is, a labor union?

GEORGETTE: Yeah!

CARPENTER: Hell, no—this here's a business. See, the union officers run us for the bosses. And we pay 'em.

GEORGETTE: Well, it doesn't have to be like that. Hey, here's a leaflet about some folks who are making a change. *(CARPENTER takes one look at leaflet, backs off.)* I wanted the union to support them. See, if we came out in favor of—oh, I know some people are going to say that's creating lots of new jobs for us, but how long are those jobs going to last?

CARPENTER: *(Takes guitar from musician, sings "Redneck's Song.")*
Don't let the blood from your bleeding heart drip on me.
Why don't you keep your nose where it belongs?
Spare me all the world's problems—
A working man has problems of his own.
(Hands guitar back, walks off.)

GEORGETTE: Hey, I can understand where you're coming from—but the same guys that want to tear down the hotel want us to take a wage cut! Gee, maybe I came on too strong. *(Music. She leaflets, sings "Come to the Demonstration.")*
Come to the demonstration,
Come and fight against eviction.
Support the Hotel Universe,
We got to fight for the Hotel Universe. *(Chorus.)*

NURSE: *(Enters, chasing bus.)* Bus driver! Bus driver! You honky sucker—you better hope I never get on your bus!

GEORGETTE: Good evening.

NURSE: Is it?

GEORGETTE: I was wondering if you wouldn't mind taking a leaflet about the Hotel Universe. You don't have to read it now—maybe later, tonight.

NURSE: Gimme one of them things. *(Reads.)* Uh huh. Mm hm. Look here. I got eight kids. I work two jobs to feed 'em. I get one day off a week when I can do my housework, and you askin me to spend it at your demonstration?

GEORGETTE: Well, yes—I mean, no—I . . .

NURSE: Well, you better ask me! 'Cause I live just round the corner—they gonna be tearing down my place next. Give me some leaflets so I can pass them out in my building. *(Sings.)*
Come to the rally and hear the facts:
Our community's fighting back.
They want to take away our homes,
They think we're weak and all alone.

BOTH: *(Sing chorus.)*
Come to the demonstration. *(Etc.)*

GEORGETTE: *(Sings.)*
They want to put me in a concrete tomb
To give their profits lots of room.
To grow from the ashes of the homes
Of the people who built the city.

BOTH *sing chorus.* NURSE *exits.* SHOPKEEPER *enters.*

GEORGETTE: Here's another neighbor. Hi, Mrs. Gallo . . .

SHOPKEEPER: Oh! You scared me—I thought you were a mugger.

GEORGETTE: Who's minding the store?

SHOPKEEPER: We close early now—it's not safe to stay open at night.

GEORGETTE: Well, if the Hotel tenants win, *(Gives her a leaflet)* maybe things will turn around in the neighborhood.

SHOPKEEPER: Yes, isn't that sad? Such nice old people. They been my customers for years.

GEORGETTE: So you'll come to the rally?

SHOPKEEPER: *(Crushes leaflet.)* But when they build a big office building here—honey, that's when we gonna sell lotsa sandwiches. We gonna stock French wine, and Italian antipasto . . . *(Music. She sings, to the tune of "Come to the Demonstration.")*
Life was bitter, now it's sweet,
All the executives come to eat.
We'll get rich like Rockefeller
Selling lots of mortadella.

GEORGETTE: Wait!

SHOPKEEPER: Prosciutto!

GEORGETTE: You can't mean it!

SHOPKEEPER: Salami!

GEORGETTE: Think it over!

SHOPKEEPER: Pasta fazoul'. *(Exits.)*

LOWRIDER: *(Enters, spots* GEORGETTE.*)* What's happening, mama? Looking good! You want me to show you how to—salsa?

GEORGETTE: You're wasting your time. I don't go out with men.

LOWRIDER: That's good—I don't go out with men either!

GEORGETTE: You don't understand. I'm passing out leaflets for this demonstration.

LOWRIDER: She wants a demonstration!

GEORGETTE: I mean a rally.

LOWRIDER: That's too many people for me.

GEORGETTE: Andale, vato . . . *(Hands him leaflet.)* Léalo! *(Music: "Manuel's Song" as* LOWRIDER *reads leaflet.)*

LOWRIDER: Hey, this is a bad poem! You got a couple extras I could give to my friends, Chuy and Louie? I specially dig that part about the longshoremen. My old man was a longshoreman! *(They slap hands.)* You sure you don't go out with men?

GEORGETTE: Hey!

LOWRIDER: Just kidding. *(Exits with leaflets.)*

GEORGETTE: *(Sings.)*

Come to the demonstration
Come and fight against eviction.
Support the Hotel Universe:
We all live in the Hotel Universe!

Be there tomorrow! Two o'clock! Save the hotel. *(Exits.)*

Scene 8: A Street

LANDLORD: *(Enters, clutching leaflet.)* Where the hell is he?

SAILOR *still drunk, enters with lamppost, following* LANDLORD. *Business of* LANDLORD *hearing, looking,* SAILOR *hiding behind lamppost.* MAYOR *enters, clutching leaflet.*

MAYOR and LANDLORD: *(Shaking leaflets at each other.)* Have you seen this?

MAYOR: The Hotel Universe has five thousand people marching on City Hall!

LANDLORD: I told you to call the Tac Squad.

MAYOR: "Call the Tac Squad." Tomorrow's the election! I've always done everything you wanted. But now I have to go with the flow.

LANDLORD: Wait.

MAYOR: What?

LANDLORD: That's it—go with the flow! Listen . . . *(Whispers.)*

SAILOR: *(Eavesdrops.)* What the hell? *(Steps forward.)* All right, Mr. Mayor! You and this big-nose, firebug landlord are in cahoots, and I'm gonna tell the whole god-damn world!

MAYOR: He knows! *(LANDLORD knocks SAILOR over the head with lamppost.)* What are you going to do?

LANDLORD: Kill him. *(Drags SAILOR off.)*

MAYOR: Oh, my God! Oh, my God! *(Follows them off. From curtain.)* Oh, my God!

Scene 9: City Hall

TENANTS, GEORGETTE, and TRUMPETER march on at demonstration. They are carrying signs—"No More Evictions," "We Won't Move,"—playing, and chanting.

TENANTS: *(Sing "We Won't Move.")*

We won't move—been moved before.
We don't move no more.
They'll have to carry us out the door.
We won't move.
Our city is people, not concrete.
Parking lots and cars aren't the only things on our street.
Lived here so long, got friends all around,
Won't let the man come and tear it down.

We won't move—we won't move.
We won't move—no, we won't move!

GLADYS: *(Terrified, pushed forward by MANUEL and MYRNA.)* Good afternoon, everybody. *(Long pause.)* One day, when I was working in Seals Stadium, Joe DiMaggio hit the ball out of the park. I stood and watched it fly way over the fence. *(She watches ball. So do others.)* A little boy tugged at my sleeve. "Are you here to sell hot dogs, or what?" *(MYRNA and MANUEL cringe.)* And that is why we're here today. *(MYRNA and MANUEL die a thousand deaths.)* To ask ourselves, "Are we here to save the Hotel, or what?" *(All cheer.)*

MANUEL: *(Addresses crowd.)* We're gonna show those bums up there in City Hall that we're gonna stay right here until they save the Hotel! *(Leads chant.)* We won't move!

MAYOR: *(Enters to chanting.)* Beautiful! Fantastic! Right on—right on!

MYRNA: Right on cue. Mr. Mayor, we have appealed to you. We have waited. We have signed petitions. Now we—and our five thousand friends here—are going to camp out on your doorstep until you stand up, step in, and save the Hotel!

MAYOR: *(Kisses her hand.)* Thank you. *(Kisses* GLADYS *hand.)* Thank you.

GLADYS: You're welcome. For what?

MAYOR: For your youthful spirit—an inspiration to us all. For this *(indicates crowd)* stirring proof of the people's true power. For giving me the strength I needed to defy the most powerful interests in this city!

LANDLORD: *(Enters snarling, brandishing contract.)* Where is he? *(MAYOR steps out.)* You expect me to sign this? *(Throws it down.* MANUEL *picks it up.)* I'll fight you all the way to the Supreme Court!

MAYOR: You'll sign it.

LANDLORD: Oh, no I won't.

MANUEL: Listen to this. *(Reads.)* "Owner agrees to sell the Hotel Universe to the city, to provide low-cost housing for its aged tenants."

All react but GLADYS.

GLADYS: Myrna, the landlord has a big nose.

MYRNA: That doesn't matter now—they're gonna give us the Hotel!

MANUEL: He's never sign it.

LANDLORD: I'll never sign it.

MAYOR: We'll see about that. Sign it.

LANDLORD: Never!

MAYOR: Sign it, or you'll never get another building permit.

TENANTS, TRUMPETER, and GEORGETTE: Oo-oo-oo.

LANDLORD: Hah!

MAYOR: I'll rezone your condominiums into mini-parks.

TENANTS ETC.: M-m-m!

LANDLORD: You wouldn't!

MAYOR: I'll plug your loophole.

TENANTS, etc. gasp.

LANDLORD: My loophole!

MAYOR: Sign it! *(LANDLORD signs.)*

TENANTS ETC.: A-a-ah!

TRUMPETER: Far out! This is the first time my side ever won.

MAYOR: That's democracy for you.

GEORGETTE: Well, this goes to show that your government has to listen to you, if you holler loud enough.

MAYOR: Let's just hope it still is your government, after the election.

MYRNA, GEORGETTE, and TRUMPETER: What do you mean?

MAYOR: Downtown business is backing my opponent. If he should win, God knows what would happen to our agreement.

MYRNA: Down the tubes?

MAYOR: I'm afraid the battleground's moved from the streets to the ballot box.

MYRNA: *(Blows whistle.)* Come on, everybody! We're wasting time sitting here in the streets! Let's break this up now, and all of you get back to your neighborhoods and canvass for the mayor!

MANUEL: Wait! We can vote, that's okay. But we got to remember: what they give us at the ballot box, we won right here in the streets. And if we want to keep it, we got to stay on the streets. Save our home!

MAYOR: And support the mayor!

OTHERS: *(Taking up chant.)* Save our home and support the mayor!

MANUEL: Save our home! Forget the mayor! *(Others march off chanting.)* Screw the mayor. *(Exits.)*

Scene 10: A Dungeon

SAILOR: *(Hops on, tied hand and foot.)* What day is this? Where am I? *(Sign appears: "In an unused BART tunnel.")* That firebug landlord and the mayor are trying to hornswoggle the Hotel tenants—and I blew my chance to blow the whistle! Drunk! I'm always drunk. I always been drunk. *(Struggles.)* If I can get out of here before the election, I swear I'll never take another drink!

LANDLORD: *(Enters.)* Hello, old-timer, I have a surprise for you.

SAILOR: What is it this time—the Malay Mangle! The Singapore Sieve? You can't scare me—I've seen 'em all.

LANDLORD: But you haven't seen the morning paper. *(Shows it, reads.)* "Mayor Re-elected."

SAILOR: That's impossible. How long have I been here?

LANDLORD: Long enough. You'll especially like this part. "Victory due to popularity of mayor's stand on old folks' hotel."

SAILOR: No more, please—no more.

LANDLORD: You look as if you could use a drink. Let me fix you something special. *(Takes vial marked "Poison," pours contents into wine bottle.)* You know, I owe you an apology. I never should have been afraid of you. *(Cuts SAILOR's ropes.)* Suppose you did rant and rave about fires and conspiracies—who'd believe a wasted old wino? *(SAILOR swings; LANDLORD puts bottle in his hand.)* Take a drink, grandpa—take a couple. Pretty soon you'll be in heaven. *(Exits.)*

SAILOR: I gotta get out of here—I gotta warn the people at the Hotel! *(Bottle pulls him back.)* Aah, he's right—who'd believe a wasted old wino? *(Struggle. SAILOR is torn between duty and drink. Finally throws bottle down, exits to "Internationale.")*

Scene 11: City Hall

MYRNA and GLADYS enter dressed up; MANUEL in giant sombrero.

MYRNA: Hurry up, Gladys. Manuel, you could have at least worn a tie.

MANUEL: It wouldn't fit over my hat.

MYRNA: We want to get to the mayor's office and surprise him before he leaves.

MANUEL: Yeah, before he sneaks out the back door. You really think he's going to keep his promise?

GLADYS: He will when he tastes this cream pie I baked for him. Lawd, what a beautiful morning. This just goes to show you, faith will have its reward.

MAYOR: *(Enters in aloha shirt with suitcase, singing.)* "I'm going back to my little grass shack . . ."

MYRNA: Good morning, Mr. Mayor.

GLADYS: *(Takes pie out.)* We come to congratulate you on your re-election.

MAYOR: That's so kind of you.

MANUEL: And to have you sign the papers about the Hotel.

MAYOR: The Hotel! We're just waiting for the final okay on our agreement. *(Drum roll.)* Here it is!

LANDLORD: *(Appears above, dressed in a judge's black robe. Gavels.)* The City's use of eminent domain proceedings to acquire the Hotel Universe on behalf of the tenants constitutes a use of public power to help people *(All nod)* . . . and is therefore unconstitutional.

TENANTS: What?

LANDLORD/JUDGE: You're going to be evicted. *(Exits to doom music.)*

MYRNA: *(Blows whistle.)* Activate the Red Alert!

MAYOR: I knew nothing of this.

MANUEL: To the barricades! *(GLADYS hits MAYOR with pie. They exit.)*

Scene 12: The Hotel

MANUEL enters with wood, nails up barricade.

GLADYS: *(Enters.)* Manuel, there's a thousand of our friends outside and more on the way.

MANUEL: Maybe with ten thousand we could do something. *(Looks out.)* I don't see no cops yet. *(Phone rings.)*

GLADYS: Hotel Universe here. Fifty police cars? On Front Street? All right, you stay there and keep us posted.

MYRNA: *(Enters in hard hat, blowing whistle.)* All right everybody—we haven't got much time. Manuel, you barricade that door.

MANUEL: *(Glancing at already barricaded door.)* I'll do that.

MYRNA: Gladys, you check the medical supply room.

GLADYS: I checked it.

MYRNA: I forgot the gas masks!

GLADYS: I remembered. *(Phone rings.)*

MYRNA: Gimme that phone. Hello? *(To GLADYS.)* Don't just do something, stand there! *(To phone.)* What? *(Hangs up.)* They're coming up Broadway.

MANUEL: I can see 'em.

GLADYS: Strengthen me, Jesus.

MYRNA: All right, nobody panic. Manuel, you're second story captain. Gladys, you're in charge of first aid. I'm—I'm, I'm—oh, who am I kidding? What's the use?

GLADYS: Myrna!

MYRNA: Oh, look—they're coming with horses! They'll break through that human chain before we even get a chance to finish these barricades. We may as well give up right now.

MANUEL: Give up?

MYRNA: We fought so long, and so hard—and for what?

OLGA: *(Bursts in, holding her head.)* I have returned.

GLADYS: Olga!

MYRNA: She couldn't miss the finale.

OLGA: I had to come back.

MANUEL: After you deserted us? *(All turn their backs.)*

OLGA: Yes, I deserted you. And as I sat alone in my room, I heard the news of your struggle on the radio. It was a great lesson to me. My friends, you are a symbol of courage to the whole city. *(As she talks, the trio takes heart, and turns towards her.)* I am so proud of you, and so ashamed of myself.

GLADYS: Olga! You're hurt!

OLGA: It's nothing. Outside, those cossacks are clubbing everyone.

MYRNA: Olga, we always knew you was a . . . *(All do a little dance step.)* trouper.

OLGA: My friends, we are together again, no?

GLADYS: Yes.

OLGA: And we still have a little time, yes?

MANUEL: Maybe.

OLGA: Now I would like to dance for you. *(Trio gives her the space. Music: "Sailor and Olga Theme." OLGA dances. As she completes an arabesque, SAILOR enters. They are face to face. Both check photographs.)*

SAILOR: Olga!

OLGA: My sailor! *(They kiss.)*

Bass drum sounds. Behind couple, hotel drop falls to stage, revealing painted drop of riot police moving forward. To drumbeat, this moves downstage, over TENANTS, holds for a second, then turns, spilling TENANTS onstage again. Back of new drop is view of boarded-up hotel, and signs "Keep out," "No Trespassing," etc.

TENANTS pick themselves up, walk slowly upstage and look at their former home; then move downstage. When they speak again, time has passed.

MYRNA: They moved us—then they bashed in all the windows. Three years later, our half-wrecked home was still standing, to remind us we have no rights they are bound to respect.

GLADYS: For a lifetime of submission, what was our reward? Nothing. But our year of struggle is a story that will live when we're gone.

MANUEL: While you live, fight: resist every injustice. Keep in practice: more blows strike more sparks of resistance. And who knows which spark is going to start the big fire?

Others enter, all bow.

The End.

"The Big Picture" from *False Promises/ Nos Engañaron*

1976

Lyrics by Andrea Snow

Why can't people see the whole picture?
We live in the Dark Ages.
Believing in little pictures,
Little fragments, all distorted.
The little pictures of
Terror and destruction.
Who said ignorance is bliss?
Ignorance is the worst tyrant of all.
We live in the Dark Ages;
On Monday we refuse to be victims.
We stand up to the powerful men who own everything.
On Tuesday, we forget who we are,
And praise the men who steal everything.
Entranced like fools by great men,
And their hocus pocus.
We believe that folks like us,
Far away, who also fight, are devils.
Why can't people see the big picture?

But who can blame people?
Powerful men, who manipulate despair,
Control the press, the schools, and our imaginations.
Little pictures are for sale instead of information.
And if you don't have much,
It's hard to take exception
With men who own it all and plainly threaten,

"You've got everything to lose."
Of course we've got the power
To overhaul the system.
But men who own the military,
Courts, police and then some,
Always have a point.

And you Casey my boy were a fool.
You sprang the trap to press a point
And frightened people whose courage was great.
But who can blame me?
I can see the big picture.
And a new age, a just, and a beautiful age,
Will be brought about
By the whole working class.
It's so close, and I became impatient.

San Francisco Mime Troupe: *Teatro Gratis en los Parques/Free Theatre in the Parks.*

Poster for *The Dowry*, 1962.

Chorizos, Duboce Park, 1964. (Photo by Jeffrey Blankfort. Courtesy of Jeffrey Blankfort.)

R. G. Davis arrest in Lafayette Park, 1965. *Left to right:* Bill Graham, R. G. Davis, Luis Valdez, Paul Jacobs. (Photograph by Erik Weber.)

"Chick and Stud" from *A Minstrel Show, or Civil Rights in a Cracker Barrel,* 1965. *Left,* Joe Lomuto and *right,* Jason Marc-Alexander. (Photograph by Erik Weber.)

The Gorilla Band, 1971. (Photograph by Gerhard Gscheidle. Courtesy of Gerhard Gscheidle.)

L'Amant Militaire, 1968. *Left to right:* Kent Minault, R. G. Davis, and Jason Marc-Alexander. *Above:* Sandra Archer as the Pope. (Photograph by Gerhard Gscheidle. Courtesy of Gerhard Gscheidle.)

The Dragon Lady's Revenge, 1971 and 1987. Poster by Patrick Lofthouse. Printed by Inkworks Press, Berkeley. Poster from the Inkworks Press Archive. (Photography and digital imaging by Lincoln Cushing.)

The Mother, 1973. Poster by Jane Norling. (Courtesy of Jane Norling.)

False Promises/Nos Engañaron, 1976. Teddy Roosevelt tells President McKinley and J. P. Morgan about the location of the Philippine Islands. *Left to right:* Melody James, Ed Levey, and Sharon Lockwood. (Photograph by Marian Goldman.)

Hotel Universe in Mission Dolores Park, 1977. *Left to right:* Eduardo Robledo, Deb'bora Gilyard, Sharon Lockwood, and Joan Mankin. (Photograph by Michael Bry.)

Factwino: The Opera, 1985. Poster by Spain Rodriguez. Printed by Inkworks Press, Berkeley. Poster from the archive of Michael Rossman, AOUON Archive or All Of Us Or None Archive, Berkeley. (Photography and digital imaging by Lincoln Cushing.)

"Factwino." Comic by Spain Rodriguez. Previously published in the *San Francisco Bay Guardian*, July and August 1982.

Factwino: The Opera, 1985. *Left*, Shabaka as Factwino and *right*, Audrey Smith as the Spirit of Information sing "Fight for Life." (Photograph by Michael Bry.)

The Reagan Supreme Court, 1985. *Left to right:* Gus Johnson, Wilma Bonet, Dan Chumley, and Audrey Smith. *Above:* Sharon Lockwood. (Photograph by Michael Bry.)

Steeltown, "Defense Boogie," 1984. *Left to right:* Sharon Lockwood, Wilma Bonet, and Audrey Smith. (Photograph by Jeffrey Blankfort.)

The Mozamgola Caper, 1987. Poster by Lincoln Cushing. Printed by Inkworks Press, Berkeley. Poster from the Inkworks Press Archive. (Photography and digital imaging by Lincoln Cushing.)

Ripped van Winkle, 1988. Arthur Holden as Rip. (Photograph by Katy Raddatz.)

Ripped van Winkle, 1988. Keiko Shimosato as Sunshine. (Photograph by Katy Raddatz.)

Offshore, 1995. *Left*, David Furumoto and *right*, Keiko Shimosato. (Photograph by David Mayes.)

Seeing Double, 1989. Poster by Salim Yaqub. Printed by Inkworks Press, Berkeley. Poster from the Inkworks Press Archive. (Photography and digital imaging by Lincoln Cushing.)

Coast City Confidential, 1995. Poster by Jane Norling. Printed by Inkworks Press, Berkeley. Poster from the Inkworks Press Archive. (Photography and digital imaging by Lincoln Cushing.)

San Francisco Mime Troupe: First Forty Years, 1999. Poster by Spain Rodriguez.

San Francisco Mime Troupe appeal letter, 1995. Illustration by Spain Rodriguez.

Appeal letter envelope, "Stolen!! Have You Seen This Truck?" 1996. Illustration by Spain Rodriguez.

3. The 1980s: National and International Recognition

If the Carter years in the 1970s had left the San Francisco Mime Troupe without a clear agenda, the Reagan-Bush era in the 1980s would galvanize the company and their audience. In 1983 Joan Holden commented: "We got an enormous recharge when Reagan and Milton Friedman's monetarism came in. Suddenly everything was very clear again."[1] The Reagan-Bush era offered grist for the troupe's mill throughout the decade, resulting in at least eight highly successful major productions and numerous awards. They took shows to Europe, Cuba, and Nicaragua. They were awarded several major grants and experienced a period of financial stability. In spite of internal and external struggles, the now mature company got to reap its rewards.

Religious fundamentalism, the economy, nuclear weapons, and foreign policy dominated the troupe's plays. In the 1980 election all three major candidates (Reagan, Carter, and Anderson) identified themselves as born-again Christians. The Moral Majority, backing Reagan, defined part of his agenda: opposition to abortion, to gay rights, and to the Equal Rights Amendment. Reagan's ascent also marked the end of New Deal liberalism. Social programs were slashed and homelessness swelled. U.S. cruise missiles were deployed in Europe while millions protested. Meanwhile Reagan unveiled his Star Wars defense plan at home. The United States sponsored "freedom fighters" to destroy popular movements in Nicaragua and Angola. The division between the rich and the poor in the nation and in the world deepened.

The Company

In 1987 the San Francisco Mime Troupe was awarded the Tony for regional theater, the first time it had been given to an overtly political theater, and to one without a theater space or a multi-million-dollar budget. The honor came with a fifteen-thousand-dollar grant from American Express. In accepting the award, veteran trouper Sharon Lockwood recalled the company's twenty-eight-year commitment to fighting for peace and freedom and added: "We perform original musical theatre about world fascism, U.S. foreign policy and the price of beans. We believe people should stand up and raise hell until every person on this planet can live a decent life."[2] Actor-musician Eduardo Robledo dedicated the award to Benjamin Linder, the Oregon engineer killed in Nicaragua on 28 April by "contras financed by America."[3] Holden noted: "We couldn't have won this Tony three years ago. We probably have Contragate to thank for this."[4]

The company began the 1980s by self-publishing several of its most successful plays from the 1970s in *By Popular Demand: Plays and Other Works by the San Francisco Mime Troupe.* They also released two albums with Flying Fish Records: *The Album* in 1984, and songs from *Steeltown* in 1985. After following the company at home and on tour in 1984, Glenn Silber and Claudia Vianello debuted their feature-length documentary film, *Troupers,* in 1985. Dan Cohen of the *Guardian* called it "a well-deserved tribute to one of the most durable left cultural institutions" prior to its airing on PBS three years later.[5] *Los Angeles Times* reviewer Patrick Goldstein wrote that the documentary offers "an intriguing glimpse at . . . the kind of exuberant political satire that has almost vanished from today's stages."[6]

The documentary contains footage of the company's first decade, including commentary by R. G. Davis, Bill Graham, and Peter Coyote, as well as an in-depth look at the midwestern tour of *Steeltown* in 1984. Consequently several reviewers compared the company in the 1960s and later. Jay Carr of the *Boston Globe* suggested "some of the establishment-sassing fun seems to have gone out of the troupe, but, on the other hand, its compassion seems to have deepened. It seems less superior in its attitudes, less patronizing to its audiences. . . . There's a respect for the intelligence of workers that often was lacking in the work of the '60s and early '70s." He also identified the Mime Troupe as "America's foremost dispenser of alternative theatre, packing political messages into its agitprop razzmatazz."[7]

Early in the 1980s the company made a decisive move away from pure collectivism by professionalizing the office rather than continuing to share administrative duties among collective members. It was a return to the structure Davis had instituted. By 1982, company finances and tour booking showed improvement. Marie Acosta-Ponce, who was a collective member in the 1970s, became the general manager from 1980 to 1986. Her successor, Patrick Osbon, remained with the troupe until 1997. Osbon managed day-to-day operations and tour booking when the company could not afford to hire a booking agent. He also did all the fund-raising and wrote grant proposals. Chris Kovatch, business manager from 1984 to 1990, handled all financial matters.

In 1984, just in time for the company's twenty-fifth anniversary, Barbara Jeppesen was hired as publicist and stayed with the company until 1995. She gave the troupe "the look"—poster art created to suit each production, designed by artists whose styles would best portray the spirit of the work. She located Victor Moscoso, an artist from the Graham-Fillmore era to design *Ripped van Winkle's* psychedelic logo and Israeli artist Salim Yaqub to design the image for *Seeing Double*.[8] Press packets rivaled those of theaters with much bigger budgets with attractive one-sheets on troupe history, awards, and critical raves.

In 1984 with *Steeltown,* the company began giving artists individual credit on programs. This decision was practical: actors receiving individual recognition might more easily get other work, and reviewers were requesting actor's names. It also suggests a return to the 1960s model that recognized individual expertise. However, it moderated the company's public image as a collective.

A major setback to the company's collective organization occurred in 1984 and 1985 when the troupe found itself in an ironic and painful conundrum with Actors' Equity. Sharon Lockwood, who had just earned her Equity card in a production of *Cloud Nine* outside the troupe, was cast in *Steeltown,* the troupe's prolabor play. The company tried to negotiate a guest artist contract for her, but at the lower salary of the other collective members. The request was denied, and Lockwood, a staunch union supporter, resigned from Equity to end the crisis. However, the Mime Troupe was added to the AFL-CIO boycott list because they did not have a union contract.

The following year, with *Factwino: The Opera,* the troupe requested guest artist contracts for Shabaka and Mike Goldner at the same $190 salary as the rest of the collective. They were again denied, and while trying to negotiate, the San Francisco Labor Council circulated a letter asking members not to patronize the Mime Troupe. This time the dispute ended with the troupe establishing guest artist contracts and paying the two actors over $300 a week.[9]

Although the troupe and Actors' Equity had discussed unionizing for several years, they had been unable to negotiate an industrial contract that would include all the artists rather than just the actors. Arthur Holden summed up the paradox of unions and collectives: "The typical contract establishes an adversarial relationship (between employers and labor) but that doesn't apply to us because management and labor is the same in our group."[10] The larger issue of unionizing the company was finally resolved when a permanent contract with Equity was negotiated in 1991. Nevertheless, the boycott and the antiunion accusation remained one of the bitterest episodes in the troupe's history, and the permanent contract divided the company into labor (actors) and management (everyone else), further undermining the collective.

A significant change in the company's financial philosophy occurred in 1984 when the troupe applied for and was selected as one of eight U.S. companies to receive a grant under the National Endowment of the Arts' new Ongoing Ensemble Program, designed for companies with a resident group of actors. Other grantees ranged from mainstream theaters such as Milwaukee Repertory Theatre and Arena Stage to the Spanish-speaking Repertario Español of New York and the Wooster Group. The Mime Troupe was awarded ninety thousand dollars as the first installment of a diminishing three-year grant to begin in January 1986. The grantees needed to apply for funding each of the three years demonstrating increased income from earned and contributed revenues.

Because applying for the NEA had been a contentious issue within the company and affected its public image, several press releases and articles followed the company's acceptance of government funding. Holden explained: "We'd gone about as far we could go being funky . . . the NEA grant was basically a question of (financial) survival. There hasn't been a major political change, just a new reality."[11] In a company document defining the goals of the NEA grant, the troupe defined this new reality as maturity: "Perhaps this swelling of ambition stems from the fact that as the Troupe's core group of artists passes through our thirties and into our forties, we realize that the company is not a fervent interlude in our lives, but our life's work."[12] Dan Chumley also explained a change in company philosophy as a paradigm shift: "Radical theatre needs to take its rightful space alongside establishment theatre."[13] Furthermore, international tours had increased the troupe's awareness of arts funding in other countries, giving them a more realistic perspective about their own. Holden noted that "theatre isn't self-supporting anywhere in the world."[14]

The troupe's primary objective in applying for NEA funding was stability, so members could have a livable wage and health benefits. Salaries had reached $140 a week in 1983 and 1984 with $175 a week for administrators. They increased to $150 in 1985, and the film *Troupers* documents a collective meeting about the pros and cons of a $40-a-week raise to $190. With the NEA grant in 1986, salaries jumped from $190 to $231 a week plus health insurance.

The troupe also planned to use the grant for ongoing training for company members and for supporting an indoor season to parallel and complement the outdoor shows. However, according to Osbon, the company found it increasingly difficult to maintain salaries of $231 as the NEA funds decreased. This pressure was exacerbated by the need to increase revenues from other sources at a time when the members persistently opposed corporate funding—a position they maintained until they relented in the early 1990s.[15]

Besides the NEA ensemble grant, Holden received a Rockefeller Foundation Playwrights Fellowship that partially funded her writing *Spain/36*, and the troupe received grants for new musical work for 1985–86 from the NEA's Opera-Musical Theatre program to help fund mid-decade shows: *Factwino: The Opera* and *Spain/36*.

For most of the 1980s, collective members were salaried on a yearly basis, whether they were working on a show or not. The company subsisted on tour bookings and ticket sales from the indoor season in winter, and donations in summer, with chief funding from San Francisco Hotel Tax Fund. By 1984 the budget had grown to $400,000, and annual attendance was up to seventy-five thousand spectators at over one hundred performances. After receiving the NEA grant, the operating budget grew to $750,000, and the company's debt grew to $11,000. Park proceeds in the middle of the decade ran about $13,000 for a summer. In 1988, due to aggressive pitches and appeals, park donations jumped to over $40,000.

A change in company membership occurred in 1982 in what Holden describes as "the second purge" (the first was in 1967 when Davis dismissed thirty-five members).[16] In 1981, collective members included Marie Acosta-Colon, Glenn Appell, Joaquin Aranda, Bruce Barthol, Wilma Bonet, Dan Chumley, Brian Freeman, Arthur Holden, Joan Holden, Sharon Lockwood, Tripp Mikich, Esteban Oropeza, Muziki Roberson, Eduardo Robledo, Shabaka, Patricia Silver, and Audrey Smith. However, tension had been developing since the late 1970s over differences in ability among members, especially as skill in singing had become essential. At a meeting in 1982, Holden proposed they establish a standard for actors—"journeyman," defined as the ability to play any role. The motion passed, and several members who did not meet the new standard were out. Some of the emotional damage to the troupe never healed. Another new policy was adopted later in the decade: working with artists for a season before asking them to join the collective.

In 1986 the collective membership reached seventeen, and several members resigned or took leaves the following year. Robert Hurwitt attributed the departures to a strain on core members after the enormous effort that went into *Spain/36* in Los Angeles and its less than hopeful critical reception.[17] However, two new actors joined the company in 1987 and remained into the twenty-first century: Ed Holmes and Keiko Shimosato.

The Productions

The company had experimented with a comic strip style with *The Dragon Lady's Revenge* in 1971. In the 1980s they explored it more fully with four shows built around a recurring character: Factperson-Factwino. The first character was a waitress with "the human frustration of not being able to respond to arguments she knew were wrong."[18] She evolved into Factwino, the alcoholic savant who challenges misinformation propaganda with the power given him by the Spirit of Information. However, if he boozes, he loses it.

Henri Picciotto, a Bay Area political activist and math teacher who is an expert about Stan Lee's Marvel comics, wrote a 1980 review of the troupe's *Factperson,* applauding the superhero format but critiquing the absence of two important aspects of the genre: secret identity and the super villain. He was invited to collaborate in the creation of its sequel, *Factwino Meets the Moral Majority,* and then its sequel, *Factwino vs. Armageddonman.* A fourth play, *Factwino: The Opera,* completes the tetralogy. *Factwino Meets the Moral Majority* became one of the troupe's most successful shows in the 1980s, winning four Bay Area Theatre Critics' Circle awards: Shabaka for performance of Factwino, Bruce Barthol for original score, Holden (and others) for original script, and the San Francisco Mime Troupe for the production.

During the 1983 summer run of *Factwino vs. Armageddonman,* Spain Rodriguez, who has illustrated many of the troupe's posters and appeal letters, created a comic strip version of the play for the *San Francisco Bay Guardian.* Each installment advertised the next park performance location. The weekly series began with a prologue summarizing the prior Factwino show.

Besides the exaggerated comics style, the troupe also began exploring realism. An unpublished troupe document from 1982 states: "We need to learn the proper uses of realism—our realistic scenes are still too long, too preachy, too schmaltzy."[19] *Mother Jones's* Clark Norton disagreed: "Plays have become somewhat more subtle and realistic, with less cartoonlike caricature and strident rhetoric."[20] In numerous troupe shows, at least as far back as *False Promises* (1976), the oppressors were written as broad caricatures, while the working-class characters were drawn with more realistic nuance.

Experiments with realism also might be attributed to an increase in indoor productions. Although most of the Mime Troupe's shows open in the parks, then play in both indoor and outdoor venues during tours, since the 1960s some shows have been specifically created for indoor sites. In the 1980s, many of the troupe's biggest shows were indoors. The company's dream, to stage a new major indoor musical every other winter and a summer park show yearly, ended with the funding crises in the 1990s. In December 1979 the troupe had launched their first indoor season at the Victoria Theatre with their critically acclaimed production of Dario Fo's *We Can't Pay, We Won't Pay*. Three winter seasons were staged at the Victoria Theatre in the Mission District early in the decade. *Steeltown*, the prolabor play about plant closures and the end of the American Dream, opened at the Victoria in March 1985 after its fall 1984 tour.

The troupe's shows also became less optimistic in the 1980s: "Happy, uplifting allegorical endings are being phased out."[21] Holden explained: "Now our shows tend to end on people struggling to keep in the struggle—people faced with the dilemma of giving up or making an immense effort and continuing the fight."[22] The 1980s was an era of despair for many leftist activists. The enormous popularity of the Reagan and Bush administrations, with their imperialist foreign policies and disastrous domestic policies, often made the struggle seem insurmountable.

In 1982, the indoor show *Americans, or Last Tango in Huahuatenango*, was the troupe's first to critique U.S. policies in Central America. Set in the fictional country of San Martin, where oppressed people struggle against a U.S.-supported junta, the play specifically attacks U.S. policy in El Salvador.[23] Mel Gussow noted in his rave review in the *New York Times* that "everything is as timely as tomorrow's headlines."[24] The troupe took up the subject of Central America again with *Spain/36*, another indoor show, coproduced with the Los Angeles Theatre Center in the summer of 1986. The production commemorated the Spanish Civil War while implying a parallel to the U.S. opposition to the Sandinistas in Nicaragua. The multimedia musical was brilliant, complex, unwieldy, and a critical failure.[25]

In 1986 and 1987 the troupe revived two hits from the 1970s, *Hotel Universe* and *The Dragon Lady's Revenge*. The latter, with its expose of the U.S. drug traffic in Southeast Asia, conveniently paralleled U.S. illegal drug running in Central America that erupted into the Iran-contra scandal in November 1986. The troupe's flyer for the 1987 revival read:

> When the evil "Mr. Big" enters the White Monkey Bar, the mysterious Dragon Lady meets her match. CIA pranks during the Vietnam War—specifically heroin trafficking—are featured in the Mime Troupe's revival of the classic *The Dragon Lady's Revenge*. The Lady's back and things haven't changed a bit. Don't miss it this time!

Another troupe show skewering U.S. foreign policy, *The Mozamgola Caper*, opened at San Francisco's Theatre Artaud in February 1987 after touring in the fall 1986. This highly successful production criticized U.S. meddling in developing countries in Africa, specifically Angola. The troupe took it to the Kennedy Center in Washington, D.C., as part of the San Francisco Festival of the Arts in 1988. The *Christian Science Monitor*'s Louise Sweeney described the mixed audience reaction in the capital to the show's final declaration of a thirty-four-nation moratorium on debts to First World banks ("After 400 years of economic exploitation, we declare those debts paid in full"): "Some members of the audience felt gulled, and looked as shocked as if they'd been mugged by the Muppets, while others raced out to the lobby to sign up their support and buy troupe T-shirts on sale there."[26]

The last show of the decade, *Seeing Double,* was created with the kind of cultural collaboration that would increasingly mark the troupe's work in the 1990s. This comedy about the Middle East was written by an Israeli, two Jewish-Americans, a Palestinian, a Palestinian-American, and an Iraqi. The multiethnic cast portrayed both Palestinians and Israelis in a play suggesting a two-state solution to the conflict.[27]

The troupe examined domestic issues in at least two successful park productions in addition to the Factwino series in the 1980s. *Secrets in the Sand* (1983) involves the government cover-up of radiation exposure near an atomic testing site in Utah in 1954. The production received three Bay Area Theatre Critics' Circle awards. *Ripped van Winkle* (1988), arguably the most popular show in Mime Troupe history, juxtaposes the values of the counterculture 1960s to the 1980s. The title character wakes up in consumer-driven 1988 after a bad acid trip taken twenty years earlier. Holden said that after shows targeting Reagan and Bush, "it's time for us to take a good look at ourselves."[28]

New collective members in the 1980s expanded the company's range of stock characters, which, in turn, influenced the writing. Shabaka played various roles between 1981 and 1986, but Factwino became his signature role and eventually came to represent the San Francisco Mime Troupe to many San Franciscans. Audrey Smith, with her powerful singing voice, excelled in angry, stalwart characters such as Rose in *Steeltown*. Wilma Bonet, also a strong singer, played comic characters and strong heroines such as Franco and Emilienne Morin in *Spain/36*. Joan Holden describes heroic leading man Gus Johnson as "Atlas."[29] He played roles such as Durruti in *Spain/36* with intelligence and compassion. Eduardo Robledo, who continued composing throughout the decade, played sympathetic Latino heros. Ed Holmes's specialty was and still is the bad white guy, frequently a CIA operative or capitalist mogul, all business, no heart. Keiko Shimosato created punk rockers and avant-garde artists. Michael Sullivan, a superb singer with physical agility who joined the collective in 1988, plays leading men, usually a love interest. He played both the Jewish-American and Palestinian-American look-alikes in the mistaken-identity plot of *Seeing Double*.

With Shimosato joining the company, Asian characters began to appear in the productions, and the 1987 revival of *The Dragon Lady's Revenge* elicited some press commentary on the troupe's ethnic bending: "The Mime Troupe defied Hollywood traditions in its casting. The familiar film pattern has Caucasian actors playing both the heroic roles and, in heavy make-up, the Asian stereotypes . . . [The original cast in 1971 was entirely Caucasian actors]. The Mime Troupe employed three Caucasians to play Asian parts, an Asian in an Asian part and—surprise—an Asian in a Caucasian part."[30] The growing Pacific Rim identity of the West Coast and the company would emphasize Asian characters and issues increasingly in the next decade.

Although the company frequently employs nontraditional casting, the practice has been uneven because it is sometimes in conflict with collective commitments to rotating leading roles and directors' casting choices. Issues of ethnicity, especially related to casting, have led to collective conflicts several times since 1974, when the company became multiracial. With *Americans, or Last Tango in Huahuatenango*, Latino company members felt strongly that Wilma Bonet, a Puerto Rican American actress who joined the company in 1980, should play Luisa, the Latina lead. Dan Chumley, the director, cast Audrey Smith, an African American actress in the role. Several company meetings about racism in the troupe followed, and Smith was retained in the role. This was bitter experience for some Latinos in the troupe, but for Smith it represented the company's commitment to nontraditional casting.[31]

Gay characters had appeared in earlier Mime Troupe productions but became more vocal in the 1980s, thanks especially to actor-director Brian Freeman. *Factwino Meets the Moral Majority* was the first troupe play with a central conflict involving gay characters. *Factwino: The Opera* includes a scene in an AIDS era gay bar. The lead roles in *Crossing Borders* are a lesbian couple. Rip's old girlfriend in *Ripped van Winkle* had become a lesbian, and the show includes two other incidental characters who are gay.

By the 1980s Dan Chumley emerged as the company's principal director. He had directed at least four shows in the 1970s and codirected several others. In the 1980s he directed the big shows: *Spain/36, The Mozamgola Caper, Ripped van Winkle,* and *Seeing Double.* Joan Holden had commented in the 1970s that with Davis's departure, the company lost its sense of style.[32] Although totally different from Davis, Chumley, an intense, indomitable perfectionist, also has a strong visual sense and tireless energy. Actor Lonnie Ford says that Chumley has "a hell of an eye," and that he learned about the physical side of acting from Chumley.[33]

Holden continued as the undisputed principal writer, scripting (her term), as part of a team or alone, all but two of the new original shows for the 1980s. Holden and Chumley, as the principal writer and director as well as senior company members, became, in effect, the company's leaders. The resulting disparity in power, exacerbated by race because Holden and Chumley are white, frustrated some younger members of the collective, who had to learn to assert themselves. Former member Marie Acosta-Colon described their leadership as "a double edged sword." She left the company temporarily because of Holden's and Chumley's dominance, but realized that part of the responsibility was her own because she had not fought hard enough to be heard.[34] In her study of collective practices including those of the Mime Troupe, Ardith Ann Morris suggests that, paradoxically, "a collective avoids a destructive consolidation of power" by encouraging the exercise of strength and power and "by trusting in the checks and balances of open discussion. The members who remain active in the company are the fittest who survive."[35] Race and culture complicate the equation.

The musical aspect of Mime Troupe shows evolved significantly in the 1980s. While music had been part of the productions since the 1960s, in the 1980s the integration of music and theater increased. Furthermore, the music became increasingly electric. By 1976 the band had included electric bass and guitar. When Muziki Roberson joined in 1981, he added electric piano. The change from battery power to a generator in the early 1980s made it possible to support a public address system to amplify the actors. While adding significantly to the quality and kind of sound, as well as the ability to reach bigger crowds, it also increased freight, set-up time, and expense. Thus the troupe became less portable—less guerrilla. In addition, musical theater requires close collaboration between composer and playwright, which the months of touring had made difficult. In 1982 the company resolved to spend more time developing fewer productions.

Music garnered increasing critical praise. Several critics singled out Barthol's "Because You're Stupid" from his award-winning score for *Factwino Meets the Moral Majority*. The 1984 Bay Area Theatre Critics' award for best original score went to Eduardo Robledo and Muziki Roberson for *Secrets in the Sand*. In his *Steeltown* review, *San Francisco Chronicle's* Bernard Weiner described songs by Barthol and Robledo as "superb, in a wide variety of musical styles . . . these songs are among the best the Mime Troupe has ever produced."[36] Robert Hurwitt commented on the authenticity of *Steeltown's* 1940s songs and praised Barthol's "National Defense Boogie" and "Stand'n with the Union" as "remarkable."[37]

The company continued to appear at rallies and political events, although less frequently. Their protest against the Performing Arts Center at the Civic Center that had begun in 1973 culminated in the 16 September 1980 opening of the $28 million complex.

In 1981 the troupe created a short play, *Ghosts,* for the 13 December 1981 opening of the multi-million-dollar Moscone Convention Center, a facility that displaced residential hotels in the Yerba Buena neighborhood south of Market Street. Borrowing from *A Christmas Carol,* they presented three visions: Yerba Buena past, present, and the future with high-priced condominiums. The following day Chief Administrative Officer Roger Boas responded in the *San Francisco Chronicle:* "We may have displaced some parking lots, but people—no way." Several responses to Boas's astonishing blunder appeared in the San Francisco press over the ensuing days.[38] One *San Francisco Chronicle* letter to the editor on 28 December 1981 pointed out that the Redevelopment Agency tore down "more than four dozen residential hotels and small apartment buildings housing 4000 low income, mainly elderly people" to create the parking lots. The writer was Chester W. Hartman, author of *Yerba Buena: Land Grab and Community Resistance in San Francisco.*[39]

On 1 April 1982, the troupe's fictional punk rock band, Mark Anthony and the Nihilists, performed at the Media Alliance's "Censorship is Foolish" anti-book-banning rally. In August 1989 the company joined a protest against NEA restrictions by performing a shortened version of *Ubu Roi* wearing the original 1963 costumes (by William Wiley). In the troupe's protest adaptation, Ed Holmes, wearing a huge phallus, played Pa Ubu. Keiko Shimosato, as Ma Ubu, "endowed with breasts akin to guided missiles," urged Pa to run for president to rid America of "fags, commies, and artists."[40]

With the Democratic National Convention in San Francisco in July 1984, the troupe created that summer's show, *1985,* specifically to address the upcoming election and the urgency of voting to defeat Ronald Reagan. The troupe had voter registrars at every park performance and estimates they registered over forty people at each show. The title, *1985,* reflects the production's focus on nightmare scenarios following the November 6 election if Reagan were reelected. Recycling *A Christmas Carol,* in *1985* a former black activist, now successful lawyer, Ebenezer Jones, dreams of visits from the past (Nixon), the present (Nancy Reagan), and the future (a Reagan-appointed Supreme Court).

The Mime Troupe has been agitating school administrators since 1966, when *A Minstrel Show* was abruptly stopped in performance at St. Martin's College in Olympia, Washington. In 1982 the Nonesuch Farm School in Sebastopol performed the Mime Troupe's *San Fran Scandals* at various Sonoma County venues including a local elementary school, where, during the performance the principal misunderstood the name of the villain of the piece, "Smellybucks," the corporate toilet-paper tycoon. Believing he had heard "Smelly Butts," the principal determined the play contained offensive language (it also includes the expression "screw you"), and in order to stop the performance he pulled the school's fire alarm. The students filed out and the show came to a halt, thus joining *Il Candelaio* and *A Minstrel Show* as the only Mime Troupe shows stopped in performance.

Ripped van Winkle agitated school officials in Cleveland in 1988. The troupe's permit to perform the show in a high school auditorium was rescinded when seven administrators from the Cleveland Heights/University Heights Board of Education who previewed a video of the play found the content "unsuitable." The play's position against drugs, they argued, was not strong enough, and the play used "extreme racial stereotypes." Interviewed by phone in San Francisco, Holden responded that the play's message was definitely antidrugs and that the characters were comic archetypes.[41]

Other troupe shows have been criticized for using ethnic stereotypes. Laura Berman, the naive photojournalist in *Americans, or Last Tango at Huahuatenango,* is Jewish, and the show was picketed by the New Jewish Agenda.[42] Holden, who is Jewish, defended the role as a caricature of herself. In spite of great care to cover all perspectives in *Seeing Double,* the show was criticized by Jews and Arabs, each thinking the other had been portrayed more respectfully. *A Minstrel Show* had offended both white and African American spectators, and *The Dragon Lady* some Asians.

Foreign touring continued and enhanced the company's growing international reputation. In May and June 1980 the troupe took *Hotel Universe* to the Festival of Fools in Amsterdam after touring it in West Germany and Switzerland. A representative of Cuba's Ministry of Culture was apparently impressed by the Dutch performance, and an invitation to perform in Cuba that October followed—the first to a U.S. company since the revolution. A week's performances of *Squash* (1979) and *Hotel Universe* (1977) at the Teatro Sala Hubert de Banck in Havana played to full houses. During the second week, the troupe joined the Teatro Escambray, touring in the provinces and visiting schools. For both shows, some lines and scenes were hastily translated into Spanish and memorized en route and on the scene.

Another bilingual version of *Hotel Universe* traveled to the National Theatre Festival in Managua, Nicaragua, in 1986, where the company was one of five international groups performing. They met with President Daniel Ortega and minister of culture, Ernesto Cardenal, and participated in a demonstration in front of the U.S. Embassy in Managua. Bruce Barthol and Dan Chumley published articles on this trip, which took place during the U.S. covert war against the Sandinista government.[43]

The troupe returned to Europe in the fall of 1981, touring *Americans, or Last Tango in Huahuatenango* in West Germany in October and November, followed by a successful British debut in December. The company returned to West Germany in 1985 with *Factwino: The Opera* and was the only U.S.

company invited to the Red Song Festival in East Berlin. They returned to West Germany again with *The Mozamgola Caper* in 1988. The Mime Troupe also began American-Israeli exchanges in 1984 and 1985. The first brought Israeli playwright Sinai Peter to the Mime Troupe, then took Joan Holden and Dan Chumley to Tel Aviv. This exchange resulted in the highly successful *Seeing Double* at the end of the decade.

In 1985 the Mime Troupe made a decision that enhanced both their workspace and their place in the Mission District neighborhood where their offices are located. A committee of local residents and troupe members selected muralist Juana Alicia to paint the history of the company and the community on the troupe's Treat Avenue building. The mural, *For the Roses/pa'las Rosas* was one of over a dozen Alicia painted in San Francisco, Sonoma County, and Nicaragua between 1983 and 1990 and is included in Timothy W. Drescher's book, *San Francisco Bay Area Murals: Communities Create Their Muses, 1904–1997*. The mural is a collage of imagery from at least ten Mime Troupe productions, as well as Fantasy Records, which had previously occupied the space, and Mission Dolores, which gives the district its name. Visitors now enter the troupe's building through a door painted with Shabaka as Factwino. Wilma Bonet, Sharon Lockwood, and Audrey Smith sing Bruce Barthol's "Defense Boogie" from *Steeltown,* and in the far upper right Audrey Smith, Melecio Magdaluyo, and Dan Chumley dance and sing "The Dictators' Song" as Mobutu, Marcos, and Pinochet in *1985.* In the far right corner, Joan Holden toils at her typewriter. In the center, eager spectators surround a stage on which Mime Troupe history is played.

Notes

1. Sullivan, "Troupe Still Has Message."
2. John Trinkl, "Mime Troupe Never Leaves Home without Its Politics," *Guardian,* 15 July 1987.
3. Jeremy Gerard, "Tony Acceptance Speech Receives Angry Reaction," *New York Times,* 9 June 1987.
4. Trinkl, "Troupe Never Leaves Home."
5. Dan Cohen, "Mime Troupe Celebrates Twenty-five Years," *Guardian,* 4 May 1988.
6. Patrick Goldstein, "'Troupers': Documentary on the Mimers of Mime," *Los Angeles Times,* 14 November 1985.
7. Jay Carr, "Honest Portrait of Some Real Troupers," *Boston Globe,* 22 November 1985.
8. Barbara Jeppeson, email to Susan Vaneta Mason, 11 June 2002.
9. "S.F. Troupe in a Bind," *American Theatre* 2 (July–August 1985): 39.
10. Bill Snyder, "S.F. Mime Troupe Accused of Anti-labor Practices, Boycotted," *West County Times,* 14 April 1985.
11. Hilary DeVries, "Politics, Humor, and a Dash of Boogie," *Christian Science Monitor,* 30 October 1985.

12. "San Francisco Mime Troupe Receives Ensemble Grant," troupe document, 1984, SFMT files.

13. Bernard Weiner, "S.F. Mime Troupe's Big Establishment Grant," *San Francisco Chronicle*, 6 September 1984.

14. William Kleb, "The San Francisco Mime Troupe a Quarter of a Century Later: An Interview with Joan Holden," *Theater* 16 (spring 1985): 59.

15. Patrick Osbon, email to Susan Vaneta Mason, 1 August 2000.

16. Joan Holden, interview by Susan Vaneta Mason, 8 May 2002.

17. Robert Hurwitt, "Don't Cry for Me, Mozamgola," *East Bay Express*, 13 March 1987.

18. Lawrence Christan, "'Factwino': Zapping with Zip," *Los Angeles Times*, 10 May 1985.

19. San Francisco Mime Troupe, "The State of Our Art," n.d., SFMT files.

20. Clark Norton, "The S.F. Mime Troupe Turns Twenty-five," *Mother Jones*, April 1984, 5.

21. Ibid.

22. Bernard Weiner, "S.F. Mime: Still Radical after All These Years," *San Francisco Chronicle*, 11 March 1984.

23. See Adele Shank, "The San Francisco Mime Troupe's *Americans, or Last Tango in Huahuatenango*," *Drama Review* 25 (fall 1981): 81–83.

24. Mel Gussow, "Theater: '*Last Tango*' from San Francisco," 27 November 1982.

25. See Janelle Reinelt, "Approaching the Sixties: Between Nostalgia and Critique," *Theatre Survey* 43 (May 2002): 37–56; and Susan Mason, "The San Francisco Mime Troupe's *Spain/36*," *Theater* 18 (fall–winter 1986): 94–96.

26. Louise Sweeney, "Sampling San Francisco's Drama, Dance, and Music," *Christian Science Monitor*, 28 June 1988; *Mozamgola Caper, Theater* 20 (winter 1988–89): 71.

27. See Stacy Wolf, "Politics, Polyphony, and Pleasure: The San Francisco Mime Troupe's *Seeing Double*," *Journal of Dramatic Theory and Criticism* 8 (fall 1993): 101–15; script *Seeing Double, Theater* 23 (spring 1993): 61–81.

28. Misha Berson, "'Ripped van Winkle': '60s Hippie in the '80s," *San Francisco Chronicle*, 17 July 1988.

29. Holden, interview, 8 May 2002.

30. Laird Harrison, "*Dragon Lady's Revenge* Plays Well in the '80s," *Asian Week*, 24 July 1987.

31. Wilma Bonet, interview by Susan Vaneta Mason, 16 June 2002; Joaquin Aranda, telephone interview by Susan Vaneta Mason, 20 July 2002; Audrey Smith, telephone interview by Susan Vaneta Mason, 30 July 2002.

32. Holden, "Collective Playmaking," 34.

33. Lonnie Ford, telephone interview by Susan Vaneta Mason, 22 June 2002.

34. Ardith Ann Morris, "Collective Creation Practices," Ph.D. diss., Northwestern University, 1989, 333. Morris quotes Joaquin Aranda describing the difficulty he had learning to assert himself at the Mime Troupe: "As a minority child in school, I was always told to sit down and shut up, or that my ideas were stupid. It took me awhile to feel safe and comfortable enough to contribute to the process in open meetings" (333–34).

35. Ibid., 331–32.

36. Bernard Weiner, "Local Musicals—Some Good Signs," *San Francisco Chronicle*, 17 March 1984.

37. Robert Hurwitt, "A Musical Comedy on Plant Closures," *Socialist Action,* April 1984.

38. Paul Liberatore, "Troupe's Bitter Skit at Moscone Center," *San Francisco Chronicle,* 14 December 1981.

39. Chester W. Hartman, "More Than Lots," letter to the editor, *San Francisco Chronicle,* 28 December 1981; Chester W. Hartman, *Yerba Buena: Land Grab and Community Resistance in San Francisco* (San Francisco: Glide Publications, 1974). Herb Caen also pointed out Boas's "quandumb leap in logic," noting that "Roger must have forgotten that the parking lots were created when the city tore down small hotels in which oldsters were living on the cheap." *San Francisco Chronicle,* 16 December 1981.

40. Nancy Scott, "S.F. Mime Troupe Fights NEA Funding Ban with Laughter," *San Francisco Examiner,* 2 August 1989.

41. Marianne Evett, "Mime Play Banished, Moves to New Site," *Plain Dealer,* 11 October 1988.

42. Henri Picciotto, one of the writers on the Factwino series and a member of the New Jewish Agenda, wrote a four-page letter to the organization defending the character of Laura Berman, especially because she changes.

43. Bruce Barthol, "In the Face of Fear and Struggle, Art," *American Theatre* 4 (June 1987): 26–29; Daniel Chumley, "Going South: The San Francisco Mime Troupe in Nicaragua," *New Theatre Quarterly* 3 (November 1987): 291–302.

Factwino Meets the Moral Majority

1981

Script by Joan Holden with Brian Freeman, Tede Matthews, Peter Solomon, and Henri Picciotto

Introduction

Sedro F. Wooley, aka Factwino, is possibly the most popular character in Mime Troupe history. He is also the hero in three out of four plays of the Factperson tetralogy. *Factwino Meets the Moral Majority* is the second play in the series. The show uses the Marvel comic book style and ends with a cliffhanger, laying the groundwork for the subsequent show, *Factwino vs. Armageddonman.* Whereas Milton Friedman was the villain in the first Factperson, and Jerry Falwell and New Right are villainous in this second installment, this Factwino develops the concept of the supervillain in the form of Armageddonman, a two-headed monster: war and business. The production was highly successful and garnered four Bay Area Theatre Critics' awards.

Commentary

Shabaka

Playing the Factwino character was one of the most fulfilling experiences I've ever had as a performer. ("Forty Years of Speaking Up," *San Francisco Chronicle,* 28 November 1999)

Audrey Smith

Factwino was discovering heaven on earth. I never tired of the amazing people I had the chance to work with. I'd pay to do that show again. (Telephone interview by Susan Vaneta Mason, 30 July 2002)

Henri Picciotto

Conventional comic book heroes tend to be white male professionals: journalist, photographer, industrialist, millionaire, doctor, student, scientist.

During the '70s comic books have featured increased numbers of black and especially female superheroes, in response to the times. But the Mime Troupe went further: with Rita [*Factperson*], we have a working class woman heroine; and with Sedro, a black wino. These choices, combined with the 'gender free' name inscribed on the superhero's cape (Factperson), are a necessary—if not original—comment on the conventions of the genre. ("Comics on Stage," in *West Coast Plays 15/16* [Berkeley: California Theatre Council, 1983], 187)

Wilma Bonet

I had a great time doing the show. It was at a time when the company was at its best artistically. As if we couldn't do wrong. The topics were timely—in fact ahead of their time. We were right on the money in attacking the Christian Right and to do it in a comic book style. It was a family show everybody could relate to. The audiences got it, and their response was unbelievable. Factwino was a great character. (Interview by Susan Vaneta Mason, 16 June 2002)

Joaquin Aranda

Working on *Factwino* was an unforgettable experience. Everything, from the writing, the mounting of the show, to finally performing it with an unbelievably talented cast was just phenomenal. It was as if the company was in an artistic zone, so to speak. (Telephone interview by Susan Vaneta Mason, 20 July 2002)

Mel Gussow

The show is, in Mime Troupe tradition, a pop cartoon that sounds the alarm against pomposity and sanctimony. ("San Francisco Mime Troupe," *New York Times*, 19 May 1982)

Paul Berman

The San Francisco Mime Troupe's new musical is a rousing comic book triumph over the Moral Majority—rousing because it speaks to one's deepest, which is to say lowest, political beliefs. A rock singer asks the public, "You voted for Nixon twice—why?" And the back-up singers chant: "Because you're stupid!" ("Zap, Wow!" *Village Voice*, 1 June 1982)

Esteban Oropeza

Factwino was wonderful. It was sharp. It was exciting. The hero is a lower class guy, a wino, who exposes what's up. It was a whole arsenal attacking the Right. I am blessed to have been in the Mime Troupe. It was a struggle, but you get through it. (Telephone interview with Susan Vaneta Mason, 12 August 2002)

Welton Jones

Factwino is the second in what may prove to be a whole Wagnerian cycle of plays. ("*Factwino* Is Irresistible in Mime Troupe Tradition," *San Diego Union*, 24 March 1982)

Dan Sullivan

Factwino, the only superhero with wardrobe by Fruit of the Loom. ("A Mellowed *Factwino* at Variety Arts," *Los Angeles Times*, 17 May 1985)

Nancy Scott

As craziness mounts, day by day, as the Rev. Jerry Falwell marches militantly backward into the dark ages of fundamentalism, as humanist reforms are stricken from the laws and bookburners hold their torches at the ready, don't panic. Factwino is here. ("Mime Troupe Tackles Falwell," *San Francisco Examiner*, 5 August 1981)

The Production

Factwino Meets the Moral Majority opened on 25 July 1981 in Mission Dolores Park, San Francisco, with the following cast:

A Librarian, Right-to-lifer	*Patricia Silver*
Georgianna, Edna, Robot	*Wilma Bonet*
Spirit of Information, Dela, Reverend Ben Kinchlow	*Audrey Smith*
Buddy	*Joaquin Aranda*
Sedro F. Wooley, Factwino	*Barry Shabaka Henley*
A Fundamentalist, Clyde	*Esteban Oropeza*
A Nurse	*Brian Freeman*
Jimmy, George, Jerry Falwell	*Dan Chumley*
Armageddonman	*Dan Chumley, Bruce Barthol*
Dick	*Bruce Barthol*
Barney	*Brian Freeman*
Mark Anthony and the Nileists	*The Band*
Book Burners, Moral Majority Members, TV Crew	*The Ensemble*

Directed by Sharon Lockwood. Musical director: Bruce Barthol. Songs by Bruce Barthol. Costumes by Patricia Silver, Wilma Bonet, and Nora Boni. Musicians: Glenn Appell, Bruce Barthol, Al Guzman, Stephen Herrick, Muziki Roberson.

Characters (in order of appearance)

A librarian
Georgianna, a single mother
Two book burners
The Spirit of Information
Sleepy, a street person
Buddy, also a street person
Sedro F. Wooley, his longtime companion
A fundamentalist
A nurse
Dela, a young woman in trouble
Jimmy, her boyfriend, the cause of her trouble
Right-to-lifer
Edna, a convert
George, her husband
Rev. Ben Kinchlow
Members of the Moral Majority
Robot, a smart machine
Armageddonman
Dick, a bar owner
Barney, a hedonist
Clyde, an activist
Working musicians
Jerry Falwell
A TV crew

Factwino Meets the Moral Majority

A sign appears from behind the curtain: "A year has passed since the Spirit of Information visited our planet to save a nation threatened by a rising tide of ERROR.*"*
The sign changes to: "The Spirit chose a champion and endowed her with the power of knowing EVERY FACT THERE IS. *But Factperson misused her gift—and*

lost it. The rest is history."
The sign changes again to: "After the Budget Cuts . . ."

Scene 1

LIBRARIAN: *(Enters, sets box at counter, calls to stacks.)* Please check out
  your books. Library hours have been shortened. Closing time is now 1
  pm.

GEORGIANNA: *(Enters.)* Can you recommend a book . . . where it talks about
  . . . on abortion?

LIBRARIAN: We're closing. Come back tom . . . go on in. Sex Education,
  shelf B12. I'd look at *Our Bodies, Ourselves.* (GEORGIANNA *hurries off.)*
  And we've also got Pope John's Encyclicals.

MAN enters with large stack of books.

LIBRARIAN: Oh, my best customer—This is your third visit today. How do
  you read so many books so fast?

MAN: Uhhh . . . Evelyn Woods.

LIBRARIAN: Wait a minute—it says here you've got 2,200 books overdue.

MAN: Must be some mistake.

*SECOND WEIRDO enters with large stack of books. LIBRARIAN pulls slips and
stamps furiously.*

LIBRARIAN: With all the cutbacks and layoffs, there's no way to keep up
  with the paperwork. The *Joy of Sex*—tell me about it—*The Origin of
  Species?*—Picasso's *Nudes*—they're wonderful, aren't they?—*Women
  Loving Women*—hmmm—*(Ends with paper flying everywhere.)* I'm not
  really complaining—I'm so glad people still want to read.

MAN: We'll be back next week to check out history. *(Exits.)*

GEORGIANNA: *(Enters with a book.)* If this is supposed to be a joke, it's not
  funny.

LIBRARIAN: The Bible?

GEORGIANNA: That's the only book on the whole shelf. It's also the only
  book under Science. I *have* a Bible—and it hasn't helped me. Right now
  I need information! *(Exits.)*

LIBRARIAN: All those books gone—the Bible—oh no! I didn't think it could
  happen here! Who's going to save knowledge? Help! Oh, who am I calling for? Nobody works here anymore but me.

OLD LADY: *(Enters with books.)* Excuse me, honey, I was putting in a little
  overtime on the top floor when I heard a voice calling for help.

LIBRARIAN: Intelligence is in terrible danger! It's the Moral Majority—
  they're clearing out every book they don't like. Pretty soon there'll be
  nothing left on the shelf. It seems as though ignorance has been on the
  march ever since Factperson left.

OLD LADY: Factperson? Who's he?

LIBRARIAN: She. I keep her picture. She knew everything. But the best part was, she made people want to know more—just the opposite of the Moral Majority. Then she disappeared—dropped out, I guess, like so many people.

OLD LADY: I fired her.

LIBRARIAN: What?

OLD LADY: She broke the contract.

LIBRARIAN: Contract? Hey—you said you were on overtime.

OLD LADY: It's a rough century.

LIBRARIAN: Cen . . . and we don't have a top floor! What a minute—who are you?

OLD LADY: I am the Spirit of Information. I run General Reference at the Big Library out there.

LIBRARIAN: You mean . . . the Main Branch?

SPIRIT: That's right.

LIBRARIAN: Then you *do* exist—just like they taught us in Library School. Thank God you've come—I was beginning to despair.

SPIRIT: Despair is the enemy of light.

LIBRARIAN: I'll be brave—if you'll stay with us now.

SPIRIT: Stay on one insignificant planet?

LIBRARIAN: Of course you can't—then bring Factperson back.

SPIRIT: She knew it, she blew it.

LIBRARIAN: But we really need someone like that—someone who can inspire people, make people think.

SPIRIT: I guess I got my work cut out. Hold the fort, honey. Help is on the way. (*Exeunt.*)

Sign: "Where Will the Spirit Find Another Lover of Truth?"

Scene 2

Wino Park on Sixth Street, that evening. SLEEPY, *a silent wino, enters, stretches out.*

Offstage, hymn singing turns to argument, which grows louder. SEDRO *and* BUDDY *are kicked on stage.*

SEDRO: Yeah? Yeah, you holy all right—you *full* of holes. You talk about saving people, ignorant as you is, you couldn't even save your ass from a hemorrhoid!

BUDDY: How come you can't just keep your mouth shut and eat? That's the third rescue mission we been kicked out of this week. I didn't even get to finish my jello.

SEDRO: Try to pose a few philosophical questions—what you gonna do with people that's only read one book? "The Bible—the only true word of God." What about the *Koran*, man? What about the *Bhagavad Gita*?

DELA : What about some Ripple?

SEDRO: Good idea. Nobody fucks with my mind but me. *(Bottle is empty.)*

SPIRIT enters with flashlight, tired and discouraged. Sees winos and shakes her head. Sits.

BUDDY: Come on, partner, we gotta fix you up. You get too sober, you start thinking about Cleveland.

SEDRO: I don't wanna think about that.

FUNDAMENTALIST: *(Enters.)* Could I ask you gentlemen a few questions? I'm a college student. We're conducting a nationwide poll.

BUDDY: Welcome to the university of the streets. My friend here, Sedro F. Wooley, knows everything. *(SPIRIT gets interested).* How much you want to pay?

SEDRO: Shame on you, man here is looking for information.

BUDDY: You tell 'em, Sedro. I'm gonna go look for some change. *(Exits.)*

SEDRO: A poll, huh? This the first time I been consulted. What is it you want to know?

FUNDAMENTALIST: Do you believe in the atheistic theory of evolution that denies God and reduces man to the level of an ape?

SEDRO: Where you say you go to college?

FUNDAMENTALIST: Reliable Bible Institute in Throwback, Virginia. Our school protects us from the confusing ideas that throw many youth today into doubt.

SEDRO: Did you know your arm is made the same as a salamander's?

FUNDAMENTALIST: It is?

SEDRO: When you were in your mama's belly, you had gills like a fish.

FUNDAMENTALIST: What would that mean?

SEDRO: Meditate for a moment on the fact that your blood has precisely the same mineral composition as seawater.

FUNDAMENTALIST: Salty?

SEDRO: Right. I don't *believe* in evolution . . .

FUNDAMENTALIST: Oh, good. *(Marks it down.)* "No."

SEDRO: Because it's only a theory. But I accept it, 'cause it's the best theory we got. Now . . .

FUNDAMENTALIST: Next question. Do you believe that licensed and practicing homosexuals have a right to preach perversion in our public schools?

SEDRO: Look here: I don't believe anybody has a right to impose their trip on anybody.

FUNDAMENTALIST: "No" again! Brother, this poll is going to prove that a majority of Americans think just like we do.

SEDRO: We who?

FUNDAMENTALIST: All of us who are joining Jerry Falwell's Christian Crusade.

SEDRO: Jerry *Falwell?* That mealy-mouthed preacher who invented the medieval-minded Moral Majority? Man want to make ignorance a national religion?

FUNDAMENTALIST: He's already converted most of the Congress. And this summer, Brother Jerry's bringing his Crusade here, to the heart of Sodom.

SEDRO: San Francisco?

FUNDAMENTALIST: You can help him clean up your city. Report any public figure you know to be an atheist, communist, feminist, homosexual, or secular humanist. *(Ready with pencil.)*

SEDRO: You talking to a secular humanist, junior. Tradition of Epicurus, Erasmus, Thomas Paine, and Mark Twain.

FUNDAMENTALIST: Who?

SEDRO: Get out of my face.

FUNDAMENTALIST: That's all right, brother—Jesus loves you, whether you like it or not.

SPIRIT: *(Steps between the two.)* You better run, son. I just saw Jesus on Fifth and Market!

FUNDAMENTALIST: He's come to join our crusade! Or could it be the end of the world? *(Exits.)*

SEDRO: *(Sings "Armies of the Night.")*
Jesus, they're using your name again,
To sanctify their means and ends,
The Inquisition is here again,
And they're doing it in your name.

Books and witches to the flames,
Bless the missiles, bombs, and planes,
The armies of night are drawing near,
The armies of the night are drawing near.

I'd stand and fight but not alone,
People just don't want to know.
I'll ease my pain and ease my mind.
And lose it all in rotgut wine.

SPIRIT: *(Approaches.)* Excuse me, mister. I been sitting here worrying . . . how much is the defense budget for 1981?

SEDRO: $700 million a *day.* Say, did you see my buddy? He's a little guy, about . . .

SPIRIT: I got to call my daughter in Tanzania. Do you know what time it is in Dar-es-Salaam?

SEDRO: Twelve hours later than it is here. *(Aside.)* Woman's crazy. *(To SPIRIT.)* Be seeing you.

SPIRIT: Seems like you already know every fact there is.

SEDRO: *(Sings.)* What good is knowledge or the facts?

SPIRIT: *(Sings.)* If you know then you must act.

　　The armies of the night are drawing near.

　　People have got to hear the warning.

SEDRO: People don't want to know.

SPIRIT: You can see the storm clouds forming.

SEDRO: I've seen it all before.

SPIRIT: The armies of the night are drawing near.

SPIRIT *and* SEDRO: The armies of the night are drawing near.

　　The armies of the night are drawing near.

SEDRO: If you was my fairy godmother, I'd only ask for one wish.

SPIRIT: Shoot.

SEDRO: Give me a way to make people think.

SPIRIT: *(Zaps him.)* You got it.

SEDRO: What was that?

SPIRIT: You know your mission.

SEDRO: I do?

SPIRIT: You know it's dangerous.

SEDRO: It is?

SPIRIT: You've got the power. But remember: if you booze it, you lose it. You know what I mean? *(Exits.)*

SEDRO: Shit! "If you booze it, you lose it." Women always want to get in somebody's business. *(Calls offstage.)* Buddy! I need a drink. *(Exits.)*

Sign: *"When will* FACTWINO *discover his power?"*

Scene 3

NURSE enters, sets scene.

Sign: *"Early the next morning, at a South of Market Clinic."*

NURSE: Please have a seat and wait for your name to be called. *(Exits.)*

DELA *and* JIMMY *enter.*

JIMMY: See you later, baby. Give me a call when it's over.

DELA: You mean you ain't gonna stay?

JIMMY: Hey, baby, this is women's business, know what I mean?

DELA: Yeah . . . you mean you don't want to deal with it.

JIMMY: Hey, who fixed it up so you could stay at my sister's house? Who got you here at five o'clock this morning?

DELA: Who got me here period? "Oh, Dela, baby, I can't stand it. Ooh, it hurts so bad. Prove you love me. I'm a *man*, Dela! I need you!" And then, "Nothing ain't gonna happen if you wash with lemon juice."

JIMMY: It ain't my fault, my brother said it would work. Anyway, Dela, I don't like what you're doing.

DELA: Me!

JIMMY: It ain't nothing but murder, baby. And it's on your conscience because I told you I would support my child.

DELA: Off of stolen TVs? *(GEORGIANNA enters.)* You can't support your habit!

JIMMY: Be cool, Dela, there's people here. Call me when you got a smile for me. *(Exits.)*

DELA: I don't even like him.

GEORGIANNA: Is this your first. . . ? I mean are you. . . ? Uh . . .

DELA: Uh huh.

GEORGIANNA: *(Suddenly noticing.)* How old are you?

DELA: I'm sixteen. My father'd kick my natural ass if he found out.

GEORGIANNA: My parents are back in Iowa. They haven't spoken to me since I got divorced. My brother's here somewhere . . . but how could I tell *him*?

RIGHT-TO-LIFER: *(Enters.)* Good morning. Have you girls thought about your choice?

GEORGIANNA: Have I *thought* about it? I haven't slept in two weeks!

RIGHT-TO-LIFER: Will you be able to sleep tonight?

DELA: Who are you?

RIGHT-TO-LIFER: I'm a counselor.

GEORGIANNA: Thank God! Help me decide?

RIGHT-TO-LIFER: Decide to kill your innocent baby?

DELA: It's not a baby yet. I want to finish school!

RIGHT-TO-LIFER: You wouldn't be in this mess if we had prayer in schools instead of sex education.

GEORGIANNA: My baby's three. This is an accident.

RIGHT-TO-LIFER: You had your fun but you don't want to pay for it.

DELA: Who had fun?

GEORGIANNA: Please. I just got a job. I get up at 5:30 every day with Miranda. 7:30, I drop her off. We don't get home till 6:00. I bring home two hundred dollars, fifty goes to the sitter. How could I double that? How could I take care of two, when I barely got time to love one? I'd have to go back on welfare.

RIGHT-TO-LIFER: Which is it going to be? This? *(Shows picture.)*

DELA: Yuk! Don't make me look at that!

GEORGIANNA: Oh, no! I can't stand it.

All freeze as BUDDY *and* SEDRO *enter.*

BUDDY: I knew it was around here someplace. Worked the street all night, made forty-seven cents. This place pays twenty dollars. You even get a glass of orange juice.

SEDRO: Hold it, partner. Something tells me this ain't the blood bank.

DELA: I can't do it! I guess this means I gotta marry Jimmy. Maybe it won't be so bad. At least we'll always have a TV.

GEORGIANNA: Thank you. Now I know what I'm going to do.

RIGHT-TO-LIFER: Quit your job, raise your two babies, and pray some nice man will marry you in spite of your past.

GEORGIANNA: No . . . go back to the sitters', pick up Miranda, and throw both of us off the Golden Gate Bridge!

DELA: No!

RIGHT-TO-LIFER: See why we need an anti-abortion amendment? If there were a law against it, you wouldn't have to choose.

SEDRO *rips off his coat. He is* FACTWINO. *He zaps her.*

RIGHT-TO-LIFER: And neither would a twelve-year-old girl who'd been raped. Senators and congressmen would make the choice for her.

SEDRO *is astonished.*

GEORGIANNA and DELA: Wait a minute.

RIGHT-TO-LIFER: Of course there'll always be the illegal options . . . back-street butchers, coat hangers. Can laws stop abortion or just make it dangerous?

GEORGIANNA: Whatever got you thinking like that?

RIGHT-TO-LIFER: I don't know . . . my brain started buzzing, and suddenly everything seems so complicated.

FACTWINO *stares, amazed.*

GEORGIANNA and DELA: Really. *(Three women sit, confer excitedly.)*

RIGHT-TO-LIFER: How many so-called "Right-to-Life" congressmen voted for all those deadly nuclear weapons?

NURSE: *(Enters.)* Dela Jimenez? *(DELA stands.)* Child, you got in under the wire. The Moral Majority is trying to get a new law passed . . . if it goes through, we'd have had to notify your parents.

DELA: Whoa! I want to be a mother . . . in about fifteen years.

RIGHT-TO-LIFER: You're making the right choice. *(DELA goes inside.)* Well, it is her right to choose.

NURSE: Georgianna Strumpf?

GEORGIANNA: Do I have a right to my life with Miranda?

RIGHT-TO-LIFER: Aren't your lives human lives? *(GEORGIANNA goes in.)* What about the right to a decent life?

NURSE: Uh, if you're here for counseling, *(RIGHT-TO-LIFER discovers SEDRO and BUDDY)* that starts at 10:00, after VD. *(Exits.)*

BUDDY: Sedro . . .

FACTWINO: You know, it's a funny thing about abortion laws . . . there wasn't any until the late nineteenth century. Not even in the Catholic Church.

RIGHT-TO-LIFER: Really?

BUDDY: Sedro!

FACTWINO: And another funny thing: those laws were passed in reaction to a worldwide women's rights movement.

RIGHT-TO-LIFER: Women's rights? Maybe I'll go to that rally this afternoon and agitate for the ERA. Hmmm.

FACTWINO: What rally's that?

RIGHT-TO-LIFER: The big one . . . the kick-off rally for the Christian Crusade.

BUDDY: Say, lady, you got fifty cents?

RIGHT-TO-LIFER: Certainly. *(Gives him money.)* Take my advice though, you wouldn't want to go in those clothes. *(Exits.)*

FACTWINO: What?

BUDDY: What are you staring at? You the one that looks ridiculous. Like those shorts, though. *(Reads the back of cape.)* "Factperson?" You got to advertise it?

FACTWINO: Holy shit.

BUDDY: Dancing around, messing in women's business . . . you embarrassing. Anyway, we got ninety-seven cents. Let's go buy some wine.

FACTWINO: Come on! I really need a . . . *(Stops.)* Buddy, I can't drink!

BUDDY: What's wrong, Sedro? What's gotten into you?

FACTWINO: The power! . . . Wait—did she say something about a rally? *(Exeunt.)*

Scene 4

Sign: "Later, on the steps of City Hall."

GEORGE and EDNA enter.

GEORGE: Edna, there ain't nothing here but bums and fountains. I'm going back to the camper.

EDNA: You'll do no such thing, George. We're going to do what we promised.

GEORGE: What you promised. I'm not going to parade myself in any born-again ballyhoo. You know, you're not the same person, Edna, since you started watching all those evangelists on TV.

EDNA: I've seen the light, George. I've found out what's wrong with America.

GEORGE: You didn't even look at America. We been in thirty-five cities and fourteen national parks, and all you want to do is sit in the RV and wait for the "700 Club."

EDNA: All right, George. You won't do this for the Lord. And you won't do it for me. But maybe, just maybe, you'll do it for the children.

GEORGE: The children! Our kids are quitters, Edna. I wouldn't give either of 'em the time of day.

EDNA: You never did give 'em much time.

GEORGE: Oh, yeah? Who bought all Georgianna's Rainbow Girl dresses?

EDNA: Because you never let me get a job!

GEORGE: Who worked two jobs and still took Clyde to Pop Warner's Football League?

EDNA: He hated football!

GEORGE: Because you mothered him half to death!

EDNA: Stop it, George. There's people watching.

Music off-stage.

GEORGE: Oh, shit.

EDNA: Feel the spirit, George! Go with it!

REVEREND *and* FUNDAMENTALISTS *march on-stage singing* "The Army of the Righteous":

> We're the armies of the righteous
> We're marching with the Lord
> We're the armies of the righteous
> We're marching off to war.
>
> If you disagree with us
> It's not just that you're wrong
> But you'll burn in Hell forever
> While we sing celestial songs.
>
> We're the armies of the righteous
> We're marching with the Lord
> We're the armies of the righteous
> We're marching off to war.

REVEREND: Thank you, thank you. Welcome to the kick-off rally for our great Save the Family Crusade. *(Cheers.)* Brother Jerry can't be with us just yet, he's *(Ad libs from headline of the day.)* But we're here to talk about love. We love! We love old people, that's why we want Social Security cut, so more old folks can move in with their children. We love the home, home the way the Lord intended it. That's why we want Mom in the kitchen, not standing in line at a unisex toilet.

CHORUS: Amen!

REVEREND: We love!

CHORUS: Love!

REVEREND: We are filled with love!

CHORUS: We're full of it!

REVEREND: We're here today, friends, in the very bowels of Gomorrah by the Bay. We are here to declare war on the enemies of love. Our forces will be felt in every classroom, every Planned Parenthood center, every pervert resort. We are going to root out those strangers, those foreign elements, those alien ideas that are eating the bud of family life like the medfly. Family life . . .

EDNA: Go on, George.

GEORGE: You do it.

EDNA: But George, I'm a woman.

GEORGE: I'll lend you my hat. *(EDNA pushes GEORGE.)* Uh, well, uh, uh . . .

REVEREND: Come forward, friend. Tell your story.

GEORGE: *(Takes out photo.)* This is a picture of our family. Our children. We gave them everything. Georgianna left first; she married right out of high school.

EDNA: It was an all-white wedding.

GEORGE: They came out West someplace . . . then she up and left the guy, six months after she married him. Like to broke her mother's heart. Naturally, I had to disown her. This is my boy, Clyde. I pinned all my hopes on him . . . then he quit college halfway through! Said he'd rather die than live in Iowa!

BUDDY and FACTWINO enter; others freeze.

BUDDY: Is this one of them anti-nukular rallies? We won't get a penny out of them.

FACTWINO: No, these people are pros. Pro-horseshit, I believe. Mmm, I have work to do.

REVEREND: Now why did such misfortune come to your home?

GEORGE: That's what I don't understand.

EDNA: Our family was destroyed by atheistic, communistic schoolteachers!

REVEREND: Now you're talking.

EDNA: By immoral TV programs.

REVEREND: I hear you.

EDNA: By government interference!

REVEREND: Tell it!

EDNA: And lured away by the false glitter of hot tubs and narcotics. *(FACTWINO can't stand it. He zaps her.)* Wait a minute . . . Do you think the economy might have something to do with it?

ALL: What?

EDNA: I mean, the family farm, like we grew up on, that's gone . . . and the factory jobs are all drying up . . . new jobs, they're for women, I guess 'cause we're cheaper—could these things be affecting the family?

REVEREND: No way.

GEORGE: Yeah—what kind of future would Clyde have in Iowa?

EDNA: Where were you supposed to find time for the kids? I mean, how many families can make it on one paycheck?

FACTWINO: Not many. Only seventeen percent of US households have a mama who stays home while papa goes off to work.

GEORGE: Who's the weirdo in the outfit?

EDNA: This is San Francisco, George. *(To FACTWINO.)* What do you think, mister—is immorality destroying the economy or is the other way around?

FACTWINO: Well, I know a very smart man once wrote, "Every age, every state of economic development invents the ideology it requires . . ." *(Aside.)* Was that Marx or Lenin?

GEORGE: What kind of economy requires a Moral Majority?

FACTWINO: Good question! You know who said that children, church, and kitchen were the only legitimate concerns of women?

GEORGE: Jerry Falwell!

FACTWINO: Adolf Hitler.

GEORGE: Whoa. It's all coming together, you know what I mean? Edna, if we ever hear from our kids, we got a lot of things to talk about.

EDNA: What do you mean if? Let's get busy and find 'em.

GEORGE: How're we going to do that? They could be any place.

EDNA: You know what it says in the Bible, George.

GEORGE: That again?

EDNA: "Seek and ye shall find."

EDNA and GEORGE: *(To FACTWINO.)* Thanks, mister. *(Exeunt.)*

REVEREND: Wait a minute! Brother, you are possessed by Satan.

FACTWINO *zaps him.* REVEREND *begins singing "The Zap Rap."*

> Am I really knocking at Heaven's door
> When I serve the rich and milk the poor?

FACTWINO: Well, devil's sure to toast your ass
> If you keep working for the ruling class.

CHORUS: Hey! What is this? *(FACTWINO zaps them.)*
> We've been told by Brother Jerry
> Questions are unnecessary

FACTWINO: If you don't ask questions, and afraid to doubt
> Your head shrinks, and your mind strikes out.

CHORUS: That's right!

FACTWINO: That's right!

CHORUS: That's right!

FACTWINO: That's right!
> Everybody knows now's the time
> To turn on the lights for the hopeless blind.
> Use your mind
> Use your eyes
> Don't listen to that mindless jive.

Be free!

CHORUS: Free!

FACTWINO: And drop your chains.

Get smart.

CHORUS: Smart!

FACTWINO: And grow some brains.

Be free!

CHORUS *exits, clapping and rapping.*

BUDDY: You had 'em all softened up. We could have scored, man.

FACTWINO: Buddy, we scored, but that was just the preliminary bout. I'm looking for the main event. Where's Falwell?

BUDDY: You know, you smell funny.

FACTWINO: What do you mean? I haven't had a drop in over twenty-four hours.

BUDDY: That's what I mean.

FACTWINO: But while I wait on him to show, we can hit some politicians' press conferences . . . school board meetings . . .

BUDDY: How 'bout hitting the bottle?

FACTWINO: Can't do it, Buddy. Some radio stations . . .

BUDDY: "Factperson" can't have any fun?

FACTWINO: You don't understand, Buddy. You see, I'm a man with a mission.

BUDDY: I understand you ain't got time for your old Buddy. Now are you going to come with me and score some wine?

FACTWINO: Guess this is where we part company, partner. Because if I booze it, I lose it.

BUDDY: Well, you just lost me. *(Exits.)*

FACTWINO: Wait—he just don't understand. I've got to fix Falwell—I got to fix him. And then, I got to figure out how he fits in. *(Exits.)*

Sign: "A big order for our teetotalling titan—bigger than he knows."

Scene 5

ROBOT enters, sets scene.

Sign: "In a Secret Shelter Underneath the Potomac"

ARMAGEDDONMAN enters. He has two heads, whom we shall call BUSINESS *and* WAR.

BUSINESS: Earth and her inhabitants, surrender your riches to me!

WAR: Let humanity cower in fright, puny insects before my boundless power. I command the most lethal war machine in history. See this button *(reaches for it)* I can destroy the whole world.

BUSINESS: *(Stopping him.)* Not yet—I'm not done with it.

WAR: Okay, Okay. But I am invincible.

BUSINESS: It helps to have a friend in the White House.

ROBOT *enters with drinks.*

WAR: To the president!

BUSINESS: To the people who make it all possible!

WAR: You mean the fifty percent who don't vote?

BUSINESS: I mean our shock troops, our little soldiers of God, who fight our battles at election time. If they didn't exist, we'd have to invent them.

WAR: Ah, yes: to the Moral Majority! *(They both laugh, drink, and then sing "Armageddonman.")*

There is less but we want more
So we take it from the poor
You can't stop us, no one can
Call us Armageddonman.

In the water, in the air
Our poison's everywhere
You can't stand us, no one can
Because we're Armageddonman.

Karl Marx predicted our demise
But it's on crises that we thrive
Find a new market or a war will do
We'll see our historic mission through.

Even though our race is almost run
When we are through, you'll all be done
What we don't use up, we'll blow away
On that Armageddon Day.

Round the world we're number one
We'll win the war that can't be won
You won't survive, no one can
Thanks to Armageddonman.
Thanks to Armageddonman.
Thanks to Armageddonman.

BUSINESS: Enough partying. There's a planet to suck dry. *(Computer alarm.)* What the . . .

ROBOT: Danger Detection System Early Warning Emergency Alarm.

BUSINESS AND WAR: It's the Danger Detection System Early Warning Emergency Alarm.

WAR: Armageddon is here! *(Reaches for the doomsday button.)*

BUSINESS: Don't do it! *(To ROBOT.)* Request more information.

ROBOT: Danger Detection System Report. Place: San Francisco. Nature of emergency: major setback for New Right.

WAR: Why can't it ever be the Russians.

BUSINESS: *(To ROBOT.)* More information!

ROBOT: Factperson II turns Moral Majority demonstration into pro-choice, pro-ERA parade.

WAR: Let's nuke the bastard.

BUSINESS: Who is this Factperson?

ROBOT: Described as elderly Negro in comic-book outfit, possessed of mysterious ability to make people think.

BUSINESS: Think! Shit.

WAR: Let's kill him.

BUSINESS: No. Give 'em something to think about. *(To ROBOT.)* Get hold of Jerry. We'll set this Factperson's facts straight.

WAR: Then we'll kill him. *(Exeunt.)*

Scene 6

SLEEPY *enters, sets scene, reclines.*

Sign: *"Unaware he is the object of a sinister search, Factwino continues to pile triumph on triumph, giving no thought to Security."*

Sign: *"or to the Buddy he has left behind. Soon, on Sixth Street . . ."*

BUDDY *enters tanked and tearful and shakes sleeping wino.*

BUDDY: How many years? How many cold nights I found him a newspaper? How many foggy mornings I made us a fire? Now he tosses me away like an empty bottle. Let's drink to friendship. *(Bottle is empty.)*

ROBOT: *(Enters.)* Good evening.

BUDDY: Good e . . . *(Aside.)* Jesus Christ! *(To ROBOT.)* Say—you got a quarter?

ROBOT: Here is five dollars.

BUDDY: Five dollars! Whoo! Hey, you're beautiful! *(Leaving.)*

ROBOT: Let's talk.

BUDDY: Uh, I'd like that—but I gotta get something at the store.

ROBOT: I have wine. *(SLEEPY wakes up as ROBOT produces bottle.)* Let's have a party.

BUDDY: Hmmm. "Chateau Rothschild 1976." You ever taste Annie Green Springs? *(Drinks, chokes.)* No offense, I like sweet wine. *(SLEEPY has bottle, chug-a-lugs.)* Hey! She give it to me! *(Grabs bottle back. SLEEPY goes back to sleep. BUDDY drinks throughout the following.)*

ROBOT: Where is your friend, Factperson?

BUDDY: I don't have a friend! The son of a bitch.

ROBOT: Why has he abandoned you?

BUDDY: I don't want to talk about it. You know what he told me?

ROBOT: What did he tell you?

BUDDY: You know, you're all right. At first I thought you was kinda hard looking.

ROBOT: What did he tell you?

BUDDY: The worst part is, I understand him. You know why? 'Cause I'm the only one that knows about Cleveland.

ROBOT: Cleveland? Recording—beep.

BUDDY: Let it all hang out! He keeps it secret. You see, he was The Rapper.

ROBOT: The Rapper? Beep.

BUDDY: On the radio. On a rhythm and blues station in Cleveland. In the '50s. He used to rap the facts . . . till they called him a communist.

ROBOT: Communist? Oh, boy. Beep

BUDDY: Turned up to work one day, they'd put a preacher on in his time-slot. I bet you think that's why he started drinking.

ROBOT: Started drinking? Beep.

BUDDY: Nope. It was because nobody out there said nothing. Total silence.

ROBOT: Total silence. Beep beep.

BUDDY: Not now! Ever since he got that new outfit, he's a big shot.

ROBOT: What did he tell you?

BUDDY: Huh?

ROBOT: What did you tell you?

BUDDY: Oh, yeah. Those words that cut me like a knife. "We gotta part company partner—because if I booze it, I lose it." *(Sobs.)*

ROBOT: "If I booze it, I lose it." Beep.

BUDDY: Aw-ww-w.

ROBOT: Can you keep a secret?

BUDDY: Link a sphinx, lady. My lips are sealed.

ROBOT: Do not tell Factperson that Jerry Falwell will invade Castro Street just after sundown tomorrow night.

BUDDY: Tomorrow night? Castro Street?

ROBOT: Do not tell Factperson. The party is over. *(Exits.)*

BUDDY: Serve him right if I didn't tell him. Yeah, but when he hears how I got the secret out of her, he's gonna learn to appreciate me. *(Shakes SLEEPY.)* Hey, Sleepy! Wake up! We gotta find Sedro!

SLEEPY: Where's Sedro? *(Exeunt.)*

Scene 7

Sign: "Deep in the Heart of Castro."
DICK *enters the Target Bar and calls off-stage.*

DICK: Hey, Bill. Did you pick up the tickets for the "Oblivion Express" dance? . . . *(Voice answers, "yes.")* Good! *(Checks cash.)* This one's stamped "Gay Money." Isn't that cute? My former stigma is now my meal ticket. If they could see me now . . . *(Checks further.)* We're out of amyl nitrate! *(Exits.)*

BARNEY: *(Enters in a huff.)* Bartender! That butch burnout of a bouncer asked me for three pieces of picture ID! I mean, really. He told me it was getting too dark in the jungle. I can be insulted on the street for free. Hey—let's have some music. *(Punk band enters.)* I just want to forget. Pretend it never happened.

BANDLEADER: *(As music vamps.)* We just want to let you know that you're right on target at Dick's Target Club. That's right, yeah. I'm Mark Antony and these are the Nihilists. *(Ad libs: introduces band members. They begin singing "Because You're Stupid.")*

These fearful times make willing slaves
Who seek their freedom in their chains.
Reagan's election was no surprise:
You voted for Nixon twice.
Why? Because you're stupid.
Stupid, stupid, stupid, stupid.
Blame it on the black folks
Blame it on the Jews,
Blame it on anyone not like you.
You can blame it on the reds,
Blame it on the greens,
But you never put the blame on the
man who pulls the strings.
You must be stupid.
Stupid, stupid, stupid, stupid.

TV preachers quote the Lord,
Say, "Beat your plowshares into swords.
Live your life in the Christian way,
Send your money and you'll be saved."
Why? Because you're stupid.
Stupid, stupid, stupid, stupid.
Stupid, stupid, STUPID!

BARNEY: I must be stupid to spend half my paycheck in this polyester paradise. Something tells me this is not the place I'm going to meet Prince Charming. Bartender! Bartender! Hey, can a lady get a drink or is this the YMCA?

DICK: *(Enters.)* Relax, Barney. You're here, the music's hot, and the night is young.

BARNEY: Yeah, and I'm not getting any younger. Give me one of your Martian Mai Tai's. I need to calm down. *(DICK makes drink while BARNEY checks out poster.)* Hmmm, "Oblivion Express," next Friday, hottest disco party of the season—fifteen dollars.

DICK: You coming?

BARNEY: What else is there to do on a Friday night in Babylon-by-the-Bay? *(Jeers and screams from backstage.)* The wolves are at the door.

DICK: No sweat, the Hulk will take care of them. *(CLYDE enters, dazed, leaflets in hand.)* Look what the ill winds blew our way.

CLYDE: Contradictions! I tried to leaflet these dispossessed youth and they started queer-baiting me. I didn't even tell them I was gay.

BARNEY: Pulleeze, honey . . . Hey, don't I know you from someplace?

CLYDE: I don't know—I meet a lot of people through my organizing. Here's a leaflet for the anti–Moral Majority rally next Friday. With the New Right trying to deny us our basic human rights, it's time we build coalitions and fight back!

DICK: Jeesus . . .

BARNEY: I'm not into politics anymore. That night I'll be shaking my booty at the "Oblivion Express." Honey, I'm gay, not glum.

CLYDE: Jerry Falwell and his gospel squad even hate disco.

BARNEY: Well, they should start a punk band.

DICK: Hey, buddy, take your rap somewhere else. People come here to forget their troubles.

BARNEY: Wanna dance?

CLYDE: I usually need a few drinks before I can . . .

BARNEY: Dick, give this man a double.

DICK: Here, this should soothe the savage beast.

BARNEY: Now darling, pretend I'm an exotic cabaret chanteuse, à la Dietrich. It's Berlin in the late '30s.

CLYDE: And we're making out in the back of a Nazi paddy wagon with pink triangles on our concentration camp drag . . .

BARNEY: That was then—in Germany. We are in San Francisco. I fled Florida to be free! Stop trying to bring me down. Want a quaalude?

CLYDE: We did meet before—in Miami, during Anita's Holy War. I had flown down to help the forces.

BARNEY: And I was in the field office, answering phones, while the men were off in the front lines.

CLYDE: One moonlit night we went walking on the beach by the Fontainebleau.

BARNEY: Then we went to your sleazy hotel room.

CLYDE: This is getting embarrassing.

BARNEY: Then, when the election was over, you winged in back to Frisco— I was just another forgettable layover in the jet-set world of political intrigue.

CLYDE: I had to get back to my anti-Bakke organizing work. They were cutting back childcare—district elections were . . .

BARNEY: See why I get bored with politics?

Shouting match outside. TV REPORTER *and* CAMERAPERSON *burst in.*

REPORTER: Wide shot. Pick up the fruit salad. *(Into mike.)* This is Dana Datsun and your Eyewitness News team at the Target Bar on San Francisco's Castro Street, where Romeo and Julian are about to be hit with a big surprise.

DICK: *(Enters.)* What's all the—TV cameras? *(Heads for* BARNEY.*)* Barney, would you get out of sight?

BARNEY: *(Preening.)* I am out of sight.

REPORTER: Who are you, sir?

DICK: I'm the owner. What you see tonight, it's not really typical. Usually we have dart games, football pools—

CLYDE: What you see is a parasite who preys on this community and . . .

REPORTER: Speak into the mike sir—you're on national TV.

CLYDE: Good! Because somebody's got to stand up and say . . . national? But—uh, Mom and Dad, if you're watching in Iowa . . . I'm sorry you had to find out like this. I always meant to write but—I didn't know how to—oh, this is terrible—this is going to kill Dad.

REPORTER: Glimpse of a family tragedy there. A bizarre scene on Castro Street tonight as—*(More shouting offstage.)* Here he comes, the mighty mullah of the Moral Majority—*(*FALWELL *enters)* the Reverend Jerry Falwell.

CLYDE: Jerry Falwell! I don't care about cameras. I have a few words to . . .

FALWELL: Let us pray. I want every head bowed and every eye closed. Oh, Heavenly Father, bless all those Christians out there who are sickened in their very souls by the filth they see on their TV screens tonight.

BARNEY: *(Waves.)* Hi there!

FALWELL: These—can I call them men?—are the enemy within that is delivering this country straight into the hands of the communists.

DICK: I'm a Republican!

FALWELL: Lord, a growing number of fundamentalists are demanding the death penalty for homosexuals.

CLYDE: You heard him.

FALWELL: But I—in the spirit of Christian forgiveness—call only for an end to all so-called gay rights. Amen, amen.

DICK, CLYDE, BARNEY *start to protest.*

REPORTER: These men don't like that message! Tell us, Reverend, why did you choose a gay bar as the site of your first personal appearance in San Francisco?

FALWELL: Well, Ms. Datsun, tonight I'm going to be wrestling with Satan. And I want to meet him on his home ground.

SEDRO: *(Enters.)* Jerry Falwell?

FALWELL: Speak of the devil.

SEDRO: *(Sings.)* Ring the bells, I have arrived
  Going to blast away all Falwell's jive.
  Say hey, boom-di-ay
  I'm back with facts, going to save the day.

DICK: It sounds like . . .

BARNEY: It can't be!

CLYDE: It is!

SEDRO: It had to be a barroom.

DICK, BARNEY, CLYDE: Factperson II!

REPORTER: Remember, you saw it here on Eyewitness News.

FACTWINO: You got your cameras cranking? *(To FALWELL.)* I am gonna make you think. *(FALWELL shakes his head "no.")* I hereby challenge Jerry Falwell to a hands-down, no-holds-barred debate—on any topic he sees fit to choose.

REPORTER: This could be the confrontation of the century. Factperson II is unbeaten! He's made opponents from every walk of life eat their words as soon as they utter an error! Will Falwell risk it?

FALWELL: I accept. *(Gays cheer.)* On one condition.

FACTWINO: I am going to allow him a handicap. Because this man has not used his mind, has not asked himself a single question in twenty-five years. Well, name your game, Falwell, and warm up your brain—you are in for an experience. Okay, one condition. What is it?

FALWELL: One problem with being a preacher, everybody thinks you're a prude. I don't like that. Let me buy you a drink.

FACTWINO: Huh?

FALWELL: Bartender. *(DICK is glad to comply.)*

FACTWINO: Thanks—I never drink when I'm working. State your proposition.

FALWELL: You haven't worked in twenty-five years.

FACTWINO: Stop—stop stalling, Falwell. Say something stupid so I can make you refute it.

FALWELL: What was it they used to call you back in Cleveland—The Rapper?

FACTWINO: Come out with it Falwell—any of that shit you spout every day!

FALWELL: Soon as you empty that glass. Bottoms up—right boys? Surely Factwino's power can't be so fragile that a little booze would cause him to lose it?

REPORTER: Factwino? The pavement philosopher is certainly losing his equanimity.

FACTWINO: You been spying on me!

FALWELL: I'm a pastor, brother, I know human nature. I know your very deepest fear.

FACTWINO: No one knows that!

FALWELL: You're afraid nobody will care what you say. Nobody cares about a communist. When they shut you up, like they did before, nothing will be heard but—total silence.

FACTWINO: No! *(Raises glass to lips. Freezes.)*

SPIRIT OF INFORMATION enters.

SPIRIT: I don't hold with entrapment. Mr. Falwell?

FALWELL: Huh?

SPIRIT: I was goin' down Castro Street collecting beer cans and peoples said you was in here, and suh, I be watching your show every Sunday but seem like I always be missing things, so I sure would like you to 'splain me what's this here sexual humorism you talks so much about on TV.

FALWELL: Sexual—secular humanism is an atheistic, amoral philosophy that destroys the American family and the great Christian principles on which our founding fathers built this great nation.

SPIRIT: I was hoping you'd say that. *(Exits.)*

FACTWINO bangs the glass down. Thunder crashes. Lightning flashes. He zaps FALWELL.

FALWELL: Since our founding fathers were founding a Christian country, why didn't they just come out and say so in the Constitution? Now I know that one or two of them were unbelievers—Jefferson . . . Franklin . . . Madison . . .

FACTWINO: And George Washington, who said—and I quote—"The government of the United States is not in any sense founded on the Christian religion."

FALWELL: Well, there may be some problems with the Constitution. Okay. Some of our friends in Congress are getting ready to rewrite it. But the true building block of this country is the Christian family: Dad, Mom, and the kids, in the order God meant. *(Zap.)* Of course, when the country was founded, it was more like Grandpa and Grandma, two uncles, three aunts, six children, and the hired man.

FACTWINO: You talking 'bout white folks now.

FALWELL: The family has evolved . . . no . . .

DICK, BARNEY, CLYDE: Evolved?

FALWELL: I mean the family's changing and . . . could I have a glass of water?

REPORTER: Falwell is feeling the strain now.

FALWELL: But one thing never changes! The inerrant, unalterable Word of God: the Holy Bible! *(Zap. FALWELL crying.)* Then how come it contradicts itself three times inside the first two chapters? Because the text evolved—no! Because men wrote down different parts at different times and naturally there were—no! If there are errors, there are no absolutes! No absolutes, no morality! What's to stop me from fornicating that fruit there?!

BARNEY: No way!

FALWELL: What's to stop me from whipping out a machine gun and cutting down the whole Osmond family as they kneel in prayer? *(Mimes machine-gunning.)* Ack-ack-ack-ack-ack-ack—

FACTWINO: Better give that boy a bourbon. *(DICK does, FALWELL belts it.)*

REPORTER: Well, champ, in another minute you'd have had us thinking that atheism is as American as apple pie.

FACTWINO: Better for you, too—it don't contain any sugar. See I believe that the human heart and the human mind keep us moral.

REPORTER: What do you call that religion?

FACTWINO: Secular humanism. *(FALWELL is raving.)*

REPORTER: *(To camera.)* Miss Muggins? *(They take FALWELL out.)*

BARNEY: What a man! That's the end of the Moral Majority.

FACTWINO: After them, what? I need to think. I need a drink.

DICK, BARNEY, CLYDE: No!

FACTWINO: I need to get out of here! *(Exits.)*

BARNEY: Let's have some music! Let's boogie!

CLYDE: It's a little soon to celebrate. There's millions of them out there. You oughta meet the jerk my sister married. You oughta meet my parents!

Music; EDNA enters.

EDNA: Oh, I hope he's still here—where's my son?

CLYDE: Mom?

EDNA: Clyde! After five long years. *(They embrace.)*

CLYDE: I'm sorry, Mom. I don't know how to explain . . .

EDNA: You don't have to dear—we saw you on TV . . .

CLYDE: We? You mean Dad's here?

EDNA: He's parking the RV. Have you seen your sister?

CLYDE: She's here? Is that why you came to California?

EDNA: It's a long story, but we like it here. We want to stay. Oh, I'm sure your father's lost—all those people on the street look alike—I'm going to go stand on the corner, you stay right here in case I miss him. Oh, we'll all be together again—*(Exits.)*

BARNEY: I wish my mom were like that.

CLYDE: Something's turned her around. Wait'll you meet my dad.

Music; GEORGE enters.

GEORGE: Clyde?

CLYDE: Yes, Father? *(Cringes.)*

GEORGE: Son—you don't know what it meant to me to hear you say right on TV how much you care about your old Dad. Now if only your sister were . . .

Music; GEORGIANNA enters.

GEORGIANNA: Excuse me, I'm looking for my brother—the TV showed him here, he . . .

GEORGE: Georgianna!

GEORGIANNA: Daddy!

CLYDE: Georgie!

GEORGIANNA: Clyde! *(All embrace.)* You mean you ran away because you were a little . . . ?

CLYDE: A lot.

GEORGIANNA: And Daddy—you mean you don't mind?

GEORGE: Funny thing—a lot of things changed in my mind since I met this old colored guy in a funny-looking suit.

CLYDE, GEORGIANNA: You, too?

GEORGE: Where's my grandchild?

GEORGIANNA: At the sitter's.

GEORGE: I want to see her!

GEORGIANNA: Where's Mom?

CLYDE: She's out looking for Dad! We better look for her. But wait—there's someone I'd like you both to meet. This is Barney.

All shake hands.

GEORGE: He's tall, isn't he?

BARNEY: *(Indicating leaflets.)* Aren't you forgetting these?

GEORGE: Anti–Moral Majority? *(CLYDE cringes.)* After we find your mother, we can all pass 'em out. These people are giving Christians a bad name.

DICK: Hey, and after the rally, everybody make it back to the Target for the big Fight Fascism Boogie.

GEORGE: *(To BARNEY.)* May I have the first dance? *(Exeunt.)*

Epilogue

Sign: "Some weeks later, on Sixth Street."

Enter SLEEPY; he sleeps. Enter BUDDY with fruit juice and newspaper.

BUDDY: Hey, Sleepy—wake up! I just scored yesterday's New York Times! Here, have a hit of this carrot juice. *(SLEEPY shudders. BUDDY reads.)* "Economy Slows—Signs of Recession." I saw it coming. "1000 Jobseekers Riot in New York." You think there could be a connection? Whoo— "Moral Majority in Fast Fade!" Did you hear that? "Moral Majority chapters nationwide are dissolving in the wake of the much-publicized mental breakdown of their one-time leader, Jerry Falwell. Falwell, arrested recently in Las Vegas while clad in a leopardskin jumpsuit, had only this to say, 'Where's Bo Derek?'" All right, Factwino!

SEDRO *enters with huge stack of books.*

BUDDY: Hey, Sedro—you gotta see this!

SEDRO: Why you think I been to the library?

BUDDY: Don't you understand, partner? You won! You done knocked out the Moral Majority!

SEDRO: I understand that somebody or something wanted the Moral Majority to keep folks' minds off the real problem. Now I got to figure out how they going to move next. Let's see here: we got George Orwell, *1984;* Fanon, *The Wretched of the Earth;* this one, *The Use of Military Power in History* by Engels—now we're getting warm . . .

ROBOT *enters.*

ROBOT: Factwino?

BUDDY: *(Shields* SEDRO.*)* He ain't here. *(To* SEDRO.*)* That's her! That's the one tricked the secrets out of me!

ROBOT: If you see him, tell him: tripling the defense budget is the only way to save our economy.

BUDDY: No!

SEDRO *can't help it—he becomes* FACTWINO. *He zaps the* ROBOT. *But the zap doesn't take. Three times he zaps; three times the zap bounces off.*

ROBOT: Your power only works on human intelligence. *(Zaps him.* FACTWINO *is paralyzed.)*

FACTWINO: What th . . .

ROBOT: Lasers.

BUDDY: No! You can't . . . *(She stops him—with a zap.)*

FACTWINO: Buddy!

ROBOT: Microwave partial lobotomy. Now you will meet Armageddon-man.

FACTWINO: Arma—who?

ROBOT: You'll find out. Come. *(He must obey.)*

FACTWINO: Buddy! Sleepy! You out there! Somebody say something!

ROBOT: Hahahahaha. *(Exits.)*

BUDDY: *(Wakes slowly.)* Hey, wasn't there somebody else here before? Seem like I—whose overcoat? What's all these books? Oh, well—come on, Sleepy. Let's go sell this stuff and buy us some wine. *(At this,* SLEEPY *wakes. Exeunt.)*

Signs appear: "Is This the End?" "Will FACTWINO *be forgotten?" "What happens when the* SPIRIT *meets* ARMAGEDDONMAN?*" "Watch This Space."*

Ripped van Winkle

1988

Script by Joan Holden and Ellen Callas, with
Sharon Lockwood and Keiko Shimosato

Introduction

Ripped van Winkle is the most charming and nostalgic of all the troupe's shows. Rip, a hippie who wakes up twenty years after a bad acid trip in Golden Gate Park to the consumer-driven 1980s, has suggested the Mime Troupe's own anachronistic presence to many observers. The troupe has, on occasion, been criticized as being too sixties, and Rip embodies those values. The power in the play is in the juxtaposition of Rip's naive idealism with the narcissism of the yuppies, and the play searches and finds a place for his principles to make a difference. The battleship *Missouri,* state of the art in 1944, is a foil for the real argument: is there a way Rip's 1960s ideals can effect change in 1988?

Commentary

Arthur Holden

As a large white guy, one of my contributions to the troupe's mission was to portray characters who in one way or another represented the patriarchs/oligarchs/exploiter types: villains who make life so rough for so many of us. This was fun, don't get me wrong, their obsessions were great material . . . but Ripped was a character with essentially my outlook and consciousness and my problems. This rare synergy intensified my pleasure in the performance as well as that taken from the response. (Email to Susan Vaneta Mason, 22 July 2002)

Joan Holden

This play is, in a way, my answer to *The Big Chill.* . . . Everyone usually either dumps on the 60s or oversentimentalizes them. I wanted to show what was ridiculous in that era without ridiculing it or reducing it to nothing. (Quoted in "Ripped van Winkle: '60s Hippie in the 80s," *San Francisco Chronicle*, 17 July 1988)

Bruce Barthol

Ripped asked the question we of the generation of '68 were asking: What the hell happened? A cathartic and fun show to work on. (Email to Susan Vaneta Masen, 3 August 2002)

Bernard Ohanian

Ripped van Winkle takes a fond look at the 1960s through the eyes of a hippie who drops some bad LSD in 1968, sleeps for 20 years, and awakes to the rampant consumerism of the 1980s. The show pokes good-natured fun at the foibles of both eras and prods the audience to greater activism. ("Fighting That Bushed Feeling," *Mother Jones* 14 January 1989, 49)

Paul Schmidt

Ripped van Winkle restoreth the soul. ("Mime Troupe Back in Parks with a Winner," *People's Daily World*, 29 July 1988)

Audrey Smith

For me, this play was a blast from the past to teach the future. (Telephone interview by Susan Vaneta Mason, 30 July 2002)

Ed Holmes

Ripped was an inspired show. Great to contrast the decades/attitudes. Makes you wonder where idealism gets a bad name. My character Benny was the essence of lost ideals. Playing the cheesy white guys is fun: I get license to chew the scenery and be over the top of the top. Having the crowd boo/hiss and being able to respond to them is a performer's delight. I don't consider myself an actor; an actor needs a script, a set, motivation, a director, etc. A performer just needs an audience. I feel very lucky to be working with the San Francisco Mime Troupe. I doubt it could exist anywhere else but here in San Francisco . . . outdoor theater needs good weather, mental and meteorological. (Email to Susan Vaneta Mason, 8 August 2002)

The Production

Ripped van Winkle opened on 23 July 1988 in Mission Dolores Park, San Francisco, with the following cast:

Supervisor, Benny, Brad	*Ed Holmes*
Wong, Sunrise, Little Fox	*Keiko Shimosato*

Anizetti, PJ, Waiter, Juice, Del	*Mark Christopher Lawrence*
Rip	*Arthur Holden*
Rock, Woman Executive, Liberté	*Audrey Smith*
Susan, Crazy Lady	*Sharon Lockwood*
Woman Executive's Date, Stone, Lead Singer	*Harry Rothman*
Rambo Dojo	*The Band*
Passersby, Cashier, Customers, etc.	*The Ensemble*

Directed by Dan Chumley. Lyrics by Bruce Barthol. Music by Bruce Barthol and Randy Craig with the band. Set by David Brune with backdrops by Kent Mathieu. Costumes by Jennifer Telford. Musicians: Randy Marsh, Muziki Roberson, Dan Hart, Barrett Nelson.

Characters (in order of appearance)

Anizetti and Wong, gardeners for the city
Their Supervisor
Rip
Rock, a crack dealer
PJ, his homeboy
Benny, a lawyer
Sunrise, a young person
Susan, her mother
A Woman Executive
A Waiter
Brad, from the Chamber of Commerce
Juice, Stone, and Little Fox: homeless citizens
Del, a comic
Rambo Dojo, a heavy metal band
Also: a jogger, a crazy lady, a crowd of consumers

Ripped Van Winkle

Park drop set. Onstage, a large, disordered pile of leaves, old newspapers, bottles. Discernible, though nearly buried, is the crown of an old felt hat, with a feather sticking out of the mess.

PROLOGUE: CHORUS OF HOMELESS *(Sings "Out of Step.")*
   You're out of step and you're out of time
   Your shoes don't fit and your words don't rhyme
   You're out of luck and you think you're going out of your mind
   It's a sign of the times.

   You still know what you once knew
   Truth has a habit of remaining true
   And the Emperor still stands completely nude
   Different face different shoes.

   Nothing, really nothing stays the same
   But nothing, really nothing seems to change.
   It's two steps forward and we're falling back
   The prophet answered when he was asked
   "He who is first will later be last."
   You make your choice and you do what you can do what you can do.

   Nothing, really nothing stays the same
   But nothing, really nothing seems to change.
   Because it all comes around again and again
   Where will you go? What will you choose?
   What will you do? What will you do? What will you do?

Scene 1: A Forgotten Corner of Golden Gate Park

SUPERVISOR, WONG, ANIZETTI, RIP, ROCK, PJ, BENNY THE LAWYER.
Birds twitter. Then, offstage, we hear voices, branches breaking, the sound of a power shredder.
SUPERVISOR *(Enters with checklist.)* Blue sky—check . . . lawn—check . . .
   audience of the converted *(ad lib)*—check . . . pile of weird stuff . . . pile
   of weird stuff? Where does it say . . . Jumping Mary and Joseph. Hey
   Wong! Hey, Anizetti!
TWO GARDENERS enter, one young, one an oldtimer.
SUPERVISOR: What's this?
Gardeners look at each other.
ANIZETTI: You mean that there?
SUPERVISOR: Yeah.
WONG: Uh—we call that the Museum.
ANIZETTI: Right.
SUPERVISOR: Galloping Jesus.
ANIZETTI: *(Picks a broken bottle out of the pile.)* See this? *(Reading label.)*
   Red Mountain. Takes you back, huh? When's the last time you saw that?

(Carefully puts it back, takes out a torn, ancient piece of newspaper.) Lookit this. Rain's faded it, but you can still see.

SUPERVISOR: *(Reads.)* "San Francisco Oracle."

ANIZETTI: The hippy paper, on Haight Street. *(Points.)* "July 22 . . . 1968."

SUPERVISOR: Mulch.

WONG: Look here—"Get out of Vietnam!"

ANIZETTI: First day I'm on this section, 10 years ago already, I'm all set to burn this stuff. Then I see we got our own La Brea Tar Pits here.

SUPERVISOR: Sweet Shivering Christ.

WONG: *(Holds up a political button.)* Hey. "Get Out of Vietnam."

SUPERVISOR: Shred this mess, now.

GARDENERS: But—

SUPERVISOR: Bunch of junk from a time that never should have happened.

VOICE OFF: Hey, Crank!

SUPERVISOR: Right away! *(To them.)* Shred it, now. *(Exit. Shredder roars off-stage.)*

ANIZETTI: You know the trouble with this country? Nobody got a sense of history.

WONG: Just be glad you got a job. *(With hoe and pitchfork, they start on the pile.)*

SUPERVISOR re-enters.

SUPERVISOR: Hold it. That was the Deputy Superintendent. Budget cuts. We're all laid off!

Offstage, shredder dies. Music up. Exeunt arguing.

The pile of leaves begins to stir, hat leading. Slowly, painfully, still half-asleep, RIP emerges from the pile, rubbing bruises. Birds twitter.

RIP: Ow . . . what . . . why'm I so stiff? *(RIP blinks at the light, listens to the birds, looks around.)* Holy shit. I been here all night. *(Remembers.)* Yeah, but that was a dynamite trip! *(Starts off, misses something.)* My mojo bag—where's my mojo bag? *(Scrabbles through pile, finds ancient woven bag.)* That's not mine! Mine's new! *(Looks inside.)* But my mojo's cool . . . what . . . that French chick switched bags on me! . . . And I thought she picked me cause I'm beautiful! Bummer. I better get back to the pad. Susan's gonna . . . *(Music up. Exit.)*

Music changes. ROCK enters, studiedly cool, takes up a spot. Pocket beeper goes off. He checks it. Takes cordless phone from coat.

ROCK: Rock Star here. You can come in for a landing. *(Resumes cool pose.)*

PJ: *(Enters.)* Rock, how you doin, blood? *(This is not who ROCK wants to see.)* What's happening, brother man?

ROCK: Ain't nothing happening, PJ.

PJ: I seen you with your new girlfriend, man—she's, uh, she's—I seen you with her. Say, man, how about just a 2–0 on the I.O.?

ROCK: I.O.?

PJ: I.O.U.!

ROCK: I said, ain't nothing happening.

PJ: Look man, that's cool, I know I owe you money, man—so make it a ten-shot, just ten more dollars, my mother's check come Thursday, man.

ROCK: Your mother's check ain't gonna be no six hundred dollars.

PJ: You making thousands, man! You got two houses, you ain't hurting! You're my homeboy—we always been partners! Gimme one rock, man. Just one 5-dollar rock, I swear I pay you Thursday, man!

ROCK: You're pitiful, man!

PJ: I wasn't pitiful when you was taking my money, man! You done sold me my first smoke, sucker! I be glad when the DOA's waste you, man!

ROCK: That's all I be hearing these days, the DOA's. I ain't worried about no DOA's, man.

PJ: (*Leaving, in tears.*) 'S' all right. You gonna worry when they come gunning for you, man! They say you be taking too much business. I'm gonna laugh when I see you laid out, motherfucker! (*Exit running.*)

ROCK *takes out a .22 pistol, checks it, puts it back. Looks offstage impatiently, checks watch.* RIP *enters.*

RIP: Power, brother. Do you have the time?

ROCK: 5 to 9.

RIP: Monday the 20th, right?

ROCK: 21st.

RIP: You sure? I tripped so far out yesterday, I was starting to wonder how long I been gone. You into psychedelics?

ROCK: Not since elementary school. Rock.

RIP: Yeah—I love music, too, man. But psychedelics make you see—the inside and the outside, the detail and the plan. You got any matches? Yesterday, me and my old lady had a fight. Next best thing to psychedelics—Panama Red. (*It goes up in flame.*) Dry. You got an old lady, man?

ROCK: Yeah.

RIP: You ever—cheat on her?

ROCK: I would never cheat on my woman, man.

RIP: Smart—nobody'll switch your mojo bag. But say you did—say you met this beautiful French chick and . . . would you tell your old lady the truth—or would you say you got stuck in Oakland, trying to buy a head gasket?

ROCK: I believe in honesty between two people, man.

RIP: Heavy. How old are you?

ROCK: Almost 18.

RIP: I'm 25. (ROCK *can't believe his ears.*) My psyche's burdened, man, carrying all this old junk from the past. You're free. You come of age the year the future was born.

ROCK: Uh huh.

RIP: The year the richest, meanest country in the world rains flaming death on a bunch of palm huts and rice paddies—and the guys in the rice paddies start winning. The big country panics—starts sacrificing its leaders.

ROCK: Yeah?

RIP: Bobby Kennedy was a bastard, but I kind of liked him. I'm not nonviolent.

ROCK: Me neither.

RIP: But I respected Martin Luther King.

ROCK: Right.

RIP: The ghettos explode. And the youth say—"That's it—it's our turn. Move over, we're gonna change all of it. We are gonna make America beautiful."

ROCK: Yo!

RIP: Not just here. You know young people are taking the streets in Paris, Rome, Prague, Warsaw, Madrid, Tokyo, Belfast?

ROCK: L.A.! I saw *Colors!*

RIP: But it's not gonna be victory overnight. It's gonna take two more years at least. You oughta come to Chicago.

ROCK: Chicago.

RIP: We're gonna hold up the Democratic Convention. 100,000 longhairs from all over the country—100,000 black people out of the Chicago ghetto. We're gonna make them listen where the whole world is watching.

ROCK: I'd like to make that, man!

RIP: Me, my old lady, and my friend Benny, we're gonna make it a spraycan run. Every small town along Highway 40 wakes up—"Stop the War" across the front of city hall.

ROCK: This old dude's into tagging! *(To RIP.)* Yeah, but I got what I got to do.

RIP: We're gonna make history. Be there. *(Elaborate handshake.)*

ROCK: Tell me something. Do your old lady dig you with that rug on your face?

RIP*: (Finding out he has a very long beard.)* Whoa. I must still be tripping. I'll look for you—peace. Power. *(Exit.)*

ROCK: *(Finds a Day-Glo sticker in his hand.)* A sticker? *(Tries to make out the words, gives up. Asks MUSICIAN.)* What that say?

MUSICIAN: "Don't trust anyone over 30."

BENNY enters.

ROCK: I like that dude! *(To BENNY.)* You took your damn time.

BENNY: *(Sniffing.)* I had a late night. *(Produces papers.)* The judge granted a continuance till the 15th of next month.

ROCK: You said you could get that mess dropped, man.

BENNY: Look, I'm working with the D.A. to get you a diversion.

ROCK: *(Hands him a quart-size ziplock bag full of rocks.)* I don't like to be out here carrying, man.

BENNY: *(Slipping bag into briefcase.)* Your bill is paid.

ROCK: How much you charge them yuppies when you sell that shit downtown?

BENNY: Hey, we all do all we can do—right, blood? *(Slaps him on the shoulder. Exeunt severally.)*

Scene 2: Susan and Sunrise's Apartment

SUSAN and SUNRISE.

Set changes to "new San Francisco" drop as SUNRISE enters, turns on radio.

RADIO: In the national news, Vice-Presidential candidate Dan Quayle, addressing a convention of Veterans of Foreign Wars, said his only regret is that he didn't die in Vietnam. *(SUNRISE exits.)* Tass, the Soviet news agency, has confirmed reports of another major accident at a nuclear plant, this time near the coastal city of Vladivos—*(SUSAN enters, turns radio off.)*

SUSAN: *(Enters.)* Where's my belt? *(Turns radio off.)* Sunrise, have you seen my lizard—*(SUNRISE points)*—ah. Hurry up, you'll be late for school!

SUNRISE: It's summer, Mom.

SUSAN: Right! What'd you do yesterday?

SUNRISE: Oh—nothing.

SUSAN: *(Dressing.)* When I was your age I had activities! Think of something creative you can do today.

SUNRISE: *(Takes book.)* How about spraypaint on glass? I hate this place! I liked our old house.

SUSAN: I've had it with crumbly plaster, cracked ceilings, and cockroaches. When a person's past 40, she deserves to be finished with funk. This is how I want to live! Now all I gotta do is pay for it. *(Phone rings.)* Put the machine on, would you? I'm too rattled to take any calls right now. *(Exit.)*

SUNRISE puts the machine on.

SUSAN'S VOICE ON MACHINE: Hi, this is Current Events, public relations and party planners! If you need a hot concept, you've got the right number! Leave a message! You can also leave a message for Susan or Sunrise. Here comes the beep! *(SUSAN is dressing.)*

Phone rings.

VOICE: Susan, this is Na'ima from Stress Management Institute. We're wondering why you've missed your last three sessions.

SUSAN: *(Enters.)* Get off my back. *(To* SUNRISE.*)* Like my new outfit?

SUNRISE: Great.

SUSAN: *(Holds up an item of trendy clothing.)* I bought YOU something, too.

SUNRISE: *(Without taking it.)* Thanks, Mom. I love it.

SUSAN: You don't like it. Why—it's too much like clothes?

Phone rings.

A VOICE: Susan, this is Paul from Central American Solidarity. You put on a great benefit for us last spring and we're hoping you can help again this year.

SUSAN: No more freebies!

Phone rings.

MAN'S VOICE WITH JAPANESE ACCENT: Moshi, moshi, Sunrise—this is your father. I have still not received your report card! Remember, I will not send you any allowance if I do not receive your grades. Also, my wife and I have agreed that you should come stay with us this summer and be with a real family for a change. Call immediately and send your report card!

SUSAN: Don't send it! So, the last tycoon wants a free babysitter.

SUNRISE: You married him.

SUSAN: He was gorgeous, Third World, he had a black belt in karate—I didn't know he had a conveyer belt in and out of his bedroom. I met him on the rebound. I'd been hurt.

SUNRISE: I'm glad something in your life hasn't changed.

SUSAN: I don't know why you're complaining. You never liked Barbara.

SUNRISE: I never liked Ginny, either. I'm trying hard to picture you with some stud named "Rip."

SUSAN: Stud? "Hi, I'm Rip, as in 'rip it off.'" Then I find out his name is Winkel Ripowitz, after his great-grandfather the rabbi. Look, I'm sorry our family life has been so—hectic—

SUNRISE: Did you think you were going change the world then?

SUSAN: Never doubted it.

Phone rings.

VOICE: Hello, Susan, this is Brad Forbes from the Chamber of Commerce. I want to hear more of your ideas about our "Homeport the *Missouri*" campaign.

SUNRISE: The nuke ship?!

SUSAN: *(Picks up phone.)* Hi, Brad, this is Susan . . . Right, see you at lunch. Bye . . . Such a pig! *(Faces* SUNRISE.*)* You look very cute. I don't need you to look shocked, I'm shocking myself. Listen, this could really turn into something. I'm sorry about dinner last night, but that party was loaded

with heavy hitters. *(Leaving.)* I promise I'll call if I'm gonna be late again.
You can always zap that leftover lasagna.

SUNRISE: Goodbye. *(Sings "It's Just Another Day in the Eighties.")*
Last night I had a dream
That took me very far away
To some strange and distant planet
That's all burnt up and grey.

Smoke is in the air
There are bodies lying everywhere
They begin to move
They're alive but not awake

They're talking loud and laughing
They don't notice anything
I realize I know them
This is Earth and I'm in school

And it's just another day in the 80's
Another day to shop at the mall.
And it's just another day in the 80's
Another day with your back to the wall.

There was once a time
When people were awake
Then they died or went to sleep
Or they just took what they could take.

People getting nowhere
Think they're all getting ahead
And everything around us
Is dying or it's dead.

And it's just another day in the 80's
Another chance to get or be got.
You did a great job, older people.
Older people, thanks a lot.
Exit with backpack.

Scene 3: A Street in the Haight-Ashbury

RIP, JOGGER, TEENAGER, CRAZY LADY, WOMAN EXECUTIVE.
Rhythm line under traffic noise

RIP: *(Enters.)* Wow, the houses—Technicolor! *(Sound of car zooming past.)* Whoa, the cars—shrunk! Through the looking glass—I'm still in Wonderland. I'd like to meet that chick's dealer! No, no, no—time to come down, now. I gotta face the music. I gotta do a valve job!

In this scene everybody is going the same way as RIP, *only faster.* STATE-OF-THE ART JOGGER *enters, moving same way as* RIP. *Shiny stretch suit, hand weights, walkman; passes* RIP, *jogs backward-forward, circles, etc. to music only he can hear.*

RIP: *(Fascinated.)* Probably training for the Olympics! Hey, mister! *(JOGGER shakes his head, exits quickly.)*

CRAZY LADY *enters with shopping cart, pushes past him.*

RIP: Hey, lady—take it easy!

CRAZY LADY: Space weapons. That's what they're sending up there. Spy satellites. They can count the snails on the nasturtiums in your backyard. No place on this earth you can hide from them, no place. Planting forts all over space so they can have laser wars. Laser wars! *(Moves on.)*

RIP: Free Clinic's around the corner—they can help you! *(She exits.)* Living science fiction. Since when do they let people that sick loose on the street?

Deafening rap music starts. KID *enters with ghetto-blaster.* RIP *is amazed at the size of this radio.*

RIP: *(Taps kid on shoulder.)* Who's the new group?

KID *turns sound up, exits.*

RIP: I'm getting to the paranoid stage. It seems like everybody's on speed.

BLACK WOMAN EXEC *enters; pin-stripe suit, tennis shoes, attache case, reading newspaper.* RIP *backs into her.*

RIP: Sorry. *(Notices the headline.)* Excuse me—

She sighs, gives him a quarter.

RIP: A quarter?

WOMAN: Usually I give flowers with it.

RIP: *(Shrugs.)* Groovy. *(Pockets quarter like a treasure.)* Have one of these.

WOMAN: *(Reads sticker.)* "Take the real freeway—don't go to work"?

RIP: Try it. Say, could I see that headline for a minute?

WOMAN: *(Hands him paper.)* Take it—take it! *(Hurries off.)*

RIP: Thanks! *(Moves folded paper closer, farther away, squints.)* Now this print's acting funny. I can't read it. *(Turns to headline.)* "Reagan Demands Death Penalty for Drug Dealers." Only in California could this man get elected Governor. *(Exit.)*

Scene 4: A Trendy Restaurant near City Hall

SUSAN, WAITER, BRAD, WOMAN EXECUTIVE, HER DATE: WHITE MALE ARTISTIC TYPE, RIP.

SUSAN: *(Enters.)* Somewhere, I missed the boat. Someplace, I got off at the wrong stop. Sometime, everybody else piled on the train and I didn't even hear the whistle. Everybody was in the Movement . . . then everybody had a baby . . . then everybody got into healing . . . then it gets vague. I was trying to do socially responsible creative work . . . suddenly, everybody else puts their kids in private school, starts remodeling the house they just bought, has a glamour job at a salary they don't even discuss—at least not with me. Is that how you know you've been left in the dust—your friends stop telling you how much money they make? OK—
(Sings "This Is the Big Time.")
This is the big time, baby.
This is where I move up.
I may have been late in blooming
But now my career
Now my career is zooming.

80 K, get some national notice
Rearrange my mind, get my life into focus
Leave the past behind and find a new beginning
Grab the brass ring and get used to winning.

This is the big time
This is the big game
This is the big time
It had to be at this address? *(Straightens her shoulders.)* This is not the time for negative thoughts.
WAITER *enters, sets restaurant scene.*
Musical number: "Grill of the Week." As song starts, SUSAN *and* BRAD, WOMAN EXEC *and her* DATE, *enter and meet, choreographed. As song progresses,* WAITER *sets places, passes menus, takes orders, serves.*
WAITER: Hello, my name is Mark and I'll be your waiter today.

It's the place for the chic and trendy
It's a must for the elite
We've hit the top of the gourmet charts
We are state of the art.

It's got a really fun location
It's got a concept that's brand new
A lush but funky hi-tech decor
That makes a statement no one's heard before
ALL: It's perfect!

It's the latest, the greatest
And oh, so unique.
We've come to dine and to shine
At the brand new grill of the week
WOMAN: When you're high-profile
    You are where you eat.
    You're not on the fast track
    If you're not known here
    If you're not seen here
    And able to criticize the cuisine here.
DATE: We belong here
    And we feel great here.
    Life is good here
    And life is sweet.
    When you're here
    You know you've made it
    All the way to the top of the heap.
CHORUS: We're the latest, the greatest
    We're oh, so unique!
    We've come to dine and to shine
    At the brand new grill of the week.
    Grill of the week.
WAITER: Fresh fashion ingredients picked on our private farm, a salad green we fly in from the Amazon, a new brand of bottled water—Eastern Europe has barely been tapped—and a dozen bright new food designs combining things you've never before seen on one plate.
SUSAN: I'll have the smoked duck quesadilla with loquat compote and hazelnuts, and the nasturtium green, baked gorgonzola and shitake mushroom salad with lime fennel cream.
BRAD: Steak tartare.
OTHERS: Ooooh!
WAITER: It's the place for the movers and shakers
    Not the spot for the casual munch.
    The portions are tiny, the prices enormous
    This is the home of the power lunch.
CHORUS: It's the latest, the greatest
    And oh, so unique!
    We've come to dine and to shine
    At the brand new grill of the week
    Grill of the week
    Grill of the week!

BRAD: You know, I'm taking a lot of heat in my department for pushing an ex-radical, but that's exactly the sensibility this is going to take. I know because I'm a sixties person myself. Were you at Woodstock?

SUSAN: I was here.

BRAD: Fantastic! You probably got your start planning demonstrations.

SUSAN: With a transition in the seventies—ecology fairs, health expos. . . . Let's see what we're up against. You want to dock a battleship loaded with nuclear missiles half a mile from the heart of this city.

BRAD: That's it.

SUSAN: You want to plant a floating atomic time bomb in one of the most beautiful places that still exists on this planet.

BRAD: You got it.

SUSAN: You want to add 5000 Navy families to this city's housing problem.

BRAD: And to its voter pool.

SUSAN: Brilliant. You're promising local people this will bring jobs, that will really go to non-union ports.

BRAD: I like a girl that's got her eyes open.

SUSAN: And to make all this happen you want to dredge the Bay floor 50 feet deep, stirring up a century and a half of accumulated toxic garbage, releasing megarems of radioactivity, and finally turning San Francisco Bay into a dead sea.

BRAD: We don't just want to do it. We want people to vote for it.

RIP: *(Enters.)* Hey—what's the address here?

WAITER: Please, sir.

RIP: Is this 540 Grove St.?

WAITER: Yes.

RIP: That's my address—where's my apartment house?

WAITER: *(Seeing him out.)* I wouldn't know.

RIP: Where's my old lady? You got a pay phone here?

WAITER: Right outside—around the corner. *(RIP is out.)*

SUSAN: Do you smell patchouli oil?

BRAD: More like compost.

SUSAN: How's this: a "Meet the *Missouri*" campaign. Take each individual sailor and officer, put their photos, names, rank on billboards, taxicabs, Muni, BART—"Meet Ensign Matthew Endicott, Gunner Enforcer." Suddenly they all have faces!

BRAD: Too much like milk cartons. We're looking for something upbeat.

SUSAN: OK—a giant concert with Michael Jackson and Diana Ross; a giant soul food barbecue in Aquatic Park; a slogan—"Make San Francisco Motown!" Get it—"The Mighty Mo"? South of Market would be So-Mo, North Beach No-mo, the Castro . . .

BRAD: Look, we've got the blacks in our pocket on account of the jobs number. We've got the unions in the bag. We've got the Dan White vote. We're concerned about Yuppies, gays, the *Big Chill* generation—people who, if we let them think about it, could vote for peace and ecology.

Meanwhile, at next table, DATE's *credit card turns out to be dead.*

DATE: *(To* WAITER.*)* I don't know—I guess I'm overextended! *(All stare at him. Furious,* WOMAN EXEC *pays.*).

WAITER: Cash? I'm going to need some I.D. *(She shows a yard-long credit card holder.* COUPLE *exits humiliated.)*

BRAD: I had a very productive session this morning with Craig de Hook at J. Walter Walter. The guy thinks big.

SUSAN: THIS big? World War II—VJ Day!

BRAD: Come again?

SUSAN: What are Yuppies all about? Winning! Where did the Japanese sign the surrender? On board the *Missouri!* We'll reenact the whole thing—I mean except Hiroshima. During Fleet Week—in October, right before the election!

BRAD: Not bad.

SUSAN: Take us back to the time this town felt good about itself.

BRAD: And loved the Navy!

SUSAN: A giant victory parade and street dance on Market Street, in '40s clothes. The retro shops will get behind it. Big bands. A jitterbug marathon.

BRAD: Great.

SUSAN: A Spam barbecue on Marina Green!

BRAD: Hot.

SUSAN: Neighborhood events—gold star for the best Victory Garden. Gay events—a Betty Grable look-alike contest.

BRAD: You're cooking.

SUSAN: A Rosie the Riveter drill-off for women in trades! It's got everything San Francisco loves—nostalgia and a great party.

BRAD: Not to mention a subtle touch of Japan-bashing.

SUSAN: Maybe, just maybe, we can get a Toyota executive to impersonate Hirohito for the ceremony!

BRAD: Get me a proposal in writing. *(They start to go.)* I'll get the Board of Supervisors on board.

SUSAN: *(Stops in her tracks.)* Am I really going to be part of a campaign to turn the most liberal city in the country into another San Diego?

RIP enters bewildered.

SUSAN: So—you going to wimp out and hand the job to J. Walter Walter? No—you're going to go for it. *(SUSAN misses RIP and exits.)*

RIP: That's a science fiction phone out there. "Beep beep beep beep" . . . 20

cents . . . and this robot voice says my number's out of service! I just paid my bill Friday cause me and my old lady are supposed to leave today for Chicago. Except my VW needs a valve job.

WAITER: So does mine.

RIP: I was supposed to do mine yesterday, except Saturday, I was helping a friend put in a transmission and I forgot to get the part. My old lady won't stop about it. Then yesterday morning, I forget to do the dishes.

WAITER: My boyfriend can't stand that.

RIP: Your boyfriend? . . . Far out! So I come to the park—Hippy Hill. A hundred people throwing Frisbees. Suddenly, there's this tap on my shoulder. It's this beautiful French chick I never seen before—tall, all in white—and two perfect, pointy breasts—bare! She opens her fingers— two purple tabs of acid. She takes my hand, and she pulls me into the bushes.

WAITER: Now that ain't safe.

RIP: I saw the universe yesterday, man. Blew my mind. But right now, I'm feeling very weird. Could I possibly use your bathroom?

WAITER: *(After some hesitation.)* OK. *(Motions him in,* RIP *exits.)*

WAITER *finishes clearing. After a moment, a bloodcurdling scream.*

RIP: *(Staggers out.)* In that mirror—oh, my God I LOOKED OLD! I want to come down now—I'm starting not to like this trip! *(Exit.* WAITER *exits, shaking his head.)*

Scene 5: The Park

ROCK, SUNRISE

ROCK: *(Enters, taking his time.)* What you looking at? I know what you be thinking. "Little jeri-curl punk, selling crack, hooking 8-year-olds, shooting guns—he the reason our streets ain't be safe!" Look here—you all got a car, right? Just like me, except I got two of em. How many y'all buyin' a house? How many wish you was? Just like me—I bought me a house, and one for my mama, too. And the chains is real. I'm a minority bidnezman. I put kids to work. I ought to get a government grant. If I live, I'm gonna build a mall in my neighborhood.

SUNRISE: *(Enters with backpack.)* Hi.

ROCK: Sunrise? Hi! Baby, you look fresh! Only we said, you don't want to be where I'm working.

SUNRISE: Rock—do you realize there's no two people in the whole world as perfect together as us?

ROCK: Couldn't be. Cause ain't no other babes as gorgeous, as smart, and crazy like you. Listen—

SUNRISE: No, cause there's no other dude as smart, brave, fine and totally cool like you.

ROCK: That first day I saw you coming out of school, I said, "She's strange—but she's the one."

SUNRISE: When I saw you standing on that corner I said, "He's wrong—but he's right!" We were meant to be.

ROCK: Had to happen. That's why—

SUNRISE: In Japan, do you know what young lovers, true lovers used to do to make their love last forever?

ROCK: Uh-uh.

SUNRISE: If they had like cruel fathers, or he was supposed to marry someone else, or she was a princess and he was poor—they would each dress in their best kimonos, then they'd pray, then they'd kneel down, face-to-face. And then he'd take his dagger and kill her, like this, and then he would cut his own guts out.

ROCK: Damn, baby!

SUNRISE: I'd rather that, than live to see the earth die—or be a sleepwalker like most people and not even see! Even cool people, if they live too long, turn into zombies, like my parents! I don't want that to happen to us. I want us to die, now, together.

ROCK: You out your mind? Sunrise, baby . . . I ain't got a dagger.

SUNRISE: You got a gun.

ROCK: Forget what I got! Look, I ain't never planned on retirement. Soon as I turn 18, my next bust gonna send me to prison. Some mother want to blow me away first, that's cool. Rock Star like a comet: blast across the sky, go down blazing.

SUNRISE: That's my man. *(Sound of car, screech of brakes.)*

ROCK: Get down! *(They hit the deck. Gunshots. Car takes off.)*

SUNRISE: *(Terrified.)* What was that?

ROCK: *(Equally terrified.)* The DOA's! *(They run.).*

Scene 6: United Nations Plaza

STONE, A WHITE HOMELESS VET; JUICE, A BLACK HOMELESS VET; LITTLE FOX, AN INDIAN WOMAN; CRAZY LADY WITH SHOPPING CART; RIP; BENNY
STONE and JUICE enter. Headbands, leather vest with no shirt, etc.; both could be mistaken for hippies.

BRAD: Uh-uh, man, no way. What she done was treason, man. Stone cold treason. She oughta be fried.

JUICE: First you say the whole war was a waste, man. Then you say Jane Fonda ought to be fried.

BRAD: I was in Hue, man. I don't forgive her.

JUICE: I was in Khe Sanh and I say, she was right!

BRAD: Hey, but that Khe Sanh doojee, man—that was out of sight.

JUICE: You know that—hoo! *(They laugh, slap backs, etc.)* Put you on the moon!

BRAD: Among the stars, man!

JUICE: You need a shower.

LITTLE FOX: *(Enters with bottle.)* Hey!

JUICE: Hey, Little Fox. Over here, darling. Where you been keeping?

LITTLE FOX: Went to visit my oil well. Had to count all my money. Decided I'd do you gents a favor and visit. How long till dinner?

BRAD: *(Looks at sky.)* 2, 3 more hours. Time to line up. *(They do.)*

RIP: *(Enters, disoriented.)* Now I'm hallucinating these monster buildings. Pyramids? When am I gonna stop crashing? *(Sees them.)* Blow my mind—normal people! What's happening?

BRAD: You know this dude? *(They don't. They regard RIP suspiciously.)*

RIP: Can you people help me? I'm on a bad trip. I'm coming way, way down. *(The 3 are filled with sympathy.)*

JUICE: It'll be OK, man.

RIP: I'll walk down some block. Everything looks new, huge, cold—I think I'm in 2001. Next street, things look right—but something's wrong. Around that corner there—this is really weird—all the stores, the signs, the people, it looked like—Vietnam!

BRAD: You ain't tripping.

RIP: People passing look the other way—they don't want to see me.

LITTLE FOX: Uh-huh. You are definitely not tripping.

RIP: And my house—it's gone! *(They can relate.)*

BRAD: Give him some wine.

RIP: Thanks. I don't know where to go.

JUICE: About the best place right here. And there's some people bring soup.

RIP: The Diggers. They're far out.

CRAZY LADY: *(Enters with shopping cart.)* Alert star command!

LITTLE FOX: Uh, oh.

JUICE: Every night.

CRAZY LADY takes her place in line.

RIP: Soup! Feels like I didn't eat for years. Groovy: get some food in me, get my head straight, maybe I can find my house, my old lady, my bus . . . Hey—Anybody need a ride to Chicago?

JUICE, STONE, LITTLE FOX: Just come from there/Too hot, man/Chicago?

RIP: We're putting on a Festival of Life outside the Democratic Convention.

BRAD: The Democratic Convention—isn't that in Atlanta?

RIP: Chicago. Only one thing wrong with hippies: nobody reads the newspapers.

BRAD: Who you calling a hippy, man?

RIP: You—me—us. People who stay outside. All us freaks.

JUICE: I'm no freak, man.

RIP: I'm proud to be a freak—starts with "free." Everybody who won't program into the system. We're the sugar in America's gas tank; we're loose rods, wrecking their death machine!

CRAZY LADY: Death machine . . .

RIP: All of us who live between the lines, bloom in the cracks, don't get degrees, don't want jobs, burn our draft cards. Call us longhairs, dropouts, protestors, freaks, I don't care—we're all in the same tribe.

There is a brief pause.

LITTLE FOX: Not my tribe.

JUICE: I'm no dropout, man. I'm a roofer.

BRAD: You burn your draft card?

RIP: Well, they haven't called my age group yet, but . . .

BRAD: Uh huh. You a Communist?

RIP: With a small "c." *(SHOPPING LADY bumps him with her cart.)* Ow! Actually I think I'm more of an anarchist.

CRAZY LADY: *(Bumps him again.)* Death machine!

BRAD: Listen to the commie, coming around saying we don't want jobs!

JUICE: That's messed up.

CRAZY LADY keeps bumping RIP.

RIP: Lady—

BRAD: He was waving Vietcong flags when we were getting killed, man! *(Grabs RIP.)*

JUICE: Take it easy, Stone, bro . . .

BRAD: Some things I can't forgive. *(Pulls knife. JUICE decks him.)*

RIP: Thanks a lot, brother.

JUICE: I ain't your brother. *(Decks RIP.)*

BENNY enters, sees this scene, hopes to avoid it.

RIP: Hey, Mr. Sloane!

BENNY: My God—Rip! Hey, folks—free stuffed potatoes at Karl's Junior! *(CRAZY LADY whirls around and starts off.)*

JUICE: Hear that? Taters!

LITTLE FOX: Come on! *(Pulls STONE.)* I want mine with baco-bits! *(They exit, ad-libbing.)*

BENNY: I don't believe this.

RIP: Thanks, Mr. Sloane. Hey—you know where I can find Benny?

BENNY: Hey. I am Benny.

RIP: Benny?! What happened to you?

BENNY: You don't look exactly fresh-faced, yourself. For Christ's sake, it's been 20 years.

RIP: 20 years?

BENNY: But you look like you never left 1968.

RIP: Wait . . .

BENNY: Where'd you go, anyway? Don't tell me—underground.

RIP: Kind of . . . I took this hit of acid, and . . .

BENNY: Ah. And then another, and then another . . . some people just can't handle drugs. Well, it's been . . .

RIP: Wait . . . what . . . you're saying . . . this is 1988?

BENNY: Smell the decaf.

RIP: 1988? *(Suddenly the day's experiences make awful sense.)* Nineteen-eighty—but . . . what happened to the Revolution?

BENNY: "The Revolution"? The Revolution. The Revolution! *(Sings "Update Bringdown.")*

> Nixon got elected in '68
> The war continued to escalate
> What we couldn't blow away
> We tried to defoliate.
> Peace with honor and napalm too
> Nixon won again in '72.

RIP: Nixon? Nixon!

BENNY: We took Cambodia, bombed Hanoi
> Lost 50,000 American boys.
> Cause the war didn't end till '75.
> And after that, the Movement died.

RIP: '75? '75? Died?

BENNY: And in Cambodia we backed some stooge.
> But his ass got kicked by the Khmer Rouge.

RIP: Right on!

BENNY: They killed more people than you'd believe
> Till they got creamed by the Vietnamese.

RIP: Wait . . .

BENNY: Then Nixon sank in a swamp of sleaze
> Now the only ones that like him are the Red Chinese.

RIP: Nixon and the Red Chinese?

BENNY: Things kept happening weird like that
> We even had a Democrat.
> You don't know about Chile or Lebanon?
> About Nicaragua or the neutron bomb?
> About the CIA and secret war
> And oil spilling off the shore?

RIP: Uh-uh.

BENNY: About liberation for women and gays?

RIP: Right on.

BENNY: Women got nothin' and the gays got AIDS.

RIP: "AIDS"? What's "AIDS"?

BENNY: What goes around, and it's gonna come around.

    Hey, we had some fights, we had some fun

    But the drug revolution is all we won.

    I don't mean reefer, talkin' bout smack

    Acid is old, try some crack.

RIP: "Crack"?

    Turn on, tune in, but the bottom dropped out

    The gravy bowl done lost its spout.

    The margin's shrunk, there ain't no fat

    And half the people think the world is flat.

RIP: No, no! It's round!

BENNY: The final nail I'll now pound in—

    Forgive us, Che, for we have sinned—

    It ain't pretty, it ain't nice:

    Ronald Reagan's been elected twice!

    President.

RIP: *(Screams.)* Y-a-a-a-ahhh!

BENNY: But it's the way it is, what you gonna do?

    The rich get richer and the poor get screwed.

    Better get hip to the way it's done

    You better look out for number one.

    Whoops—that's me. Later. *(Going.)*

RIP: Wait—what happened in Chicago?

BENNY: Chicago? Ah, the Democratic Convention. 20,000 cops beat the shit
out of 10,000 demonstrators—

RIP: Only 10,000?

BENNY: On national TV—and the whole country cheered. *(Going.)*

RIP: Benny, wait, Benny—Where's Susan?

BENNY: You better forget Susan. Well, I—*(Going.)*

RIP: Benny, Benny—I really need to get my head together—can I crash at
your pad for a few days?

BENNY: I don't think it would work. But I'm in the book—leave a message.
Ciao, dude. *(Exit.)*

RIP: I thought, by the time I'm middle-aged, we'd be living in this beautiful
country. "Farmers will grow things, city people will make things—we'll
trade. We'll dismantle all the corporations. We'll all work—4 days a
week. We'll have trains going everywhere—we won't need many cars.
We'll only need a very tiny amount of petroleum. We can clean up the
rivers. We can save the rest of the redwood trees. Americans will be
happy—we can stop proving how great we are. We can let the rest of the
world breathe." So now? What am I supposed to do? What do I do?

CHORUS OF HOMELESS: *(Backstage sings "Out Of Step.")*
He never thought he would be so alone
What was familiar is now the unknown
Can he survive? Will he find his way home?
RIP goes very slowly off.
   Nothing, really nothing stays the same
    But nothing, really nothing seems to change.
   Where will he go? What will he choose?
   What will he do? What will he do? What will he do?
Musical interlude and sign: "Time Passes."

Scene 7: A Popular Buying Spot

CASHIER, FIVE CUSTOMERS, RIP.
Sign: "Whole Earth Excess." Customers enter and exit, shopping.
#1: Carol—over here, I found it! *(Exit.)*
#2: Sherry, where are you? I found it! *(Exit.)*
#3: *(Enters.)* Excuse me, where can I find the personal remote phones?
CASHIER: Right over there next to the porta-gyms, in our porta section.
#3: The porta section! Thank you. *(Hurries off.)*
CUSTOMERS #1 and #2 enter carrying boxes, followed by 3, 4, & 5. The more boxes, the better.
#2: I am just loving this graphite-coated earthenware. I can't believe what a great price—only $39.95 a place setting! And you just can't find these Bavarian toaster ovens—they can't keep them on the shelves. Look—it even has a special setting for defrosting tofu. I love it! So convenient!
CASHIER: Next, please.
#2: I know—so's this Swiss garbage disposal. Frankly, I just burned out on composting. Those stinky buckets, always attracting flies . . . too time-consuming. I came to buy socks—but this is something I can really use!
CASHIER: Cash, check, or charge?
#1: Charge. Let's see—*(examining the box)*—the sale price is marked here somewhere. Wait—what's this? *(Discovers Day-Glo sticker.)* "Do you really need this? *(Looks around; half to self.)* Do I really need this? Well, gosh, I don't know. I want it. But I guess I don't really need it. *(Hands box to CASHIER.)* Never mind—I changed my mind. I'm going to aerobics. *(Exit.)*
CASHIER: *(Annoyed, tears up charge slip.)* Next!
#2: *(Finds another Day-Glo sticker.)* "You are what you buy." What? You are what you buy? Where did this come from?
CASHIER: I don't know, ma'am. Do you want the trash masher or not?
#2: No—no, I don't think so. *(Exits. CASHIER is exasperated.)*

#4: This is great. A combination pasta maker and food scale! It's perfect for me. Now I can weigh out my complex carbos as I make them. The ultimate in portion control. I'm so happy.

CASHIER: I can take you here.

#1: Great. *(Hands card.)* Just take it out of my ATM, please. *(Turning back to mate.)* Yeah, and can you believe . . . this phone is waterproof so I can call from the shower. That's really going to give me a jump on my day. *(Reading.)* "Guaranteed . . . made in Korea . . . ." "Caution: conspicuous consumption may be hazardous to your soul."

#4: *(Reading.)* "Your purchase today will be toxic waste tomorrow." Honey, this is creepy.

#3: *(Grabs his card from* CASHIER*'s hand.)* Let's get out of here! *(They go.)*

#5: *(Slams down package.)* I come shopping to relax! And now this? "A Life Full of Things is a Life Full of Nothing"? What's that supposed to mean? My guru never said anything like that! *(Exit.)*

RIP enters.

CASHIER: I suppose you have a message!

RIP slaps sticker on counter, flashes him v-sign, exits.

CASHIER: Thanks for stopping by. *(Reads.)* "Shopping is the opiate of the '80s"? I knew that!

Scene 8: Susan and Sunrise's Apartment

SUNRISE, ROCK.

Sunrise enters, turns on radio.

RADIO: . . . predicting a record high of 92 degrees! On the international scene, Scientists for Global Responsibility, meeting in Geneva yesterday . . .

SUSAN'S VOICE OFF: 'Bye, honey—try to find something to do! *(Door slams.)*

SUNRISE: She's gone—you can come out now!

RADIO: . . . that at current rates of carbon dioxide emission, by the year 2010 the Greenhouse effect will turn inland areas of the Northern hemisphere into desert, while melting of the polar icecaps will flood coastal . . .

ROCK: *(Enters, turns off radio.)* I don't know how much longer I can take this—hiding out in your mama's house.

SUNRISE: Can you believe what my mother's doing?

ROCK: Can you believe what's happening to me? DOA's all up in the park, selling big as life on my corners. PJ's in Juvy, I bet he running his mouth . . . Cops been three times to my crib. I missed my court date. By the time I get done saving my ass, I'm be fucked!

SUNRISE: You know what happens from here? We get older and things get worse. You wanna get high?

ROCK: No! *(Paces. Phone rings.)*

SUNRISE: Hello . . . Who's calling, please? . . . Yes, he's here. It's your sister.

ROCK: Kanisha? *(Takes phone.)* Didn't I tell you not to call me here? . . . Possible—might be some people looking for me . . . What? When? . . . No—Uh uh—No! Shit! How's mama? . . . Don't do nothing till I get there. I'm coming. I'm coming right now! *(Hangs up.)* DOA's came by my mama house, shooting. They shot my baby sister! I'm outta here.

SUNRISE: I'm coming with you!

ROCK: This is my business.

SUNRISE: I thought you didn't believe in suicide!

ROCK: I'm gonna take a lot of folks out with me. Goodbye, Sunrise. Don't ever forget I loved you. *(Exit.)*

Scene 9: Fleet Week, Aboard the *Missouri*

Drop changes to deck of battleship. Stage Manager in sailor hat sets American flags. SUSAN enters in 40s dress with clipboard and walkie-talkie.

SUSAN: I'm really doing this . . . *(Into walkie-talkie.)* Main deck, Susan here. Pier 39—Brian, all systems go with the fireworks? . . . You know your cue . . . right. Embarcadero Plaza—what's your crowd count? . . . 50,000? Did Bob Hope get there? . . . I know, I know . . . one joke, that's all. Roll him on, roll him off. *(BRAD enters in navy uniform, pinches her.)* Brad, I've asked you not to do that.

BRAD: You look so cute in that outfit, I couldn't help myself. Like my uniform?

SUSAN: Gorgeous. What's your wife wearing?

BRAD: I didn't notice. You have done one hell of a job. The Chamber's ecstatic. You've got people dancing in the street, chanting "Mighty Mo, Mighty Mo"—this is bigger than the Corporate Olympics!

SUSAN: Aren't you supposed to be greeting Hirohito?

BRAD: Asking Steve Bechtel to play MacArthur—that was genius! From here on out you can write your own ticket. Tell me one more time, nothing's gonna go wrong.

SUSAN: Market Street—did the Dorsey band start? . . . Fabuloso. *(To him.)* Nothing's gonna go wrong.

BRAD: There've been a lot of weird happenings lately. Homeless sleep-ins at the Hyatt Regency and the St. Francis. "Stop the *Missouri,*" spraypainted across the front of City Hall. . . . If whoever's doing that stuff somehow got aboard here—

SUSAN: *(Into walkie-talkie.)* . . . Already? Hang loose, I'll deal with it. *(To him.)* We've got great security, plus I chilled all the radical artists. I hired them. Look, I've got a show to put on here . . .

BRAD: You are the strongest woman I ever met.

SUSAN: Go! Susan calling Copter Unit, Susan calling Copter Unit. . . . Rob, Marina Green's out of Spam. I want you to airlift two hundred dozen hot dogs . . . *(Exit.)*

BRAD *watches her go. When he turns to exit, we see a Day-Glo sticker on his back: "No Mo." Trap door opens, revealing sign, "Engine Room." RIP enters, closes trap, makes sign to audience to keep secret, tiptoes off. Enter* SUNRISE *with backpack. As she talks, she unpacks kimono and puts it on.*

SUNRISE: No problem getting backstage. I told them I was playing a Japanese diplomat. They said, "Ah, you've come to surrender." That's not how I think of it. I called my father. I said, "Dad, I'm getting into my cultural identity. I'm looking for my roots. You know those two seppuku knives of great-grandfather's? I'd really like to have one for my room." And Mom—thanks, you're giving me the perfect intro. I really hope you like the show. *(Exit.)*

SUSAN: *(Enters as M.C., to music.)* Welcome, San Francisco, to a time past and future when the country we love is on top of the world and the City That Knows How knows how to welcome the Navy! *(WOMAN EXEC from street and restaurant scenes enters ad libbing enthusiasm, sits in front row.)*

This day's about greatness, about winning, about victory. And I know that victory ceremony is what you're all waiting to see: Japan bowing to the United States! But first, our all-new USO show! San Francisco is home to a unique art form, New Vaudeville! For those not in the know, that's old vaudeville with existential angst. What our first guest does is better seen than described—please help me welcome: The Regurgitator! *(Fanfare. Nobody enters.)* The Regurgitator! *(Fanfare. Hand sticks through curtain, waving Day-Glo note.)* A slight delay, ladies and gentlemen. *(Reads.)* "The Regurgitator regrets he will not be able to perform for you today, but there are some things he can't swallow. Scrap the *Miss*—." He's been taken sick. And he's gonna to have an accident. Our next guest will make it up to you—a young man who has clawed his way from the Other Cafe to the David Letterman show, let's have a big hand for America's favorite hardball comic, Del Delmonte!

DEL: *(Enters.)* Thank you, thank you. It's great to be here aboard the U.S.S. *Missouri*. What a day, what a celebration, what a ship. The *Missouri* and San Francisco—what a fit. Just what this city needs, more unruly seamen. Do you realize that this ship has a double hull construction? That means it is unsinkable by any torpedo attack. Ain't that great, considering how often torpedoes are used today—good thing nobody's come out with that Exocet missile. *(SUSAN is taking notice.)* But hey, I love this boat. It's kind of like the "Love Boat." Although with all the stuff they'll be stirring up it's more like the "Love Canal Boat."

WOMAN EXEC *loves* DEL*'s act, vociferously.*

SUSAN: Del? Del!

DEL: Speaking of romance, I just saw a couple of glowfish in the water down there, and the guy glowfish says to the girl glowfish, "Baby, you light up my half-life."

SUSAN: Shut up, Del.

DEL: Thank you. But really folks, I think this homeporting's great. I think it's terrific that San Francisco is following the illustrious example of Alameda. Alameda, that sounds like some kind of venereal disease. "Del, what's that itch?" "Nothing, just a touch of Alameda, I'll be OK." Yeah— welcome the Navy into your town, make it your religion, base your entire economy on it, then one day, get left high and dry.

SUSAN *hits him in mouth with microphone. He stumbles off mumbling.*

SUSAN: A fresh, ironic voice! A unique sense of humor! I thought he was gonna to tell you this whole thing is a plot to change our voting patterns—forget I said that. Well! If you think old-fashioned patriotism is going out of style, wait till you meet our next guests: three boys from Crockett who are on the cutting edge of hardcore. Let's give them a big welcome, I know they need some time to set up—Rambo Dojo!

BAND *enters in torn camouflage, bandoliers, etc., carrying various pieces of metal.* BRAD *enters, frantically signaling* SUSAN.

WOMAN EXECUTIVE: *(Ad libbing.)* "Isn't this great? I'm just thrilled," etc. *(Takes place near stage.)*

BRAD: Things are falling apart. All the concession food came wrapped in these. *(Shows Day-Glo paper.)*

SUSAN: "Stop the *Missouri*"?

BRAD: That's nothing—the Blue Angels flew over dropping leaflets that say "Battleships Suck"!

SUSAN: I will personally dismember whoever's responsible for this.

BRAD: Who's this band?

SUSAN: Nobody could get to these guys, I swear—they're absolute fascists!

BRAD: Great.

SUSAN: I'm on top of this—just make sure everything's OK for the ceremony. Ladies and gentlemen—let's hear it for Rambo Dojo! *(Exeunt* BRAD *and* SUSAN.)

LEAD SINGER: Hit it! *(Percussion starts.)* We like to shoot sharks. But today, we rowed out on the Bay, and there wasn't none. Then we met this hippy-looking guy backstage, and he told us all about Mr. Big Fish, and Mr. Little Fish . . . and like that. So we wrote this song, and we'd like to dedicate it to him. We call it—Big Mo. *(Sings "Big Mo.")*

Meanwhile, SUNRISE *enters slowly, carrying knife in scabbard.*

Save the plankton
Save the fish

Send that Big Mo
Back to St. Louis.

SUSAN *enters, in a state.*

Save the sharks
Save the Bay
Keep the Missouri
Very far away.

Don't need no Navy
No toxic waste
Get that Big Mo
Outta my face.

SUNRISE *kneels, draws knife. meanwhile* SUSAN *is trying to stop* BAND.

Big Mo
Just Say No!

Big Mo
Just Say No!

Big Mo
Just Say No!

Big Mo
Just Say No!

SUSAN *sees* SUNRISE *in nick of time, grabs knife.*

SUNRISE: Mom?

SUSAN: Sunrise!

Chant resumes.

BRAD: (*Enters oblivious to* SUNRISE, *grabs* SUSAN.) The Japanese are refusing to surrender! What's going on? (SUNRISE *escapes.*)

SUSAN: Sunrise! (*Tries to follow.*)

BRAD: (*Holds on.*) Do something!

SUSAN: Stuff it!

BRAD: You want to work in this town?

SUSAN *karate-chops him, follows* SUNRISE.

WOMAN EXECUTIVE: (*Jumps up onstage.*) I love this city! And I love the Bay! Are we going to let them kill it? Let's all say it: "Big Mo, Just Say No!" We're taking this to the streets! (*Exeunt* BAND *and* WOMAN *chanting.*)

BRAD: (*Picks himself up. To audience.*) Don't say no! All right, have your fun—in November, when Bush is elected, we're going to get everything we want. And that dyke will never work in this town again.

(*Exit.*)

Scene 10: The Park, Immediately Following

RIP: *(Enters.)* "Big Mo, Just Say No," "Big Mo, Just Say No" . . . groovy—but how long will you keep it up? Seems like, you start a fire under people, it goes out unless you stay right there with the match. I used to think everybody had their own pilot light. "I used to think."—now I'm a middle-aged weirdo. A one-man Movement. Trying to save the rain forest, the ozone, the underclass . . . I gotta seriously evaluate my place in the scheme of things. I gotta sit down someplace quiet and think. *(Exit.)*

Enter PJ and ROCK, hiding under dried-out bushes.

PJ: How come we couldn't get no bushes with no leaves on it?

ROCK: It's a drought, man.

PJ: This is stupid.

ROCK: Shut up—it worked in Rambo.

PJ: You ain't him. *(ROCK bristles.)* I been studying you, blood. Now don't get mad. I'm gonna tell you something about yourself. Don't get mad. You don't wanna die.

ROCK: I'm ready! I seen the baby in the hospital—she's OK. I asked my mama's forgiveness. I said goodbye to my woman. I'm prepared to go down anytime, facing the enemy.

PJ: Then how come, when no DOA's ain't been by since this morning, we're still hiding out under these naked-ass bushes?

ROCK: Because I'm working on a plan.

PJ: Um-hm. *(Pulls out a comic book, starts reading.)*

ROCK: What you doing with that—looking at the pictures?

PJ: I'm reading this, man. *(ROCK disbelieves.)* They got me in a program. I made third grade already, going for fourth!

SUNRISE: *(Off.)* Rock? *(Enters.)* Rock?

ROCK: Sunrise?

SUNRISE: *(Very relieved.)* Where are you?

ROCK: S-h-h—over here! Quick! *(She joins them.)*

PJ: There goes the neighborhood.

ROCK: I was scared I'd never see you again.

SUNRISE: Dummy, I'll be around. I just marched from the Embarcadero to Civic Center with 3,000 old people chanting "Big Mo, Just Say No"!

ROCK: What that mean?

SUNRISE: They woke up. But my Mom's gonna be really mad at me. I don't even know where to go.

PJ coughs.

ROCK: This my homeboy PJ. If my plan works out, all three of us gonna have someplace to go. I'm looking for this man.

RIP enters.

ROCK: That's him! Hey! Yo! Hey, dude! *(RIP is alarmed.)* Hey, it's cool—peace, power!

RIP: Oh!

ROCK: I'm the one you was rapping to that day, right near here, remember?

RIP: Rock. I remember.

ROCK: All right—you ain't left yet! Hey, tell my friends here about Chicago!

RIP: Chicago?

ROCK: They having a riot there. It's gonna be the biggest thing to come down in history. All the young people, black, punk, whatever—the youth gonna take over! Not just here. It's gonna be a worldwide youth revolution. So I figure, DOA's nothing but hoodlums, small-time; I be a chump if I get killed over some crack. If we gone go down, let's go down big—

ROCK AND SUNRISE: Chicago!

RIP: Listen—I hate to tell you. We missed that one.

PJ: That's too bad.

ROCK: Aw, what, you didn't make it, neither?

RIP: I got hung up. But listen—I think you guys could help me. I been thinking a lot about this crack.

PJ: That's nice.

SUNRISE: So why ask us?

ROCK: You better off sticking to psychedelics. Stuff that show you the inside and the outside.

RIP: I don't know what I think about drugs anymore. But I'd like to see inside the crack trade. Like—how's so much of the stuff get into the country?

PJ: Pay somebody off, fool.

RIP: Who? And how come it all flows into the black community?

ROCK: Hey, maybe we turn into detectives! Cokebusters! Miami Vice!

PJ: "We belong to the city, we belong to the night."

ROCK: Supersleuths, following the crack trail!

SUNRISE: Through the FBI, CIA . . .

PJ: Hey, you know what somebody write on a wall by where I stay? It say "The real crack house is the White House."

ROCK AND SUNRISE: Wooo.

RIP: I been learning stuff about the cocaine trade that would blow your minds. *(They are all ears.)* Say, I'm in the library every Saturday, catching up on my history. Meet me there, 12 o'clock, I'll turn you on.

SUNRISE: History club!

PJ: All right.

SUNRISE: Okay. *(They notice ROCK has walked off a ways.)*

PJ: Hey man—you want to check out this program tomorrow? Get some free comic books?

ROCK: *(After a dignified pause.)* I might come with you, if Sunrise want to come, just to see.

SUNRISE: *(With equal condescension.)* Cool.

ROCK: My man . . . *(He and RIP do their handshake.)* Yo—what's your name, anyway?

RIP: Rip.

SUNRISE: "Rip"?

RIP: As in "Rip it off."

SUNRISE: Wait—

SUSAN *(Enters.)* Let her be in her favorite place in the park. Oh, God—let her be in the park . . . Sunrise?

SUNRISE: Mom?

SUSAN: Sunrise!

SUNRISE: Hi, Mom. *(Keeps her distance.)*

SUSAN: When you weren't at home, I was terrified.

SUNRISE: I'm OK.

SUSAN: I'm not.

SUNRISE: Your event went kind of crazy.

SUSAN: I know—wasn't that great? *(They hug.)*

SUNRISE: Um—this is my Mom. This is Rock—

ROCK: Hello, little mama. *(They shake hands.)*

SUNRISE: This is PJ—

PJ: *(Shaking hands.)* Very nice. I see the resemblance.

SUNRISE: . . . And I think you two know each other.

It is the shrug that convinces SUSAN. Music: "Yesterday." Dumb show: ROCK and PJ excuse themselves from family reunion, exit.

SUSAN: Where the hell did you go?

RIP: Oakland—to find a head gasket. It's—it's kind of unbelievable—can I tell you at home?

SUSAN: Home? . . . Look, it's been a while, you know . . . Things happen . . . *(SUNRISE indicates: "like me")* . . . And other things . . . But I'm really glad to see you—I'm dying to hear . . . This is my card, our address—till the end of the month. I've got to get this kid home—come by sometime! *(Exits with SUNRISE, returns.)* Make it dinner—8 o'clock tonight.

RIP: Okay—I'll wash the dishes.

SUSAN: Don't be late. *(Women exeunt.)*

RIP: *(Holding SUSAN's business card.)* Is that what we get for smashing monogamy? A dumpy room on Valencia Street . . . No family . . . no old lady and I'm funny-looking. French lady, wherever you are—how come you did this to me?

LIBERTÉ: *(Enters behind him, taps him on the shoulder.)* Rip?

RIP: You!

LIBERTÉ: C'est moi.

RIP: Who are you?

LIBERTÉ: You don't know French painting? The Spirit of 1789. Of the Revolution—Liberté. *(He doesn't get it.)* Of Freedom.

RIP: Wow. You've been away.

LIBERTÉ: I have good and bad seasons, like the wine. '68, it was an excellent year. I knew a bad time would come after, and all the good vintage would be consumed. So I bottled some.

RIP: . . . ?

LIBERTÉ: Not just you—there are many, many, all over the world. And now a better time is on its way. I am letting you out.

RIP: What should I do?

LIBERTÉ: Shave. And continue—especially with the youth. Au revoir, camarade. The '90s, it looks like a promising decade.

The End

"The Dictators' Song" from 1985

1984

Lyrics by Bruce Barthol

CHORUS: *(ragtime)*
Hey we're glad to see ya, Come on and say Hi!
We're the best friends that your money can buy
We're glad to be working for the US of A
We're fighting for freedom and getting paid!

MOBUTU: *(West African drum intro)*
Patrice Lumumba was a very bad man
He took the Congo from the Belgian hand
Mr. Lumumba him go away
Thanks to yours truly and the C.I.A.

CHORUS:
Hey we're glad to see ya, Come on and say Hi!
We're the best friends that your money can buy
We're fighting for freedom and getting paid!
We're Marcos, Mobutu, and Pinochet!

MARCOS: *(Tinkling intro)*
Mr. Aquino got what he deserved
Don't know why everyone's so concerned
But I don't care what anyone say
I got Yankee soldiers in the Subic Bay

CHORUS: *(repeat second chorus)*

PINOCHET: *(Tango intro)*
Mr. Allende he make me sick
He tried to take the money away from the rich

He wouldn't surrender so I blew him away
With help from the AFL-C.I.A.

PINOCHET:
Jimmy Carter he was some kind of Red

MARCOS:
Always worried 'bout the tortured or dead

MOBUTU:
With this Administration things are better than before

ALL:
We don't even hafta say we're sorry anymore

CHORUS:
That's why we're glad to see ya, American guy!
We're the best friends that your money can buy
We're fighting for freedom and getting paid
We're Marcos, Mobutu, and Pinochet
We're Marcos, Mobutu, and Pinochet.

"Jingo Rap" from *The Mozamgola Caper*
1987
Lyrics by Bruce Barthol

Don't be looking at me that way
I'm doin' what's right for the USA
You know if it weren't for people like me
We'd be adrift in a bright red sea

Third world countries got to learn
About the way the world really turns
Ashes to ashes, dust to dust
The whole damn world belongs to us.

Arbenz in Guatemala got out of hand
Allende in Chile with his Marxist band
So Kennicott Copper and United Fruit
Said, "Send those assholes down the chute."

We killed Lumumba, we killed Che
Tried to get Fidel but he got away
We even gave Khadafy a whirl
And killed his little baby girl.

Third World countries got to learn
About the way the world really turns
If God had meant them to be free
They'd have been born here like you and me.

We know exactly what to do
In Nicaragua and Angola too
We keep them living on their knees
And watch them while they slowly bleed.

It's a low intensity conflict scene
We just spend money, our hands are clean
We hire some psychopathic apes
Send them out to kill and rape.

And if events should go off course
We've got the Rapid Deployment Force
The whole Third World better learn the rule
If we don't dig it; it ain't cool.

(Dance break: break dance)
Self-determination, that's OK
Everybody needs an Independence Day
Run your country in your own way
But first you better clear it with the USA.

To the African people I make this plea
Better ask us if you want to sneeze
To my Latin friends I'd like to say
Come on, greaseball, make my day.

4. The 1990s: Turning West

Joan Holden has said that Mime Troupe plays always tell the same story, "people finding the strength to keep going in the face of insurmountable odds."[1] Although this could describe the company for four decades, it was especially relevant in the 1990s, when the odds against their survival mounted with the right wing's successful assault on arts funding. In 1996 there was a real possibility the troupe's thirty-three-year run of free theater in the parks had ended. Members were disheartened by the constant need to raise funds, complicated by the shift in arts funding from government grants to corporations. Asking for funding from corporations the Mime Troupe had long derided was a bitter defeat. Still, the 1990s rivaled the prior decade in the number of major productions and exceeded other decades in international outreach, with productions traveling to Asia, Europe, the Middle East, and Latin America. The company ended the 1990s with a huge fortieth-anniversary event including scenes from fifteen past productions and a symposium, "The SFMT and the Counter Culture," organized by R. G. Davis.

Show topics in the 1990s ranged from San Francisco elections to the global economy. Operation Desert Storm in 1991 boosted the ratings of former president Bush and caused public patriotic fervor to soar. Iraq became a primary U.S. target for most of the decade. The General Agreement on Tariffs and Trade (GATT), the North American Free Agreement (NAFTA), and the World Trade Organization (WTO) all revised or established in 1994, supported open international markets and promoted a McWorld future. Globalization became the new imperialism, leaving millions of the world's poor more destitute than ever before. Zapatistas in Mexico rebelled in 1994 by seizing seven villages in Chiapas, demanding land reform. Violence erupted in Somalia, Rwanda, Liberia, Zaire, and Nigeria. The Soviet Union disintegrated in 1991. Yugoslavia dissolved into ethnic conflict. In spite of a Democrat in the White House for most of the 1990s and the defeat of many of the most conservative aspects of Newt Gingrich's "Contract with America," leftist optimism soured. Slashed social programs, the Los Angeles riots, rising housing costs, the health care crisis, and disenchanted youth, surfing the net and watching television 24/7, left little to celebrate at the millennium.

The Company

In May 1990 the company received its third Obie for *Seeing Double,* their "tragic farce" arguing a two-state solution in Israel and Palestine, performed to critical praise in New York in November and December 1989. Ross Wetzsteon, critic for the *Village Voice,* explained that the troupe won the award for "their courage and their ability to address the issue . . . [demonstrating that] a company so often labeled agit-prop could deal with both sides of the issue, and could show feelings on both sides."[2]

In 1992 the troupe's *I Ain't Yo' Uncle: The New Jack Revisionist Uncle Tom's Cabin* received the Dramalog Critic's Awards for outstanding achievement in production, direction, musical direction, and writing. The troupe also received two Lifetime Achievement awards: San Francisco's Media Alliance Golden Gadfly Award in 1993, and *San Francisco Bay Guardian's* Goldie in 1995. The Golden Gadfly, a coveted journalism award, had never before been awarded to a theater company.

The troupe's business office was relatively stable in the first half of the decade even as funding diminished. Barbara Jeppeson and Patrick Osbon remained full-time as publicist and general manager until 1995 and 1997, respectively. Since their departures, publicity and development have been jobbed out. Osbon's successor, Jerome Moskowitz, has been working with the troupe since 1998. He runs his own fund-raising agency and works for several San Francisco performing groups.

Peggy Rose was hired as business manager in 1992 and, at this writing, is still with the company. Before her, an accountant had come in once a week and produced monthly financial statements. Rose's position, like many others in the 1990s, has fluctuated between full-time and part-time.

Booking is a complicated job at the Mime Troupe with multiple park shows in the summer and national and international tours in the fall and winter. Osbon handled booking on and off during his tenure. Anke Mueller was hired in 1999. Her work included assisting presenters in applying for state funding for tours, negotiating contracts, and developing booking materials as well as working closely with the production manager on tour itineraries.

Since the 1980s, the troupe has followed a pattern of booking the prior year's show for the long-distance tours in the spring and summer while the new summer show is being created. Summer shows generally tour to Bay Area parks and other venues within a one-hundred-mile radius of San Francisco, that is, from Santa Cruz to Sacramento to Sonoma, sometimes as far as Eureka and San Diego. Throughout the decade booking was handled in various ways: in house, through booking agencies, full time and part time.

Greg Tate was a jack of all trades during his thirteen years as a collective member: production manager, stage manager, youth project director, designer, writer, director, and actor. Ellen Callas has also worked in various capacities since joining the collective in 1986. She is a teacher for the Youth Theatre Project and has been production and company manager in addition to writer.

During the 1990s the collective decided to become multigenerational. Holden recalls: "I looked around one day and said, 'Oh my god, we're middle-aged.'"[3] Like many theaters concerned with the graying of the American audience, the troupe wanted to take its message to younger spectators and to represent their concerns. Consequently, the troupe began recruiting actors in their twenties so the younger members could contribute their perspectives and affect the company's direction.

In 1994 the Mime Troupe accepted its first commission. The eighty-thousand-dollar grant, from the Tobacco Free Project of the San Francisco Department of Public Health, went into the creation of a play to tour in California schools. The fifty-five-minute show, *Revenger Rat Meets the Merchant of Death,* exposes tobacco company manipulation. The emphasis on corporate culpability satisfied Bruce Barthol, the holdout troupe member who, from a civil liberties perspective, insisted the production could not oppose drugs. In the play, a cigarette company offers a young artist a huge financial inducement to publish his comic based on an antiauthoritarian character, Revenger Rat, but with the proviso that he will be seen in each frame smoking their product, a "Duke" cigarette. The artist agrees and uses the money to give scholarships to inner-city kids. However, tobacco sales to teenagers soar, and the young artist is forced to make a moral choice. An article in the *San Francisco Chronicle* noted the parallel between the plot of the play and the troupe's position as artists selling antitobacco propaganda. Holden maintained with some irony that the troupe had not been "bought" but was "paid for."[4] The show was so successful that the company created an abbreviated version that toured through the rest of the decade.

In the 1990s the troupe faced a major obstacle obtaining NEA funding because of a change in the parameters for grants. Whereas formerly companies had been able to apply for overall financial support, in the mid-1990s funding was reduced to a project-by-project format requiring detailed proposals submitted months in advance. Recalling the compulsory approval by the park commissioners of shows in the 1960s, this approach to funding also disregards the creative process in original work. Because the troupe's method is to create summer shows in the spring based on social issues of immediate concern, writing adequate descriptions of productions nine months in advance is impossible.

Right-wing slashing of the NEA budget seriously threatened the free summer shows in the parks and devastated touring subsidies. Each of the park seasons cost the company about $120,000: "The audience puts a third of the cost in our hats; Grants for the Arts [the former Hotel Tax Fund] covers another third; . . . NEA grants have made up the rest."5 In 1996 the troupe faced a real possibility that for the first time the free summer park show might be canceled, and began spring rehearsals of *Soul Suckers from Outer Space,* a show examining how far to the right the country has moved since the 1950s, without knowing if the show could open. Aggressive fund-raising eventually retained the summer season, reduced by half: five parks in five weekends. Scoop Nisker at KFOG radio asked listeners to send $10 donations, and ninety did. Individual donations from a total of about seven hundred people raised $20,000. The funding crisis was reported in the press, and approximately two thousand people attended the 4 July opening, giving twice their usual contributions at the end of the performance.

In 1990 the company received $140,500 from the NEA (25 percent of their $540,000 budget). By 1997 NEA funds had been cut to $45,000 (6 percent of their $718,000 budget) resulting in a shorter summer schedule and a 50 percent layoff of staff. In 1999 NEA funding fell to $28,000. Whereas most arts organizations facing similar cuts turned to corporate funding for survival, the Mime Troupe's staunch opposition to most corporations meant they needed to rely on individual donors.

According to Osbon, the collective objected to major arts funders "whose assets were generated by profiteering, manufacture of munitions, environmental degradation," such as the Zellerbach Family Fund. The troupe had attacked Zellerbach in the press in the 1970s and had ridiculed the family patriarch in *San Fran Scandals* because of his support of the Performing Arts Center. The largest funder of arts in the Bay Area, the Hewlett Foundation, was off limits as well because their "assets were partly generated by the manufacture of the detonation devices for pineapple bombs used by the US in Vietnam."6 However, as NEA funding plummeted, fund-raising and fund-raisers became an all-consuming concern, and soon the troupe was turning to foundations they had long scorned. Funds were eventually solicited and received from Zellerbach and Hewlett. Still, the troupe's slow acceptance of foundation support "in the face of mounting financial difficulties" frustrated Osbon, making his job as general manager all but impossible.7

Because of the NEA cutbacks, touring, which had lasted sixteen to eighteen weeks a year, was reduced to eight to ten weeks by 1997. To compensate for the revenue lost from touring, Pat Osbon and Joel Schechter, theater professor at San Francisco State University, created a youth theater program beginning in 1996. The two-phase workshop process involves at-risk teens from various San Francisco youth service agencies and educational institutions. Scripts are developed and then performed at a festival in early spring, then given full professional support by the Mime Troupe and San Francisco State University theater students interning with the troupe.

The company developed other educational outreach, including four intensive workshops with the California State University's Summer Arts Programs, and summer intern workshops in San Francisco for college students. Each project created plays and culminated in productions. The large turnout for these student training programs suggests a growing interest in the Mime Troupe and their collaborative methods among college-age students.

During the 1990s the company established a regular procedure for soliciting funding. Appeal letters, at first one a year, then two (usually with Spain Rodriguez's remarkable illustrations), were sent to the company's mailing list: a spring letter for funding the summer show and a second at the end of the year appraising supporters of accomplishments of the current year and plans for the future. Aggressive fund-raising led to a substantial increase in individual contributions from appeal letters and postshow hat donations in the 1990s.

The troupe's budget deficit grew from $63,000 in 1992 to $100,000 in 1997 and to over $200,000 by 2000. In the winter of 1991, the same year the Equity contract was put in place, all twelve members of the collective, who were earning $300–$375 a week year-round, laid themselves off for four weeks. Soon after, everyone except the office staff was paid weekly on a show-by-show basis. By the end of the decade collective members, still paid show-by-show, were making about $350 a week. The troupe paid full health insurance premiums for laid-off members and half for working members.

Hardship escalated in 1996, the worst year of the company's financial crisis, when in November, during the fall tour, the troupe's truck was stolen off a street in Los Angeles. The company was able to continue scheduled performances of 13 Dias/13 Days on the UCLA campus, but a truck had to be rented to return the set, costumes, and equipment to San Francisco. Insurance covered only half the value of the truck, and the troupe had to buy another. As late as the summer of 2000 they were still making payments on the stolen truck. The 1996 year-end appeal letter was sent in an envelope with Spain Rodriguez's sketch of the truck captioned: "STOLEN!! Have You Seen This Truck?" The only sighting was reported by a Tucson actor from 13 Dias/13 Days, who received a call from an actor elsewhere in Arizona saying he had seen the truck heading for Mexico.

Major and minor financial crises continued to plague the company through the late 1990s, from funding decreases and soaring housing costs for company members and interns, to building maintenance and repairs. On 22 August 1998 the *San Francisco Examiner* solicited donations to raise at least twenty-five hundred dollars for the company to repair damages to their building from freeing a cat trapped between the troupe's offices on Treat Avenue and the building next door.[8] The story drew a response from cat lovers and the cat's owner, who contributed generously to the troupe.

At the beginning of 1990, the ten-member collective included Bruce Barthol, Ellen Callas, Dan Chumley, Arthur Holden, Joan Holden, Ed Holmes, Sharon Lockwood, Keiko Shimosato, Michael Gene Sullivan, and Greg Tate. In the middle of the decade two long-term troupe members retired from the company. Sharon Lockwood began an extended, then permanent leave in 1995 after twenty-seven years, most of it playing leading roles. Arthur Holden, the senior member of the company, who joined in 1963, retired in 1996.

By 1999 the collective included twelve members, three-fourths of whom had joined since the late 1980s: Liberty Ellman (1995), Victor Toman (1994), Velina Brown (1992), Amos Glick (1990), Michael Sullivan (1988), Greg Tate (1988), Keiko Shimosato (1987), Ed Holmes (1987), Ellen Callas (1986), Bruce Barthol (1976), Dan Chumley (1968), and Joan Holden (1967). In June 2000, Holden retired from the company after authoring or coauthoring ("scripting" she calls it) about forty of the company's productions. Thus the troupe moved into the twenty-first century with only one member, Chumley, from the precollective first decade, and one, composer-lyricist-music director Bruce Barthol, from the early collective-defining years. In 2001 Chumley took an extended leave and has, as of this writing, not returned.

Early in the decade, Holden wanted the younger members to eventually take over: "I hope they take it away from us actually because that's the only way the theatre would go on living—if somebody really wants it badly enough to do it, like we wanted it when Ronnie left."[9] By the end of the decade, when the younger members did begin to assume control, Holden became concerned about the troupe's survival. At a time when many arts groups have been driven out of San Francisco by exorbitant rent and housing costs, she worried that financial constraints would make it impossible for the younger members to fully commit to the company.[10]

The Productions

The troupe's use of style has always been eclectic, even when one specific style dominated a production, such as melodrama with *The Independent Female* and Marvel comics with the Factwino plays. However, at no time in the history of the Mime Troupe has their style been as eclectic as with *Offshore* (1993), an Asian-fusion musical about free trade. Created as part of a three-year international, intercultural collaboration (1993–95) with the Asian People's Theatre Festival, supported by one hundred thousand dollars in grants from the Rockefeller Foundation, *Offshore* borrowed from Kabuki, Chinese opera, Filipino martial arts, and Tai Chi, in addition to troupe staples—melodrama and commedia.

Following in the tradition of *Seeing Double*, *Offshore* was created by an international team including troupers Joan Holden, Keiko Shimosato, and Michael Sullivan working with San Francisco artist Patrick Lee and poet-playwright Chung Chiao of the Taiwan People's Cultural Workshop, who developed the script. Dan Chumley directed with director–cultural activist Mok Chiu Yu of the Hong Kong People's Theatre as dramaturge. San Francisco choreographer Kimi Okada and actor David Furumoto worked with Philippine Educational Theatre Association's Maribel Legarda and dancer-choreographer Keiko Takeya of Tokyo's Black Tent Theatre on choreography. The music also incorporated Asian melodies and a variety of Asian instruments. Similar to the troupe's work in the 1960s, movement was at the creative core of the production. Scenes were developed from scenarios first as dance, then with dialogue.

In addition to the breadth of its stylistic influences, *Offshore* was one of the most timely shows in the troupe's history, on tour during the debate in Congress about NAFTA. Its warning about the dark side of globalization earned its Washington, D.C., performances mention in the *Wall Street Journal* and on the *Today Show*.[11]

Director Chumley described the politics that inspired *Offshore* and its stylistic innovation:

> *Offshore* was created in the early days of open markets, as global trade agreements required every WTO nation to eliminate international trade barriers, tariffs and subsidies to domestic industry and agriculture. Joan Holden saw the trade battles of California farmers wanting to sell rice to Japan and Japanese industrialist selling cars to the US, altering economy and culture in both countries, as the spine of an epic vision of little people caught in the gears of world trade. We enlisted the support of theater artists from Japan, Hong Kong and the Philippines with a poet from Taiwan, to help evolve the style and story. After a season in the parks and a period of rewrites that perfected the style and translated the script into iambic pentameter, we toured the work to Hong Kong, completing a circle of inspiration and creators that marked a high point in the Mime Troupe's history.[12]

Holden considers *Offshore* and *False Promises* (1976) to be the troupe's two successful original productions in epic style. Both were big shows on a grand scale. Other epics, such as *Congress of Whitewashers*, *Spain/36*, and *13*

Dias/13 Days she describes as "noble experiments that didn't work on stage."[13]

Offshore was also the troupe's first Asian show. Although *Dragon Lady's Revenge* included Asian characters, it was originally created and performed by Caucasians. For troupe member Keiko Shimosato, representing part of the Asian world on the Mime Troupe stage in *Offshore* was simultaneously joyous and deeply personal. She cowrote one scene about her relationship with her "very traditional Japanese father" and discovered the play gave her the opportunity to look at the cultural conflict in her upbringing in a positive way.[14]

Another timely production, *I Ain't Yo' Uncle: The New Jack Revisionist Uncle Tom's Cabin* (1992), coincided with national discussions about race following the Los Angeles riots in spring of 1992. The show was intended to be a collaboration between Holden and Ntozake Shange for a festival at the Lorraine Hansberry Theatre, but ended up written by Robert Alexander, who had collaborated with Holden on three other shows. Alexander's primary goal was to transform the long-maligned Uncle Tom into a hero. In the play, the stereotyped characters created by Stowe get to confront the author with their own realities. "Meanwhile," says Alexander of Stowe, "she's tired of black anger and tired of the noise, she's tired of being guilty, she's tired of being the accused, and she's even started to question affirmative action."[15]

The production was not without some of the racial conflict that had accompanied the writing of *False Promises* and the casting of *Americans, or Last Tango in Huahuatenango.* Director Chumley took the blame suggesting he had naively expected performers to defer to his choices since he was the director.[16] However, with a white male in a position of authority working on a play challenging white notions about black people and replacing them with a black point of view, conflict was inevitable. One of the struggles involved casting the role of Little Eva. Chumley wanted an Asian actress from the troupe, while Lonnie Ford, who played Uncle Tom, insisted that she be white. Ford staked his participation in the production on this choice, and his position eventually prevailed. In a play about race, especially about white oppression of African Americans, nontraditional casting of one role in an otherwise race specific production could have undermined meaning.[17] Chumley admitted that making the show work taught him to "listen in a different way, to hear people."[18]

The company's economic despair was reflected in several plays in the decade expressing a more pessimistic vision than ever before in their history. In *Rats* (1990), their nightmare adaptation of *Alice in Wonderland,* Alice is an artist who has "run out of vision" in "the mean-spirited, free wheeeeling [*sic*] dealing America of the Reagan-Bush era."[19] With *Social*

Work: An Election Year Fantasy (1992), the troupe tapped into the public's collective rage in the character of a despairing social worker who, in dream sequences, brutally murders corporate CEOs. In an early draft of *Damaged Care* (1998), the troupe's show about managed health care, Nurse Basil began killing her patients out of frustration with the system. In the final version she tried to kill herself instead.

While most of the shows in the 1990s dealt with domestic issues, two besides *Offshore* looked beyond U.S. borders: *13 Dias/13 Days* and *Back to Normal*. *13 Dias/13 Days* (1996), a coproduction with Borderlands Theatre in Tucson, Arizona, about the Chiapas uprising, was marred by excessive complexity. Created as an indoor multimedia production, it tried to "blend theatre, film and projected images and yet maintain the Mime Troupe's low-budget, people's theatre production panache," in the words of Robert Hurwitt. However, the result was "a mess."[20] The *San Francisco Chronicle*'s Steven Winn concurred, describing the production's "multimedia dazzle, chaotic time sequence and tangled story lines . . . [as] a circuit-breaking overload."[21] Holden blames her script for the show's failure, but technical excess was also a factor.[22]

Back to Normal, the troupe's response to the first Gulf War, was one of the most successful productions in the 1990s. The show's target is a media-induced "We're Number One" patriotic frenzy that distracts Americans from the economic insecurity lurking just beneath the surface. Director Ed Holmes noted that at a time when the polls registered 91 percent support for the war, the troupe could not get bookings to take the show on tour.[23] Like *Ripped van Winkle*, the show pokes fun at the Left as well as the Right. Talk radio host Hetty is as fanatical about her conspiracy theories as is the country in its patriotism. The human cost of her political extremism has been damage to her relationship with her son, who, in the ironic twist at the heart of the play, comes home a Desert Storm hero.

Four new actors who joined the collective refocused the direction of shows in the 1990s. Rebecca Klingler joined in 1989, playing sexy leading women and narcissistic characters about to be politically awakened *(Coast City Confidential)*. Velina Brown, who joined in 1992, has emerged as a strong leading woman playing the stressed-out leads that used to be written for Sharon Lockwood. Less earthy than Lockwood, she also excels at stealthy female villains and is a strong singer. Amos Glick joined the collective in 1990. He is a versatile actor with excellent comic timing and often shares the bad-guy roles with Mime Troupe veteran Ed Holmes. Victor Toman, who joined in 1994, plays intense characters in their twenties.

The troupe continued other activist activity. In January 1991, San Francisco held massive antiwar demonstrations (the largest since the Vietnam War) as the Gulf War escalated. The troupe brought out huge puppets used in the 1960s for protests against the Vietnam War, and a mask of George Bush. Theirs was a somber procession with bloody soldiers carrying a huge yellow gas pump. Holden explained: "Skits at large rallies just don't work. It's going to be like a Roman triumphal procession; you know, when the generals returned from war with their captives and booty. Well, this is the new world order, with Bush and his generals leading the soldiers, bringing the oil home, and the captives are the civilians. But the soldiers and the captives are dead. 'Blood for oil,' is what we're saying."[24] The troupe joined groups of others artists such as the Haight Street Puppet Theatre, marching from Mission Dolores Park to the Civic Center on 19 January and again the following weekend. That summer the troupe opened *Back to Normal.*

In February 1995, the company performed an *acto* about Keith McHenry (organizer of Food Not Bombs) on the steps of the Hall of Justice in San Francisco. The Mime Troupe piece, *Captain Bob's Hungry Heart, or A Bagel in the Hand's Worth Two in the Bush,* written by Michael Sullivan, included three actors portraying police arresting McHenry for illegally giving out food. The performance ended with two Food Not Bombs servers giving out food and real police officers arresting them, thus following the staged arrest with a second-act actual arrest.[25] This event recalled the troupe's guerrilla theater days by blurring the distinction between theater and life.

In response to San Francisco's soaring housing prices at the end of the 1990s, Joan Holden and her daughter, Kate Chumley, wrote *City for Sale,* the troupe's sixth production about displacing working-class housing. Lofts in industrial zones, especially in the heavily Latino Mission District where the troupe has their studio, were intended as low-cost housing for artists. Because "artist" is undefined in the zoning laws, developers have used that loophole to sell the spaces to dot-comers and Silicon Valley yuppies, thus pushing artists out of the city. At the end of *City for Sale,* the musicians in the play who are being displaced join with their neighbors to fight eviction. The show helped lay the ground for a grassroots alliance of artists and community activists, who raised one hundred thousand dollars to fight development with Proposition L in the election in the fall of 2000. Although the proposition was defeated by less than 1 percent, the slow-growth movement in San Francisco has escalated and *City for Sale* ended the 1990s with an extremely successful summer show.

The troupe had at least one problem with public schools in the decade. In 1996 they booked an auditorium on the grounds of the Fort Bragg Middle School for an evening performance of *13 Dias/13 Days.* The principal consented to a free midday performance for students, thinking it would be an innocuous piece about Mexican history. He was not prepared for the play's rough language in a school with a policy against swearing. The principal ended up apologizing to dozens of parents and the entire community and the troupe apologized for not adequately describing the contents of the play.[26]

The Mime Troupe continued to expand its international work in the 1990s by turning west to the Pacific Rim. Their three-year intercultural collaboration (1993–95) with the Asian People's Theatre Festival resulted in an exchange of artists with the Philippine Educational Theatre Association in 1992; *Offshore*, which subsequently toured the United States and then Hong Kong, in 1993; and *Big Wind*, created and performed in several Asian countries, in 1995. Also in 1995, Bruce Barthol, Joan Holden, and Dan Chumley worked with the Third World Movement against the Exploitation of Women in Manila in creating a play, *They Are So Sweet, Sir*, about criminal trafficking in Filipina women for prostitution. Later in 1998, the company took their production *Damaged Care* to the Kwachon International Open-Air Theatre Festival in South Korea in September and, returning to Europe for the first time in a decade, to Belgium that October.

The company took *Seeing Double* to the Jerusalem Street Festival in Israel in May and June 1990. It was supposed to be staged at the Tower of David, but fears of potential violence during the performance caused the venue to be changed to a walled courtyard. Both Israelis and Palestinians attended performances that were followed by fervent discussions, with both sides talking openly about the issues. According to an appeal letter from the Mime Troupe, "We performed it five times, in both Jerusalems, to a divided response; got great press coverage and descent reviews, and played demonstrations for the Israeli peace movement and Palestinian hunger strikers."[27] One significant change had to be made in the performances in Israel: the final tableau of the crossed flags of Israel and Palestine was cut because it is illegal to show the Palestinian flag in Israel.

In 1997 the company created a new Spanish-language version of Holden's feminist play from 1970, *The Independent Female, or A Man Has His Pride*, translated by Marlene Ramirez-Cancio and Carlomagna Garcia, for theater festivals in Bogota and Manizales, Colombia. Dan Chumley directed the low-budget production with Mime Troupe actors and guest artists from San Francisco's Latino theater community. Although the company had previously performed bilingual versions of their plays, this Spanish translation was their first production entirely in another language.

The Mime Troupe's century ended with the fortieth-anniversary celebration, a two-day event bringing former company members and supporters together for a celebration and retrospective titled "The San Francisco Mime Troupe: The First Forty Years." The event began on Sunday, 6 December at Cowell Theatre, Fort Mason, with an all-day symposium organized by R. G. Davis: "The SFMT and the Counter Culture: A Day of Assessment and Analysis." Davis drew together former Mime Troupe members to discuss how their experience in the company affected their later work. He suggested that today's counterculture may be found in the ecology movement, and various former troupers spoke about their performance work with environmental issues.

The following night the San Francisco Mime Troupe presented "The SFMT: The First Forty Years," directed by Dan Chumley, at the Palace of Fine Arts. Scenes from fifteen shows from almost half a century, most with original cast members, played to a packed house and received a long standing ovation: *A Minstrel Show, or Civil Rights in a Cracker Barrel* (1965), *Olive Pits* (1966), *The Independent Female, or A Man has His Pride* (1970), *The Dragon Lady's Revenge* (1971), *False Promises* (1976), *The Hotel Universe* (1977), *Factwino Meets the Moral Majority* (1981), *Americans, or Last Tango in Huahuatenango* (1981), *Steeltown* (1984), *Ripped van Winkle* (1988), *Seeing Double* (1989), *Social Work* (1992), *Offshore* (1993), *Escape to Cyberia* (1994), and *City for Sale* (1999). Act 1 (1959–79) also included a prologue with Charles Degelman as Brighella, "The Carrot Speech," inspired by *The Congress of Whitewashers,* and Larry Pisoni, who brought circus to the Mime Troupe in the early 1970s. The prologue for act 2 (1980–99) was the Troupe's fictional punk rock band, Mark Antony and the Nile-ists (Bruce Barthol, Glen Appell, with Melody James as Shockin' Con).

One notable aspect of the two-day event was bridging the first ten years with the last thirty. The title of the event: "The First Forty Years," refers to Davis's book, *The San Francisco Mime Troupe: The First Ten Years,* and the logo gave homage to the original company. The first San Francisco Mime Troupe logo was Jacques Callot's flying griffin with the words "Engagement, Commitment, and Fresh Air" on a banner held in its beak. Spain Rodriguez's anniversary logo illustrated the spirit of synthesis with a similar griffin carrying a cornucopia on which is written "Engagement, Commitment, Fresh Air" and from which pours a multitude of recognizable characters from forty years of Mime Troupe plays.

Notes

1. John Boudreau, "S.F. Troupe: The Last Angry Mimes," *Los Angeles Times,* October 14, 1992.

2. Nancy Scott, quoting *Village Voice* critic Ross Wetzsteon about the award, "S.F. Mime Troupe Bags Obie," *San Francisco Examiner,* 15 May 1990.

3. Bernard Ohanian, "Fighting That Bushed Feeling," *Mother Jones,* January 1989, 49.

4. Leah Garchik, "Mime Troupe Gets a Hand," *San Francisco Chronicle,* 15 April 1994.

5. San Francisco Mime Troupe, appeal letter, 1996, SFMT files.

6. Patrick Osbon, email to Susan Vaneta Mason, 1 August 2000.

7. Patrick Osbon, email to Susan Vaneta Mason, 18 June 2002. The troupe now receives sixty thousand dollars a year from Hewlett.

8. "Performers' Kindness Is Costly," *San Francisco Examiner,* 22 August 1998. The cat had apparently fallen two stories into a tiny space and was wedged between the buildings. After the SPCA failed to retrieve the cat from the roof, the San Francisco Fire Department's only solution was to demolish part of the downstairs studio wall. The cat was liberated but the company was left with a hole in their wall, some damage to the roof, crooked gutters, and thanks from the cat's owner.

9. Nancy Scott, "Celebrating the Presence of Mime," *San Francisco Examiner,* 5 July 1992.

10. Joan Holden, letter to Susan Vaneta Mason, 27 October 2000.

11. Rachel Englehart, "Read Their Lips: Mime Troupe Sings Out against a Trade Pact," *Wall Street Journal,* 11 October 1993.

12. Dan Chumley, email to Susan Vaneta Mason, 12 July 2002.

13. Joan Holden, email to Susan Vaneta Mason, 20 June 2002.

14. Keiko Shimosato, email to Susan Vaneta Mason, 17 August 2002.

15. Nancy Churnin, "A Renovated *Cabin,*" *Los Angeles Times,* 16 October 1991.

16. Ibid.

17. Lonnie Ford, telephone interview Susan Vaneta Mason, 22 June 2002.

18. Churnin, "Renovated Cabin."

19. Hal Gelb, "Theater," *The Nation,* 15 October 1990, 428.

20. Robert Hurwitt, "Chiapas Challenge," *San Francisco Examiner,* 21 March 1997.

21. Steven Winn, "Burnt Out on Revolution: Multimedia in '13 Days' Distracting," *San Francisco Chronicle,* 22 March 1997.

22. Joan Holden, interview by Susan Vaneta Mason, 6 May 2002.

23. Boudreau, "Last Angry Mimes." In 2002, with the Bush administration pushing for war with Iraq, the San Francisco Mime Troupe received numerous requests for the script.

24. Robert Hurwitt, "Troupe's Piece for Peace," *San Francisco Examiner,* 21 January 1991.

25. Joel Schechter, "The Arrest of the Anarchist Keith McHenry," *Theatre Journal* 47 (December 1995): 541–42.

26. "School Upset about S.F. Mime Troupe," *San Francisco Chronicle,* 11 November 1996.

27. San Francisco Mime Troupe, appeal letter, 1990, SFMT files.

Back to Normal

1991

Script by Joan Holden, Ellen Callas, Elliot Kavee,
Gregory R. Tate, and Isa Nidal Totah

Introduction

In 1990 Iraqi troops invaded Kuwait. Over the next several months the
United States led a buildup of troops in the Gulf; on 17 January 1991, a Tom-
ahawk cruise missile was launched against Baghdad, and Operation Desert
Storm, under the command of Norman Schwarzkopf, had begun. For forty-
two days an international audience watched the war live on CNN. President
George Bush rejoiced that this victory buried forever "the specter of Vietnam," and his ratings soared while celebrations across the United States
welcomed the heroic troops home. *Back to Normal* examines the jubilant
homecoming of Jimmy, one Gulf War hero, to the small fictional town of
Normal, California. The greater conflict is between appearance and reality:
the media gloss politicians use to distract us contrasted with the genuine
problems faced by working-class people.

Commentary

Steven Winn

Back to Normal . . . peels back the red-white-and-blue veneer of Anywhere,
U.S.A.—the fictional Central Valley town of Normal, in this case—and
probes the deep-seated ambivalence and malaise the war left behind. ("It's
the Post-Gulf Troupe," *San Francisco Chronicle*, 6 July 1991)

Isa Nidal Totah

I first worked with the Mime Troupe on *Seeing Double* in 1989 as both an
actor and writer. The Middle East conflict was a subject the company had
avoided for years, and when they finally decided to take it on, they wisely

chose a team of Jewish and Palestinian writers and actors. The collaboration was a mini peace conference of sorts—we argued about every line—but the final result was a play we were all proud of. Two years later, the U.S. invaded Iraq, and I was so enraged I called the troupe and insisted they do a show on the Persian Gulf War. The result was *Back to Normal*. Both *Seeing Double* and *Back to Normal* were special plays for me because both had great stories and characters along with the comedy and politics. Today things haven't changed much with regard to the Middle East. This is an unusual time for Arab Americans. But when I get frustrated, I turn to art. I believe art has the power to enlighten and affect people, to penetrate walls more than any other political activism I've done. I like to think someone out there was changed by those plays, and perhaps took an action to improve the lives of others. (Email to Susan Vaneta Mason, 26 July 2002)

Robert Kohler

Back to Normal gives every political wing pause for reflection while at the same time serving up a delicious example of charmingly handmade theatre. From the ultra-low-tech scene shifts to a wicked send-up of the postwar TV galas . . . director Ed Holmes never allows this show to stand still for very long. ("Mime Troupe Gets *Back to Normal*," *Los Angeles Times*, 10 September 1991)

Ed Holmes

We attacked the Persian Gulf War . . . as a big sham, and the polls said 91% of the country supported [the war]. We represent 9%. We wanted to take the show on the road, but people didn't want to touch it. (Quoted in John Boudreau, "S.F. Troupe: The Last Angry Mimes," *Los Angeles Times*, 14 October 1992)

Robert Hurwitt

Back to Normal is as good as its name, with the Mime Troupe confronting Gulf War Syndrome euphoria with the complexity of the issues at home that need to be resolved. ("Mother Knows Bush," *East Bay Express*, 2 August 1991)

Michael Gene Sullivan

I remember when Arthur Holden told me I wasn't going to be in *Back to Normal*. Sharon Lockwood was playing Hetty and no one thought there was a part for me. I said, "What if Hetty had a son?" "You'd be Sharon's son?" "Yeah, well . . . okay, so she had this affair with a black musician years ago." (Email to Susan Vaneta Mason, 22 July 2002)

The Production

Back to Normal opened on 4 July 1991 in Mission Dolores Park, San Francisco, with the following cast:

Iraqi, Frank	*Isa Nidal Totah*
Jimmy	*Michael Gene Sullivan*
Virgil, Delbert, Mr. Johnson, Arnold Schwarzenegger	*Dan Chumley*
Muffy Chang, Fumiko	*Keiko Shimosato*
Hetty	*Sharon Lockwood*
Mayor	*Arthur Holden*
Anchorman Arthur Pent of CNN, George Bush	*Elliot Kavee*
Celebrities	*The Ensemble*
Genie	*Greg Tate*

Directed by Ed Holmes. Music and lyrics by Bruce Barthol. Set and backdrop design by Kent Mathieu. Costume design by Callie Floor. Special effects by Dan Chumley, Ed Holmes, and J. W. Rocket Science. Technical director: Greg Tate. Musicians: Eric Crystal, Dan Hart, Eliot Kavee, Dred Scott.

Characters (in order of appearance)

Jimmy, U.S. Marine
Virgil, his buddy
An Iraqi captive
A TV team
A Military Press Officer
Hetty, Jimmy's mom
Mr. Johnson, her employer
Farid/Frank, owns the diner
Delbert, a farmer
Fumiko, owns the beauty parlor
The Mayor
A second TV team
A Genie

tion into foreign languages, are strictly reserved. All inquiries should be addressed to San Francisco Mime Troupe, 855 Treat Avenue, San Francisco, CA 94110.

Back to Normal

Preset: America drop. Overture ends. Band plays medley of Nightline-type phrases as scene changes to Kuwait desert.

Scene 1: The Desert

JIMMY, VIRGIL, IRAQI TV TEAM.

Many large warlike sound effects. Trapdoor opens. Magic music. A mysterious IRAQI *peers out, then disappears. A really huge explosion blows our two soldiers,* JIMMY *and* VIRGIL, *onstage. They are loaded with gas masks, backpacks, minesweeping equipment.* JIMMY *is confident,* VIRGIL *is a nervous wreck.*

JIMMY: Whoa, that was close!

VIRGIL: Must have been ours. This is really happening!

JIMMY: *(Detecting a mine and de-activating it.)* What's happening is we gotta get this road cleared now cause those tanks are already rolling!

VIRGIL: Right!

JIMMY: De-activated. Hey, this one's French.

VIRGIL: "La Petite Ruine." I mean, this is finally it!

JIMMY: I'll say. Finally seeing some action.

VIRGIL: Yeah!

JIMMY: I'm so pumped. *(Deactivates mine.)* De-activated.

VIRGIL: "G.E. Mr. Explosive."

JIMMY: I can feel the sweat popping through my skin. We're the first.

VIRGIL: I know!

JIMMY: We clear the way. Without us there is no ground war. *(Deactivates mine.)* De-activated.

BOTH: "Der Kaboomeister"? *(Puts mine in sack and continues.)*

IRAQI *emerges enters waving white boxer shorts and carrying a sack.*

IRAQI: American! *(A surprised* VIRGIL *spins around raising his gun.)* No, no, do not shoot me. I love George Bush! I love George Bush! *(Moves toward them with his hands extended.)*

VIRGIL: Aw, hell, not another one! *(Disarms him.)*

JIMMY: Watch out, buddy, this place is covered with m—*(There's the very audible sound of a mine being triggered. All freeze. The* IRAQI *is terrified.)* Great, just great. Okay, man, just stay there. Don't move.

IRAQI: Move? *(About to.)*

JIMMY: No!!

IRAQI: No. *(*JIMMY *gets to work.)*

VIRGIL: Whata'ya doin', man?

JIMMY: Whata'ya think? I'm gonna de-activate it.

VIRGIL: Are you crazy? The minute he steps off that thing it's gonna blow halfway to Kuwait City.

JIMMY: He's not gonna step off it. (*To* IRAQI.) Are you? (IRAQI *furiously shakes his head.*)

VIRGIL: We don't have time, man. I say leave him there.

JIMMY: Trapped on an activated mine?

VIRGIL: You think that raghead would do the same for you? These guys aren't like us. I say let him blow.

JIMMY: (*Examining the mine.*) Russian.

IRAQI: Odessa 2000. In two minutes—Kaboom! (*Panic.*)

VIRGIL: Man, these things were recalled before they left the factory. Oh, man, we got one minute and forty five seconds. (*Backing away.*) Jimbo, one minute thirty. One fifteen. Jim, the way I see it, man, you got one minute.

Enter TV reporter MUFFY CHUNG *and* CAMERAPERSON *led by* MILITARY PRESS OFFICER.

MPO: Set up here, Miss Chung.

MUFFY: Look, Captain—my viewers have had it with sand. They've waited 6 months—they want to see action.

MPO: This'll make a great wide shot when the 1st Armored Car comes through. Terrific satellite feed.

MUFFY: You said that about the chowlines, the women mechanics, the interracial folk singing. Where's this "turkey shoot" I hear pilots talking about?

MPO: Off limits. (*Sees our trio.*) Miss Chung, I'm going to give you an exclusive.

VIRGIL: Hurry up, Jim.

MPO: Go for it.

MUFFY: (*To* CAMERAPERSON.) Great. Get this.

CAMERAPERSON: Rolling.

MUFFY: Get a close-up on me, then go wide.

CAMERAPERSON: Speed.

MUFFY: (*On camera.*) Ground War—Day 3. U.S. Marines thrusting deep, penetrating Iraqi-held territory. As the sun over the Kuwaiti desert is blackened by smoke of burning oil wells, I stand witness to an act of individual heroism.

JIMMY: Alright, here we go. One . . . Two . . .

MUFFY: This young American risks his own life to save an Iraqi soldier as I, Muffy Chung, risk my life to bring you this story. (*Has them in frame.*)

JIMMY: Three! (*De-activation cue. Great relief for a moment, then the mine starts ticking.)* Stand back. It's gonna blow! *(Picks up the mine, runs, tosses it just as it explodes, blowing him back onstage.)*

VIRGIL: Wow, Jim. You're a hero, you're on TV, and—*(noticing)*—you're bleeding!

MUFFY *approaches* JIMMY *who is stunned.*

IRAQI: Hello, CNN!

MUFFY: Carving a swath of safe road through heavily mined desert, this Marine completing his mission is severely wounded as he saves the lives of 5 others! What was going through your head, soldier?

JIMMY: Well . . . ma'am . . . I thought like any Marine: "There's a job to be done," and I did it. Our war's with Saddam Hussein, not with his people . . . Knowing I could help the little guy, for an American there was no other option.

MUFFY: "No other option." What's your name, soldier?

JIMMY: Corporal James Jamal Counts from Normal, California, ma'am.

MUFFY: That wound may just get you back to Normal on the first plane.

JIMMY: I don't know if I want to go back. I haven't been back for three years.

MUFFY: Corporal Counts, your heroism will be seen tonight all over America. If your Mom is watching, I bet she's very proud.

JIMMY: My mom? She won't be watching. She doesn't even have a TV.

THE OTHERS: WHAT?

MUFFY: *(Recovers.)* A proud black mother—

JIMMY: Um—

MUFFY: A home too poor to afford a TV set—

JIMMY: Um—

MUFFY: And Corporal James Jamal Counts—a special breed.

IRAQI: *(Crowding into the frame.)* I love America. I love George Bush. I love my mother. Too many bombs. I hope she is alive!

MUFFY: *(Cutting him off.)* This is Muffy Chung bringing you more desert drama as U.S. Marines sweep into Kuwait.

MPO: *(Whisking* MUFFY *away.)* Now back to base: it's time for the briefing. *(Exeunt.)*

JIMMY: *(Taking charge.)* Get a move on. *(Noise off.)* They're coming through! Let's get Omar here to the stockade.

VIRGIL: We better get you to a medic. Gee, Jim, I can see why you don't wanna go home—your Mom don't even have a TV?

JIMMY: My mom's . . . different, all right? And who said I don't wanna go home? I said I don't know, OK? OK?

VIRGIL: OK, Jimmy.

IRAQI: American—I must to give you something. *(Fumbles in sack.)*

VIRGIL: *(Taking aim.)* Hold it right—*(Magic music.)*
With a motion, IRAQI freezes him in place.

JIMMY: *(Hasn't seen.)* I don't need anything. Just watch where you step.

IRAQI: *(Resumes fumbling.)* When I go Kuwait City, I see other Iraqi soldiers. Have many things. VCR, Mercedes, food. I go there . . . only this. *(Pulls out old middle eastern oil lamp.)* It lamp . . . to light your way. *(JIMMY takes lamp, Iraqi lifts spell from VIRGIL.)*

VIRGIL: *(Sticking gun in IRAQI's back.)* Let's go, Aladdin.

JIMMY: *(Sardonically studying the lamp.)* Open sesame! The perfect present for Mom. *(Exit.)*

Scene 2: The Radio Station

HETTY, CALLERS, MR. JOHNSON.
Preset: box that now becomes radio station console. Jazz plays.

HETTY: *(Enters with equipment & cup of coffee, sets up. Cuts music.)* Lennie Tristano, live at the Blackhawk, San Francisco, 1956. Four A.M. here in Normal, this is the second Wednesday of the month, this is station KUBU, the Voice of the Valley: time for "Reality Sandwich" with your host, Hetty Counts. "Where was George?" Chapter 19. But first, as the ground war heads into Day Three—recognize this? No official body count; massive air strikes; blinders on the press; Administration claims our casualties light and no, repeat no, civilians bombed! Panama, 1989. Operation Just Cause. Just 'cause Manuel Noriega had the goods on George Bush—or explain why Drug Enforcement agents spent two and a half days in the Panama City bunker, alone with Noriega's files! *(Phone rings. She is amazed. She grabs it.)*

HETTY: Good morning, this is "Reality Sandwich" and you're on the air! *(Fumbles with equipment.)* I think.

CALLER #1: Hello, Hetty—remember me?

HETTY: Berkeley, 1958? Tangiers, 1965?

CALLER #1: I'm the fella that followed you tonight.

HETTY: That pickup with the lights out? I figured you for the fuzz.

CALLER: Nope. Our preacher talked about you in church last Sunday. You ain't a bad gal at heart. You just need a little husbanding, heh, heh, heh, and I'm gonna give it to you. What you need to fix your sandwich is my nice fat sausage! I'm gonna stuff it in your big fat mouth!

HETTY: *(Hangs up.)* A lot like poetry. First call since a wrong number in '89, and it's a crank. But: "Where was George" on November 22, 1963—the day JFK was blown away? Where were you? I was in the Deux Magots reading *Naked Lunch*. Every American who was over 5 that day knows where they were—except George Bush. I hear he told Bob Woodward, "I don't remember." Here's a memory-enhancer, George, took me two years to run down. (*Holds memo up to microphone.*) A secret FBI memo identifying George Bush as a CIA agent interviewing anti-Castro Cubans about the Kennedy killing on November 23, 1963! Why does Bush not remember what no one else can forget? Hey, if I had a fairy Godmother to grant me one wish, it'd be to hear our President tell his true-life story. That'd be a real naked lunch. (*Phone rings, she picks up.*) Reality Sandwich. You're on the air!

CALLER #2: Hetty, this is Donna Burkitt and I'm a senior at Normal High School and my parents say you're a Communist, but I couldn't sleep tonight so I called because I want to tell you I don't think you'd be talking this way if you had a son or husband over there.

HETTY: Yes, I would.

CALLER #2: Well, my boyfriend John is over there. And I stay up every night and pray for him.

HETTY: I hope it works, Donna. And hey, I have a son, but not in Iraq. My son's different. He didn't sign up for Uncle Sam's death machine. He took off three years ago, and he's on the road, on his own, digging different countries, grooving on different cultures, learning to see other colors besides red, white, and blue. Do yourself and the country a favor, Donna—try and do the same when you graduate.

CALLER # 2: I'm getting married when I graduate! (*Hangs up.*)

HETTY: Good luck. Where was I? 1973, Bush Republican National Chairman. (*MR. JOHNSON rushes on, a little old man in bathrobe and slippers.*) Bill Liedeke, Bush partner Zapata Oil, finances Watergate break-in. (*JOHNSON frantically signals her to cut.*) Already? Time for me to say "later." Tune in in two weeks. Coming right up, the farm report. (*Cuts off sound, jumps up to shake JOHNSON's hand warmly.*) Mr. Johnson! You're out early. (*He is panting.*) Your heart condition!

MR. JOHNSON: I heard your program.

HETTY: Wild—I got two calls!

MR. JOHNSON: Got three at home myself.

HETTY: The show's taking off. Sometimes you get the feeling nobody's listening—but tonight proves there's people out there, picking up on what I'm putting down!

MR. JOHNSON: Hetty, I stood behind your Watergate story. And your assassination investigation. But my Dad started KUBU, and it's just a little, small, home-town station.

HETTY: (*Collecting her things.*) Not for long. (*Sings "Boppus Conspiratorus."*)
The day is coming we've been waiting for
We'll shine a lamp behind that secret door
The whole damn country's gonna freak right out

When the real story comes out about
Malcolm and Martin and Jack and Bob
And who ran the drugs and who's tied to the mob

There's a secret club, a bunch of boys
Who play with people like they play with toys
And on the day when people shout
"Enough is enough, throw the bastards out"
It will be because of me and you
And radio station KUBU

MR. JOHNSON: You always say that!

HETTY: Just think of the day when Ronnie's inside
And Nancy's doing 1 to 5
And George Bush tells no more lies.
I gotta go now, I gotta go now.
Gotta do that breakfast thing, then I better get home to take calls.

MR. JOHNSON: Hetty, I don't like to ask this, but I'd like to see a script of your next broadcast before your next broadcast.

HETTY: "Where was George" Chapter 20: the Cuban connection. You're gonna flip. *(Pats him on the back, leaves.)*

MR. JOHNSON: Hetty . . . *(Strikes equipment, follows hopelessly.)*

Scene 3: The Diner

FRANK, HETTY, DELBERT, FUMIKO, MAYOR.
FRANK, in apron, sets up, exits. Bell rings, HETTY *enters.*

HETTY: (Anxious.) Farid? Hey! *(FRANK enters. She is relieved.)* Cool, it's you. Farid, man, what's happening? What's the new sign—"Frank's Yankee Doodle Diner?"

FRANK: *(Pours coffee.)* I'm redecorating.

HETTY: Crazy—hit a flag sale? Eggs and falafel.

FRANK: No falafel. New menu. Eggs and bacon. *(Works.)*

HETTY: Just coffee. Who the hell's Frank?   .

FRANK: I am. I'm an American citizen. I should have an American name.

HETTY: Try Geronimo. Anyway, I got a special for you. April, 1990, the White House.

FRANK: Not now, Hetty, I have a headache.

HETTY: But dig—secret meeting. Bush is there, Thatcher's there. What's on the table? Just the future of the whole Middle East. I sent this one to 20/20.

Bell rings. DELBERT *enters*

DELBERT: Morning, folks!

HETTY/FRANK: Morning, Delbert. *(FRANK pours coffee.)*

DELBERT: Looks like we're going all the way! Next stop, Baghdad! Unbelievable. Saddam Hussein's big, bad army goes bye-bye without even a fight. D'ja see 'em all yesterday, crawling over that desert, waving their dirty drawers for white flags? Way to go, America! (*About to give* FRANK *high 5, stops.*) Where'd you say you were from?

FRANK: I'm Armenian.

DELBERT: All right! (*They slap hands. Pulling change from pocket.*) Ham and eggs. (*Looks at change.*) Uh—no, toast and coffee.

HETTY: How were they gonna fight? We dropped 5 Hiroshimas on 'em first.

DELBERT: Hey—if you're gonna go in there, go in good: hit 'em with all you got and get out. Like we didn't do when I was in 'Nam. Tryin' to fight our way out of that jungle with one arm tied behind our back.

HETTY: News to a million dead Vietnamese.

DELBERT: Then we come back home and people spit on us.

HETTY: Who spit? I bought you a drink!

DELBERT: One Budweiser.

Bell rings. FUMIKO *enters.*

FUMIKO: Good morning, people!

HETTY: Fumi!

DELBERT: Morning, Fumiko. (FRANK *nods, not knowing her well.* HETTY *kisses her.* FUMIKO *is cool.*)

HETTY: I never see you eat breakfast out!

FUMIKO: I had to be with people this morning. It's so moving: all those young boys and girls ready to give their lives. Gives you something to have faith in—(*snubbing* HETTY)—right, Delbert? (*They clasp hands. To* FRANK.) Waffles and coffee, please! (*To* DELBERT.) How's the farm?

HETTY: (*To* FRANK.) Used to be her father's farm before the War—the real one, I mean.

DELBERT: Bank gets hardnosed just when prices get soft—but heck, we'll make out OK . . . How's the beauty business?

FUMIKO: Well—the young girls go to Supercuts out at the mall. And I guess ladies are economizing, going back to home perms. But I'll be fine. (*To* FRANK.) On second thought—just give me a donut.

HETTY: Frank, get her some waffles.

FUMIKO: No, thank you.

HETTY: Fumi, hey, I've been meaning to come in for a trim, but my scene has been truly—

FUMIKO: I couldn't sleep. I heard your program. I don't think it's right.

Bell rings. MAYOR *enters.*

MAYOR: Howdy, folks.

ALL: Morning, Mayor.

MAYOR: Well—redeye gravy and biscuits—I was a doubter.

FRANK/DELBERT: Right!/Yeah!

MAYOR: These fellas know, cause all these months, I argued with 'em.
(They corroborate.) I was afraid we'd get stuck in some quagmire, napalming babies like in Vietnam. But I have watched my set night and day now for 3 days and nights, and I have seen how smart our weapons are, and not one single person got killed! So God Bless our troops and God Bless our President: they're giving America the jumpstart God knows we need. *(Displays envelope.)* Now if you were a teacher say, or a custodian or the librarian: would it spoil the victory for you to get your pink slip tomorrow, or would tomorrow be a good day cause it'd soften the blow?

HETTY: You blow my mind.

MAYOR: *(Sings "We're Number One.")*
It's hard being Mayor in times like these
Revenue cuts brought me to my knees
But amid the potholes and shut down schools
One thing keeps me from feeling like a fool

DELBERT: What's that, Mr. Mayor?

MAYOR: We're Number One

HETTY: *(Speaks.)* Oh, come on

MAYOR: We're Number One
We're out from under the shadow of Vietnam
I'm proud to be a nephew of my Uncle Sam

FUMI: Even though my life seems to be collapsing
We're gonna give ol' Saddam a bashing

ALL BUT HETTY: He's just like Hitler
He's just like Hitler
He's just like Hitler

HETTY: *(Speaks.)* Where do you get this stuff?

ALL BUT HETTY: We're gonna thrust
We're gonna probe

FUMI: We're gonna seek out the soft spots
I want to explode!

HETTY: Fumi!

ALL BUT HETTY: We're gonna thrust

HETTY: I'm gonna vomit!

ALL BUT HETTY: We're gonna probe
Gonna push real hard
Get in real deep
'at ol' Saddam's gonna lose a little sleep

HETTY gives up and listens, horrified.
He's just like Hitler

He's just like Hitler

He's just like Hitler

HETTY: *(Stops the music.)* It's a little more complicated.

ALL BUT HETTY: You can tell that Saddam

You can tell King Tut

America's coming and we're

Gonna kick butt.

We're Number One (*3 times*)

All slide almost into slow motion as they return to their seats. They seem to be under a spell.

FRANK: More coffee, Mr. Mayor?

HETTY: You look at pictures on TV and you think you got the facts? You people sound like you've been brainwashed!

There is a brief, shocked silence.

FUMIKO: When you went away, I thought you were gone for good. Why'd you come back here?

HETTY: Because I could work here! Because this is my home!

MAYOR: Because your Mom and Dad left you a house here. And we welcomed you. And put up with ideas that aren't Normal.

DELBERT: You wouldn't have so many ideas, if that son of yours were over there fighting for freedom, instead of bumming around Europe or wherever he is.

HETTY: Tangiers, Cadiz, Gibraltar, Naples, Athens, Malta—he sends me a postcard every week! And when he comes home, you're gonna see what a free person really is!

Bell rings. TV anchorman enters.

PRODUCER: Is there a Hetty Counts here?

F, F, D, M: That's her.

ANCHORMAN: Ms. Counts, I'm Arthur Pent of CNN.

F, F, D, M: The Scud Stud!

ANCHORMAN: I've got a camera crew outside, I wonder if you'd give us an interview.

HETTY: An interview—about my Desert Scam packet! At a secret meeting in the White House last April—

PRODUCER: Lady, I don't know what—

HETTY: Oh, right—I sent that to ABC! CNN—my Bush in Miami story! In 1973—

PRODUCER: Hold the phone? I'd like to ask you some questions about your son.

HETTY: . . . About Jamal?

PRODUCER: You must be very proud, Ms. Counts. He's a hero.

HETTY: He is?

PRODUCER: You mean you haven't heard? *(Checks watch. To FRANK.)* Could you turn on the morning news? *(FRANK does.)*

FUMIKO: Look—it's Jimmy! *(HETTY staggers back.)* And he's hurt!

JIMMY: *(On TV.)* There was a job to do, and I did it.

DELBERT: Way to go, Jimmy, boy!

JIMMY: I don't know if I want to go back—My hometown wasn't too home-like. I haven't been back for three years. *(All feel responsible, but everybody looks at HETTY.)*

PRODUCER: Ms. Counts?

HETTY: It's unbeli . . . I don't . . . He's in the m . . . the m . . .

ANCHORMAN: She doesn't know what to say! Fabulous, the first shock. Come right this way.

HETTY: He's in the Marines! *(ANCHORMAN bustles her out.)*

The rest look at each other.

MAYOR: I'm gonna call the U.S. Marine Corps. I'm gonna make darn sure Jimmy comes back!

ALL: Yeah!

MAYOR: Now—which of you wants to be on the committee to organize his Welcome Home Celebration?

FRANK: I'll be on!

FUMI: I will!

DELBERT: I'll help!

FUMI: But I wonder how she's gonna take it?

Scene 4: The Airport

JIMMY, MAYOR, HETTY.

INTERCOM: Welcome to Blisterville International Airport. *(JIMMY enters with gear.)* All persons waiting to greet returning military personnel, please proceed to the Executive Waiting Room. To greet returning military personnel, proceed to the Executive Waiting Room.

JIMMY: *(Sings "Jimmy's Song.")*
Me and my buddies
We sat in the sand
For months without beer
In an Arabian wasteland
Hoping for something and
Hoping for nothing
Wondering when we would
Hear the command

And it came and we went
We moved up and moved out

Into the face of our fears and our doubts
We were brown, we were white
We were yellow and black and
We stood united and
We pushed the enemy back

And together we faced the question
That is past all right and wrong
But we all stood together
And together we were strong
And for the first time in my whole life
I knew what it was to belong
And for the first time in my whole life
I knew what it was to belong

Me and my buddies drew a
Line in the sand
Protecting the world from a
Murderous madman
Hoping for something
Hoping for nothing
Hoping that we'd make it
Back to our own land

I never thought when I left here
That everything would work out right
and I never thought when I lived here
that the future could be so bright
that the future could be so bright.

So why do I feel like I want to throw up? I'm the only Marine getting back from the Gulf, that's got to apologize to his mother! (*Rehearses.*) "Look, Ma—I had to do what I had to do." "It's a guy thing—you wouldn't understand." She's gonna see inside me with those X-ray eyes! She's gonna ask piercing questions! By now she's figured out every time I ever lied to her. She'll be all, "Only one rule I laid on you: No jive."

MAYOR: (*Enters.*) Jimmy, boy!

JIMMY: Mr. Mayor?

MAYOR: (*Pumps his hand, puts wreath on him.*) You look fine, son! And you did a terrific job!

JIMMY: Thanks, sir. I was surprised when I got your telegram.

MAYOR: I understand you also got one from Washington.

JIMMY: Yes sir. An invitation.

MAYOR: To receive a medal from the President of the United States! Normal's awful glad you made it back, Jimmy. You're the kind of young man can give a town back its pride.

JIMMY: You didn't used to think that, sir, when I wanted to date Mary Lou.

MAYOR: (*Winces.*) I deserved that, son. And I know you didn't have the smoothest path, growing up. But today, we're all bending overboard to let you know Normal loves you.

JIMMY: That means a lot, sir. . . . I was wondering if you've heard from my mom.

MAYOR: Now there's someone drove over with me. Someone that's worked extra hard to make this a great day. (*Calls off.*) Come on! Meet the chairlady of Welcome Home Jim! HETTY *enters, wearing yellow ribbon and carrying a sign.*

HETTY: We're Number One. We're Number One. We're Number One.

JIMMY: Mom . . . MOM?

MAYOR: Surprised everybody.

HETTY: Hey, kid—what's happening?

JIMMY: Mom, I—

HETTY: It's cool.

JIMMY: It is?

HETTY: You don't have to explain.

JIMMY: I don't?

HETTY: That Saddam Hussein, why he's just like Hitler. And you're one of a few good men. You wanted to thrust.

JIMMY: Yeah . . .

HETTY: You wanted to probe.

JIMMY: Yeah!

HETTY: You hit real hard.

JIMMY: Yep!

HETTY: And now we're in real deep. (*JIMMY takes this as praise.*) It's not every day my son's a big hero.

MAYOR: Your Mom's busting her buttons! She's worked day and night, cranking out press releases, staying on the phone. . . . We're throwing a big jamboree for you, Jimbo, and not just some little one-horse, hometown parade: we're having us a national media event here! "Back to Normal!"

HETTY: I've got all the networks coming.

MAYOR: We got Main Street parked up with TV trucks, and the merchants are making out like weevils cause the town's crawling with some of the biggest celebrities you ever seen! Frank and the other restaurant owners, they had to send over to Bakersfield for an emergency shipment of Chardonnay!

JIMMY: I think I could use a shot of Wild Turkey.

MAYOR: I'll get the car. You two deserve a minute alone together. *(Warning.)* We only got half an hour until the parade! *(Exits.)*

JIMMY: Mom, I don't know what to . . .

HETTY: Say.

JIMMY: I go against everything you believe in . . . then you do all that for me?

HETTY: Hey—isn't that what a Mom's for?

JIMMY: Yeah, but you never—

HETTY: There is one thing I'd like you to explain.

JIMMY: . . . Why I lied?

HETTY: No. . . . Hopping from invasion to invasion like that, how'd you manage to send all those postcards?

JIMMY: *(Biting the bullet.)* Left stacks of 'em with girls I met in different ports.

HETTY: I hope you used condoms. I did the same thing!

JIMMY: Mom!

HETTY: Left a stack of letters with a cat in Zurich when I didn't want your Grandma to know I'd gone to Tangiers!

JIMMY: You lied to Grandma? . . . Mom, I need to tell you something. When I was little . . . the whole town but you knew I was a Cub Scout. *(Every sin confessed is a knife in* HETTY's *heart.)* Then I was an Eagle Scout. Then I joined JROTC.

HETTY: I guess a man's got to do what a man's got to do.

JIMMY: You know what, Mom? Semper Fi. You're outstanding. *(They hug.)* I brought you something. *(Fishes lamp from backpack.)*

HETTY: A magic lamp! *(Magic music.)* Used to have one when I was so broke, I wished it was magic. Bought it in the souks in Marrakech in '65—or '66—lost it when my stuff got ripped off in Istanbul! I used to rub and rub it, but I never could make it work!

JIMMY: I already got my three wishes: we beat Saddam Hussein, I'm a hero, and my Mom understands! *(Exeunt.)*

Scene 5: The Celebration

ALL AND THEN SOME.

March music. Parade, led by DONNA BURKITT *twirling baton.* DELBERT *drumming,* FRANK & FUMI *carrying signs "Welcome home, Jim," "We love you, Jimmy."* JIMMY *and* HETTY *waving to crowd;* MAYOR *bringing up the rear. All but* MAYOR *exeunt.*

MAYOR: Welcome, folks. And howdy all you strangers watching in different places—this is Normal! It's the first time we've been on TV! You businessmen looking to relocate: we got prime industrial sites real cheap, and plenty of folks eager to work. *(To audience.)* Everybody wave. Well, I've thought a lot here, about what this day means. "Back to 'Normal.'" Since Vietnam, things haven't been right in this country. We've been acting like a pitiful, beaten giant; lost our self-respect and our hope, and just kinda started to slip and slide. Jobs going away, crime, no money to fix anything. But this Just War has changed all that. Our young fighting men—and women—proved America's still got the right stuff! We Can Do! They've put our country back on top—Back to Normal! And we thank 'em.

You'll meet our young fighting man, Jimmy, in just a bit. He's kinda shy, but he has agreed to speak a few words. But first, there's a lot of famous folks here come to celebrate with us, and I know you're all dying to see 'em, and they're dying to come out on stage, and I believe they're gonna sing us a song. *(MAYOR has a list.)* Let's see. *(He doesn't know all the names. He finds some difficult to pronounce. Introduces celebrities one at a time. Each enters, bows, does some signature bit.)* Mr. Mike Tyson. Mr. Kenny G? Kenny G. Mr. Tony Orlando. Ms. . . . Joan Rivers. Mr. Arnold Schwarzenegger! Mr. Arsenio Hall. Miss Brooke Shields.

Celebrities prompt BROOKE *forward.*

BROOKE: My agent said "Back to Normal." I said, "Love to—Not" but then he told me it's for one of our heroes and I'm so glad to be here and we're all so, so grateful, Jimmy, and all our troops, and we thank you, and we love America, and we'd like to sing a song.

JOAN RIVERS: Oh, shut up and sing, ya stupid bimbo!

ALL: *(Sing "Voices in the Air.")*
We're voices in the air
We're over here
You're over there

JOAN: Don't know who is right or who is wrong
You go fight
We'll sing this song

BROOKE: Doesn't matter where you're sent
Could be Salvador, Korea
How 'bout Tashkent?

TONY: If you're hit, or blown up in the air
We'll be here
Not over there

ARSENIO: Don't know why we fight for some emir
But what the hey
Can't hurt my career

MIKE: War's a fluffy, cuddly thing
Can't hear the bombs
Over our singing

ALL: We're voices in the air

We're glad we're here

Not over there. *(Repeat 2 times.)*

Music continues over bows. Exit all but SCHWARZENEGGER.

SCHWARZENEGGER: How 'bout that Saddam Hussein? Thought he was tough? Thought he was Conan Barbarian? He was girly-man! America was tough! I also made myself strong. Then I made myself American. I was too strong for Europe! Europe is weak! And now I am fery, fery proud to introduce a tough man, a fit man—Jimmy! *(JIMMY and HETTY enter.)* He is no girly-man! And his strong Mom, who fit dis whole day togedder. Put your hands togedder! Vay to go, Jim! *(Exit.)*

JIMMY: *(To vanishing* ARNOLD.*)* Thank you. . . . *(To crowd.)* Thank you. Whoa, there's a lot of you. Hi. Uh. *(Gets it together and makes a great start.)* It's great to be home! But I feel fortunate that I got to be over there. With a great bunch of guys—and women—doing the best job we knew how. Standing tall. Bringing freedom to a small country that needed our help. *(Blanks.)* And . . . uh . . . We helped them. Uh . . . We had a job to do, and we did it! . . . um. I had some more to say, but . . .

HETTY: Could I say a couple of words, son?

JIMMY: My mom.

HETTY: Why is my son a hero? Are we celebrating a victory for freedom? Or freedom's latest defeat by a bunch of rich vampires, who—while we were all watching television—have taken over the United States? I have proof George Bush planned the Gulf War. And I have proof he is part of a conspiracy—*(JIMMY starts to move toward her)*—which beginning with the assassination of President Kennedy, has carried out a silent coup. *(He reaches her, she shoves him aside.* MAYOR *starts to move toward her.)* Before the glazed eyes of citizens, behind the turned back of Congress—*(MAYOR reaches her, she kicks him aside)*—a secret government now actually rules this country. *(MAYOR and JIMMY pick up podium with her in it.)* But we can vote them out—we elected them! *(MAYOR and JIMMY carry off podium, but HETTY evades.)* 1963: Secret group in CIA assassinates Kennedy. This photo, I just received. CIA agents Howard Hunt and Frank Sturgis busted behind Book Depository! Never reported. *(MAYOR and JIMMY re-enter. They approach, but she dodges.)* 1968: Same crowd assassinates Robert Kennedy. Nixon fundraiser George Putnam, amateur hypnotist: employer of Sirhan Sirhan!

They pick her up and start to carry her off log-style.

HETTY: *(Continues undaunted.)* Nixon wins: vampires take White House.

FUMI, FRANK *rush on.*

FRANK: This is America! You can't say those things here!

FUMI: And I thought you were my best friend!

MAYOR: *(Blocks them.)* No violence—we're on national TV! *(Meanwhile HETTY exits. All pursue.)*

HETTY: *(Enters with megaphone.)* 1972: Watergate break-in—because Demos have this Dallas photo! 1980: Bush in Paris . . . Deal with Iran: "Sell you weapons if you keep hostages, make Carter lose!" *(Sees crowd coming, hides.)*

FRANK/FUMI: Make her shut up! Arrest her!

JOHNSON: H-Hetty—

JIMMY: This is between my mother and me! I'm going to deal with her!

HETTY: *(Emerges when they have crossed.)* 1990: Country sucked dry, complaining. Bush plans Gulf War to keep vampires in.

MAYOR: There she is! *(They chase her off.)*

HETTY: *(Pops up through trap door.)* Last April, four months before Saddam's invasion, White House meeting: Bush, Baker, Thatcher. Decide to demilitarize the Mideast—starting guess where.

MR. JOHNSON: *(Entering.)* H-Hetty?

HETTY: Saddam falls for mother of all setups!

MR. JOHNSON: H-Hetty!

HETTY: Mr. Johnson!

MR. JOHNSON: H-

HETTY: You TV watchers out there—meet the best crusading journalist in the Central Valley, Homer Johnson, owner of radio station KUBU

MR. JOHNSON: I was l-listening to you on the s-station. *(HETTY strikes "Rocky" pose.)* H-Hetty, you're f-f—you're fired. You're off the air.

Crowd enters. MAYOR and JIMMY enter and grab shocked HETTY. JIMMY covers her mouth.

MAYOR: Take my keys, get her out of here the back way.

HETTY: *(Rallying.)* Who made you shut me up?

FRANK: Shut her up!

HETTY: Call (916) 285-I-N-F-O! *(JIMMY gags her. He and JOHNSON hustle her off.)*

MAYOR: *(Shepherds FRANK and FUMI off other way.)* Go and chow down. We got barbecue, we got hot dogs, we got fajitas! *(Resumes MC role.)* That's all folks, show's over—go on! *(ARTHUR PENT and CAMERAMAN enter, leaving.)* Mr. Stud, I'd like to explain to my fellow Americans out there that what they just saw, that wasn't Normal!

ARTHUR PENT: Don't worry about it. *(Exit.)*

Scene 6: The House

JIMMY, HETTY.

Piles of boxes, files, newspapers, clutter, phone, fax.

JIMMY: Home Sweet Home. Like our furniture? *(Reads titles on boxes.)*

"JFK," "MLK," "Bobby," "Watergate," "Grenadagate," "Iranscam," "Burning Bush." *(Throws stacks of newspapers around.) New York Times. Le Monde. London Observer. Washington Post. Anderson Valley Adver-tiser? Covert Action Information Bulletin.* Doesn't everybody's Mom sub-scribe to 35 newspapers?

Phone rings, machine answers. First jazz, then HETTY'S *voice.*

HETTY: Blue Monk! Hetty's hotline. Leave a message. *(*JIMMY *takes a bag from backstage, starts packing it with boy stuff—old catcher's mitt, football, etc.)*

SECRETIVE-SOUNDING VOICE: Hetty? David here. New angle on Bush-Noriega. They were lovers. I got pictures. Be in touch. *(Hangs up.)*

JIMMY: Mom's got interesting friends all over the country, and look how much mail she gets! *(Holds up bunch of letters, opens one.)* "Saw your ad. Enclosed is $3.98. Please send packet #35: 'Jesus a myth—see the photos.'" It's a living.

HETTY *enters, towelling her hair.* JIMMY *has set bag down and she doesn't notice it.*

HETTY: Rotten tomatoes—feh! I haven't been this big a hit in town since I showed up at Senior Prom with that blues player Blind Willie Washing-ton. But I tore up the picture—Yeah! I busted the screen! I hipped peo-ple all over America—they've got Bush's number now—and my num-ber! Any new calls? *(*JIMMY *shakes his head.)* Too soon yet—people are still in shock. Mr. Johnson, though . . . that kinda wasted me. I always thought he was this cool, brave old cat. Poor bastard's probably halfway through a fifth of bourbon, trying to drown the fact he copped out. But I was cooking, yes sir, I wailed! How mad are you?

JIMMY: Me? What would I be mad about?

HETTY: I dunno—I thought maybe—because I kinda—

JIMMY: Lied?

HETTY: Well, yeah—but you lied to me for three years!

JIMMY: And you used me.

HETTY: For a good cause. You know how long I've waited for a chance like that? You couldn't expect me not to take it.

JIMMY: Set me up. At the biggest moment of my life, made a fool of me. Humiliated me and destroyed me!

HETTY: Oh, everybody'll get over it.

JIMMY: What kind of mother would do that to her son?

HETTY: One who has a serious gig! One who thinks about the good of the country, not just "Me and my family."

JIMMY: What family? You and me and who? The kind of mother who when I ask who my father was, goes, "It was a hot weekend at Monterey Jazz"?

HETTY: I've told you over and over, there are only three possibilities! Dizzy

Gillespie's bass player, or Charles Lloyd's drummer, or this guy with John Handy that played electric violin.

JIMMY: Why'm I complaining? After all, you used to put on an album: "Hear those high notes? That could be your Dad."

HETTY: *(Touched.)* You remember that?

JIMMY: An album isn't a father, Mom. And clipping newspapers isn't a culture.

HETTY: You loved helping me!

JIMMY: Not since I was 11. And Mom—"Afro-Okie" isn't a race!

HETTY: It's YOUR race! I made sure grandpa took you hunting and grandma took you to ball games—and I played jazz, I read you African stories, I sent away for dashikis—

JIMMY: You never took me to Oakland! Think the crackers in boot camp thought I was one of them, cause I said "My grandpa came out of the Dust Bowl?" And the black dudes—soon as I opened my mouth, "Catch you later, bro." I thought extensions meant a cheap kind of college! I thought a drive-by was a quick-service bank!

HETTY: *(With great dignity.)* I rented a television so you would watch *Roots*.

JIMMY: Roots! I am the only person in my generation who wouldn't recognize the Six Million Dollar Man! The only person who grew up without a TV!

HETTY: Blame me for not feeding you a mind-altering drug. That's part of the conspiracy! They addict people to pictures so we'll stop wanting information!

JIMMY: The kind you push. The kind you're hooked on so bad, never mind joining PTA or coming to ball games: half the time it'd be midnight before you'd go, "Did I feed the kid?"

HETTY: If I'd cooked for you, maybe you wouldn't have joined the Marines. But you think I chose this work? It chose me. *(As she continues JIMMY resumes packing.)* I was in Paris minding my own business, picking up French, hawking the *Herald Tribune*. Some nut shot the President. So? Then some expatriate showed the film. Well, my daddy had guns. No bolt-action rifle fires four rounds in six seconds—but I was on my way to Ibiza. Five years I made the scene: Montmartre, Morocco, Greece, the Dalmatian coast, time to time reading in some French or English paper, how one more witness had been wasted—still just trying to write poetry, living on dubbing and dealing. Then King was killed. Then Bobby. Then I had to come home, when I read how Sirhan's seven-shooter left sixteen bullet holes. *("Click." JIMMY is pointing a toy gun at her.)* What's that?

JIMMY: My toy AK-47, Mom. See? Meet my GI Joes.

HETTY: Where'd those come from? Jamal!

JIMMY: Jimmy—the name's Jimmy. Twenty-three years of research, and you don't even know your own son. You did your best to raise a weirdo, but I'm an American. 100% now. I've killed for my country. (*Enjoys her reaction.*) Right. Panama. All you do is try to tear America down. (*Indicating room.*) 500 boxes full of poison that's not going to work—dead, boring shit nobody wants to know.

HETTY: Since today, they don't have a choice.

JIMMY: Oh, you think you laid it on them? One time you're glad there's a TV? I saw the cameras cut off the second you started talking.

HETTY: But . . . what . . .

JIMMY: Get a life, Mom. I'm history. Just tell me one thing: why'd you have a kid if you didn't want to be normal?

HETTY: I love you!

JIMMY: (*Hesitates for only a second.*) It isn't enough. (*Goes.*)

Phone rings. HETTY *answers.*

VOICE: Hetty? Did you catch this one? Bush Junior's big holdings in Harken Oil—exclusive drilling rights in Bahrain? Two weeks before Saddam invades, he unloads all his stock! Buys it back yesterday. Think he knew something?

HETTY: Get a life! (*Hangs up. Sings "Boppus Lamentus."*)

I wish there was a pill that I could take
To be a normal member of the human race
So when they yell "Yay team" I'd go "Rah-rah"
I wish that I could say "Just call me Ma"—
Now I've lost my show, my son is gone
And the TV cameras weren't even on!
Is this the day that I've been working for?
Ending up alone behind an open door?
Didn't stop to think about how people feel
I thought they'd get with it when I said, "Get real!"
Now I've lost my show, my son is gone
And the TV cameras weren't even on!

Scene 7: Immediately Following

HETTY, THE GENIE.

HETTY *cries over the lamp, rubs the tears off. Magical music. The* GENIE *appears.*

GENIE: Ha, ha, ha—free at last! Who are you?

HETTY: Who are you?

GENIE: I asked you first.

HETTY: I'm . . . uh . . . Hetty Counts . . . I could swear I saw you come out of that lamp.

GENIE: I'm the ghost of Christmas past.

HETTY: Wait . . . '64 . . . no, '65—the casbah in Tunis—you're that oud player that knew Silent Night!

GENIE: No, dimwit. I'm the genie of the lamp!

HETTY: And I'm Tinker Bell. I rubbed the lamp before—nothing happened.

GENIE: You had to cry on it. I've been locked in there for 900 years! You got anything to eat in this dump?

HETTY: *(Suddenly hungry.)* I wish. *(Magical music.)*

GENIE: That's one.

HETTY: One what? *(Doorbell rings.)* Jamal! I knew he'd come back. *(She opens the door.* FRANK *enters, walks past* HETTY *to* GENIE *in a daze. He is holding an extravagant pizza.)* Farid. I mean Frank. You made pizza!

FRANK: I did?

GENIE: *(Takes the pizza.)* Thanks.

HETTY: Cool. I didn't know you delivered.

FRANK: I don't.

GENIE: Mu-neer I-bin Wah-had lk'beer lk'teer. Muneer, son of a Really Big Guy.

FRANK: Ib-tih-kee Arabee! Ahlan. Meen in-ta? Hello, who are you?

GENIE: Beh Khus, Aksh! None of your business!

HETTY: Meen in'ta? Khun-zeer! Who do you think you are, you big pig?

GENIE: Shut up. Frank—

FRANK: . . . Farid . . .

GENIE: *(Speaking slowly to disoriented* FRANK.*)* Farid, you have to go now.

FRANK: OK. Where?

GENIE: *(Shoos him off.)* Yalla! *(*FRANK *exits. To* HETTY.*)* You've got two wishes left, and make them quick—I got plans. Got a score to settle with a little short wizard—short like him. *(Gazes after* FRANK.*)*

HETTY: Wishes? Yeah, sure. If you're a genie, let's see you get rid of this junk. I wish you'd make all this stuff disappear. *(Magical music.)*

GENIE: You got it. Im-she. *(A pile of junk disappears.)* Im-she. *(Another pile goes.)* Im-she. *(And another.)* Im-she. *(And another.)*

HETTY: My files! Twenty-three years of research!

GENIE: You got one wish left.

HETTY: And I blew two wishes!

GENIE: You want everything back the way it was?

HETTY: Yeah.

Magical music starts. Junk starts to reappear.

GENIE: Is that your last wish . . .

HETTY: No! *(Junk freezes halfway on.)* I do not wish that! *(Junk disappears again.)* I've got to wish for something bigger.

GENIE: Well, make it snappy, I'm late for an ass kicking. Which way to Chaldea?

HETTY: You mean Kuwait?

GENIE: Never heard of it.

HETTY: Right . . . I know—I wish for ten more wishes!

GENIE: Ah-ah-ah-ah. Genie don't play that. You got one wish.

HETTY: To get Jamal back! . . . No, too selfish. There's so many things that need to happen . . . I could end hunger . . . but that wouldn't bring peace. I could end warfare . . . no—no, there's still a few scores to settle.

GENIE: Hey! (HETTY *stops.*) Tell you what. You think about it: I gotta go. First wish you say—done. (*Magic cue.*) Better hope you don't talk in your sleep. Hee, hee, hee. Boo! (*She jumps.*) Hee, hee, hee. I'm out of here. Look out, Habibi, I'm coming for your ass! (*Prepares for takeoff.*) Look— (*points*)—Bird Lives! (*She looks, he exits.*)

HETTY: Wait! Wait! He's gone! Oh God—I'm an emotional mess—I'm in no shape to handle this responsibility! I could save the environment, but that won't feed the hungry . . . I could feed the hungry, but what'll that do to trees? . . . I could end racism . . .

VOICES OFF: Commie bitch! We know you're in there! Get out of town!

HETTY: What th—? (*Exit.*)

Scene 8: The Diner, the Morning After

FRANK, DELBERT, FUMI, MAYOR, HETTY, BUSH, JIMMY, SECRET SERVICE MAN.

FRANK *sets up. Bell.*

DELBERT: (*Enters.*) Morning.

FRANK: Morning, Delbert. Ham and eggs?

DELBERT: Just coffee. You at that mess last night?

FRANK: (*Shakes his head.*) I saw the flames around midnight, but I stayed inside. Terrible.

DELBERT: People lost their heads. But I can't say she didn't ask for it. (*Bell.*)

FUMI: (*Enters.*) Good morning.

FRANK, DELBERT: Morning.

FRANK: Waffles?

FUMI: Just coffee, please. After the—(*they nod*)—I couldn't go back to sleep. (*To* FRANK.) It reminded me of when they put us in the camps. I don't say she didn't ask for it, though! (*Bell.*)

MAYOR: (*Enters.*) Howdy.

OTHERS (*Subdued.*) Howdy, Mr. Mayor.

FRANK: Redeye gravy and biscuits?

MAYOR: I couldn't eat—just coffee. Five minutes till the morning news? (*They check watches, nod.*) We're on it.

FUMI: On, no! / DELBERT: That's all we need!

FRANK: Great.

MAYOR: Way those limousines and TV trucks lit out after the rally, I thought "Well, at least no strangers saw what happened here last night." Turns out one camera crew checked into the Bide-a-Wee, right next door to her house! Caught the whole thing, big as life. Make one jim-dandy ad campaign: "Relocate to Normal and get a warm greeting. A burning cross—(*all shake their heads*)—on your front lawn!" 'Course I won't say she didn't ask for it. Way I see it, she's got to leave town.

DELBERT: Yesterday.

FUMI: For her own good. She isn't safe here.

FRANK: She stays, make more trouble for everybody. (*Everybody waits for a volunteer to take the next step.*)

MAYOR: I know—we'll form a committee.

OTHERS: Right./Good idea./OK.

MAYOR: Make it official. "Hetty, there's no place for you here. We want our town back to Normal." (*Bell.*)

HETTY: (*Enters.*) Good morning.

FRANK: More coffee, Mayor? (*All turn their backs.*)

HETTY: . . . I know I wrecked your day. (*Grim looks.*) Look, I wish I— (*catches herself*)—arghh! . . . I was selfish . . . I'm sorry. (*Raised eyebrows, but no answer.*) I just came to watch the morning news.

DELBERT: You want to see 'em make this whole town look bad—

FUMI: —And you get to play the innocent victim!

HETTY: No. I want to see Jimmy get his medal. (*Everybody jumps up.*)

FUMI: Jimmy's medal!

MAYOR: I plumb forgot!

FRANK: Go, go, Jimbo!

DELBERT: Turn it on! (*FRANK does.*)

BUSH *appears, followed by* JIMMY, *who takes his place behind and to one side.*

BUSH: My fellow Americans. . . . (*Audience nods proudly.*) Saddam Hussein walks amid ruin. America did the right thing. (*Audience sniffles.*)

HETTY: (*Aside.*) Oh, please.

BUSH: Our troops: we followed them with our prayers, as they punished aggression. (*Audience shares pride.*)

HETTY: (*Aside.*) I can't stand this.

BUSH: Operation Desert Storm dawn of a New World Order of justice and liberty, where might no longer makes right.

HETTY: (*Aloud.*) God, I wish you'd can the jive. (*Thunder and lightning.*) Oh, no!

BUSH: . . . But it sure makes some of us a helluva lotta money. All you hicks, micks, and spicks, I mean fellow Americans: think you're winners now, right? War is great, war is OK! Keep thinking that. Saddam baby, you made my day! Hey, I had problems. S & L's. You forgot! Kicked my ass in the polls. This cameljockey volunteers to be my bad guy! We mess with him. "Piece of Kuwait? No problem." Crosses that border, bam! The New Hitler. You buy that; we buy the U.N.! Congress rolls over like a dead dog. Nobody hears Saddam say Uncle. Bomb his sadass country back to the Stone Age! Poor towelhead still don't know what hit him—he thought he was part of the club! *(By now* JIMMY *is frantically signalling backstage.)* Is it hot in here? Baker. Waving at me. Hey Jim: read my flips! Best club in the world. We ain't Republican or Democrat or American or Jap or German! We're bidnessmen. We got brains, bucks, and balls. Take a look at this! *(Mimes unzipping fly.)* Hey, go wide!

JIMMY: It's his thyroid! Mr. President, you're not feeling well.

BUSH: I feel fucking great! What are you lookin at? I got better things to do than give Sambo a badge. Here, catch: pretend it's a basketball.

SECRET SERVICE MAN enters, helps JIMMY *off.*

BUSH: This is my third term as President. *(SSM listens to message on cordless phone.)* Next time I need a hit: who's it? Who's left? Cuba! Time to mess with Fidel. *(SSM taps him on shoulder.)* Hey buddy—watch and learn. New World Order. *(SSM taps again.)* Who's gonna stop me? *(SSM grabs him and carries him off.)* Hey—somebody's gotta run the goddam real world!

FRANK *turns off TV. Silence. People look uneasily at one another.* HETTY *is in suspense: will anybody say anything?*

MAYOR: *(Coughs.)* I think—I'll have some more coffee, Frank, please.

FRANK: *(Pours.)* Fumi, Delbert—a refill? *(They murmur acceptance.)*

FUMI: Well. I think it's going to be hot today.

MAYOR: That's—what they said.

FRANK: How 'bout—those 'niners? Very sad. Should have never let go Craig and Lott!

FUMI: It's a shame—Montana's getting old.

HETTY *despairs. She has blown a chance to save the world. She tiptoes out. They watch her off.*

MAYOR: Something I never really understood, though. Sanctions could have worked!

FRANK: Of course!

FUMI: You think Jimmy was right?

MAYOR: About what?

FUMI: About it being his thyroid.

DELBERT: No god-damn way. That was him. That prissy-lipped, Ivy League son of a bitch, bouncing around in his sailboats and his golf cart, setting one draft-dodging son of his up in the oil business, the other in savings and loan, cutting taxes on rich people, to where the farmer can't hold onto his land! I knew he was a crook, and I voted for him.

MAYOR: I didn't! *(They look at* FUMI *and* FRANK.*)*

FUMI: I didn't vote.

FRANK: I couldn't!

DELBERT: I was trying to believe I had fought for something. Now the bank give me 30 days to pay back last year's loan. I got 3,000 bales down at the gin, but the way the price is, that won't even cover storage.

FUMI: I've had three customers in the last two weeks. I'm in default on my second mortgage.

MAYOR: The county's closing the hospital.

FRANK *throws a towel to the floor. Silence.*

DELBERT: Think anybody'll try to impeach him?

ALL: *(Think silently.)* "Nah!" . . . "Well?" . . . "Could it be possible?"

DELBERT: *(Drops out.)* I got 5 miles of fence to mend whatever happens.

FUMI: Time to open up shop.

MAYOR: Got a town to run.

FRANK: Might as well close early. *(Exit.)*

Sign: Time Passes.

Scene 9: The Radio Station, Sometime Later

HETTY, JIMMY, CALLER.

Music. HETTY *enters and sets up as before. On the console: the lamp.*

HETTY: This is KUBU, the Voice of the Valley, it's 6 A.M., our new time slot, and this is your weekly Reality Sandwich—with your host, Hetty Counts. Today, Where Was George? Chapter 40. But first the headlines. "Cholera Epidemic Rages in Iraq." I guess we did the right thing. "President Still Confined—After numerous public appearances marred by unexplained outbursts." *(Pats the lamp.)* "There have been no appearances by Acting President Dan Quayle, reported seen yesterday gesticulating wildly from an upper window of the White House." And the $64 question: "Will Democrats Do Anything?" *(Phone rings,* HETTY *answers.)* Reality Sandwich, you're on the air.

DONNA BURKITT: *(Appears.)* Hetty, this is Donna Burkitt, and my grandpa just died.

HETTY: My sympathy, Donna.

DONNA: And you know how you've been asking for back issues of newspapers? Grandpa had 37 years of the *Los Angeles Times!*

HETTY: I could use 'em, Donna! Bring 'em on over.

DONNA: See you after school. *(Hangs up.)*

HETTY: And local news: foreclosure sale today, junction of Blisterville Highway and Zopilote Road, Delbert Stokes' ranch. Let's show him he has neighbors. *(Phone rings.)* Reality Sandwich, you're on the air.

It's JIMMY, *in civvies now. He sings "Telephone Blues."*

JIMMY: Hello, Mama
   Thought I'd call you on the phone
HETTY: *(Speaking.)* Why . . . hello, Jamal.
JIMMY: Hello, Mama
   Hope everything's all right at home.
HETTY: Everything's fine.
JIMMY: Anyway—I got a buddy in the service
   And that is why I called
   He got hold of some secret documents
   I know you'll want to read them all
   I better not tell you on the phone
HETTY: We both know where that's at
JIMMY: I could just drop them in the mail
HETTY: No, you better not do that.
JIMMY: Maybe I better bring them
   You know I'll head on out your way
   I'll just drop in for a minute
HETTY: Maybe stay a couple of days
JIMMY: I'm hangin' here in Oakland
   I'm stayin' with that friend
   I got my discharge papers
   Won't be doin' that again
   You know mama things here are not so great
   We really need a change
   And I hope it comes tomorrow
   Cause it's certainly not today
BOTH: And I hope it comes tomorrow
   Cause it's certainly not today
JIMMY: Yes, I hope it comes tomorrow
   Cause it's certainly not today!
BOTH: Bye-bye. *(JIMMY exits.)*
HETTY: This is KUBU, the Voice of the Valley, and this has been Reality
   Sandwich. *(Exit.)*

The End

The "Red Heart" Scene from *Offshore*

Act 2, Scene 3

1993

Script by Joan Holden, Chung Chiao, Pat Lee,
Keiko Shimosato, and Michael Sullivan

GUANGZHOU. *CARLTON enters with tie loose around his neck, holding a beer to his head.*

CARLTON: Chairman Mao said, in his Little Red Book, "Revolution is not a tea party." These days here in Guangzhou, they say "revolution's a dinner party." (*Indicates beer.*) For my head. Check the suit. Hong Kong. My broker takes one look—bam, straight to the Armani boutique. I walk out feeling like a million bucks—poorer. I'm "This is borrowed money I'm spending." He says Men's Wearhouse opens no doors in China. Sets me up in a 5-star, hundred buck a night, Kanemochi hotel—30-dollar Chinese hotels open no doors either—and an appointment to give a banquet for Mr. Wing. After 10 courses, "Your proposal is interesting. But first you must meet Mr. Mok." Mr. Mok gets me Mr. Chiu, Mr. Chiu gets me Mr. Yu . . . plus their brothers and sisters, uncles and aunts, cousins and neighbors: I wine and dine them all: it's an investment. I can call these people next time I come back.

Mun wu hoi fong: Open door. Wide open! Boomtown—when's the last time you saw that in the States? Everybody zooming around on motorcycles, trying to get rich. Dudes peddling bitter melons and sneakers. Fish balls and pagers. Fake Rolex, 20 bucks. Everybody wants to be an entrepreneur. Everybody wants joint ventures, foreign investment. The train station, hundreds of guys with leather faces hang out day and night,

266

waiting for jobs. I don't know where the hell they come from, but they're there, and they're ready—and I'm gonna put 'em to work.

The Great Wall Restaurant. Tang Dynasty decor. I'm waiting for Mr. Wang. Mr. Wang is my man. With his seal on the deal, I'm in business. Fly home, collect my commission, start looking for the next deal. Mr. Wang gets more than dinner. *(Displays red envelope.)* Lucky money. 3,000 bucks.

RED HEART *arrives. He wears a Mao suit buttoned tightly around his neck.*

RED HEART: Mr. Carlton Lee?

CARLTON: Yeah! *Tsho Sun,* Mr. Wang.

RED HEART: I'm sorry. I am not Mr. Wang.

CARLTON: Oh.

RED HEART: I am the new official charged with your Investment case.

CARLTON: Terrific, Mr.—?

RED HEART: Chou.

CARLTON: Where's Mr. Wang?

RED HEART: He left his post. Perhaps you know
    The proverb, "One who walks too often
    On dark streets will someday meet a ghost?"

CARLTON: No . . .

RED HEART: Chinese are fond of proverbs. That one
    Is not encouraging.

CARLTON: I know a proverb . . .
    "A journey of ten thousand miles begins
    With a first step." You have my letter.

RED HEART: I have read it well.
    Have you heard our expression,
    "Cage Economy?"

CARLTON: No.

RED HEART: My favorite
    Metaphor. What some officials call our
    "Open Door," is really cage economy.
    The cage: our market that has been opened.
    The bird: entrepreneur.

CARLTON: He's in a cage.

RED HEART: Opened cage: not only
    Free market: also, socialist system
    Controlling bird, protecting national profit.

CARLTON: Ah.

RED HEART: Too few benefit now from the fast change
    Of life in China. We must keep the bird

In a cage, so all can enjoy his song.

CARLTON: Gotta think global today, Mr. Chou: no cages.
I am here—

RED HEART: I know why.

CARLTON: Right. As a Chinese-American, I want to help China's
Industry! Could we—

RED HEART: You want cheap labor,
Freedom to pollute. Release your solvents
To our ground water, and heavy metal
Into our rivers.

CARLTON: Beh—

RED HEART: Our sky was clear once.
Now you can't see. Our seas were full of fish.
Now they're dying. World Bank will help us
build the Yangtze River Dam—uproot a million people
Drown the valley best-loved by our painters!
Have you seen the farmers who abandon
The countryside, pour into the cities
Seeking cash?

CARLTON: Hoping to enjoy the song.
They want the good life.

RED HEART: Like Chinese-Americans.
Mr. Lee, tell me about your good life
In America.

CARLTON: Life is great. We're making
Big strides. Specially my generation.
Lotta folks doin' very, very well.

RED HEART: Here, only dirty food, flies on the street.
Dirty toilet without door.

CARLTON: But here
Is China! You don't know what that means. My past!
My lichee nuts, my water buffalo.
My warm ocean of Chinese faces. All
My life I had to fight the tide. Here,
I can close my eyes and float.

RED HEART: You can
Help China. We will accept your pollution,
Which brings the good life that our people want.

CARLTON: Great!

RED HEART: In return you share your high technology.

CARLTON: Can't help you there. Strictly the business side.
But countries can get rich without technology.
Taiwan, Brazil—*(Offers the red envelope.)*

RED HEART: Those countries are your factories.
  If you leave, they will have no industries.
  China must do more than assemble bodies
  Of logic chips. We must be able to create
  The brains. *(Pushes away the envelope.)*
CARLTON: I'm just an agent, Mr. Chou.
  I don't handle technology. Look, I've spoken
  To lots of people on this trip . . . excuse me,
  I need to make a phone call.
RED HEART: To your broker.
  In Hong Kong.
CARLTON: Yeah.
RED HEART: He will call somebody.
  Another somebody will come, and take your envelope.
  No need to disturb them. *(CARLTON readies papers.)* In 1970's,
  My friend Mr. Lin was a successful
  Nuclear scientist in the U.S.
CARLTON: Really?
RED HEART: But he decided to return
  To China, to share his knowledge of physics.
CARLTON: And?
RED HEART: He's now
  An ordinary teacher in Beijing
  Because in great things, he is ignorant.
  Does not know how to treat superiors
  To banquets; does not know how to accept
  Red envelopes.
CARLTON: You know if we don't do this
  The next guys will. The paper needs a stamp.
*RED HEART stamps the papers, but does not take the red envelope. CARLTON
exits.*
RED HEART: Open Door! Open Door!
  They say the moon above the western sky is fuller.
  I want to fly over the huge ocean following the tide of trade.
  Stand on the Statue of Liberty to see what the people on
  The other side are doing.
  Open door! Open Door! I see future in the past,
  Those most inspiring days
  When peasants broke out of their landlord-built cages
  Laborers waved the sun-red flag crying, "China has risen!"
  Open Door! Open Door! Let me fly to the top of the world
  To see the shining coins floating down the heavy-metal river.

"80–20" from *Offshore*

1993

Lyrics by Bruce Barthol

NEGOTIATOR: One future, one world, one border.
 Dividing the bottom from the top
 The New World Order, The True World Order
 On the top are the winners
 The jet-setting, sushi-eating, credit card users.
HOSTESS: *(Indicates "like me.")*
NEGOTIATOR: On the bottom is the labor pool, the losers.
 80–20, that's the split.
HOSTESS: What?
NEGOTIATOR: 80–20, that's the deal
 80–20 means you won't get shit
 That's the split, that's the deal
 You'll get minimum wage or you'll beg or steal.
HOSTESS: Not me, baby—I'm gonna be in that 20.
NEGOTIATOR: 20 percent live on dry land
 While 80 percent drift out to sea.
HOSTESS: Waterproof!
NEGOTIATOR: 20 percent have more than they need
 While 80 percent have next to nothing.
 On a good day you will assemble chips
 On a bad day you'll wash windshields and beg for tips
 Or go out to the dump and pick through the trash
 And scheme and dream of any way to get some cash.
 80–20, that's the split

That's the deal
That's the deal . . .

"We're Rich Folks" from *Social Work*
1992

Lyrics by Bruce Barthol

We're rich folks.
Really rich folks.
We're the kind of people that you never see.

We're rich folks.
Filthy rich folks.
We're the kind of people that you'll never be.

Our world is much different than yours.
Got persian carpets on our marble floors.
Your world is grey and you're always whining.
But for us the sun is always shining.

Rolled back the unions.
Hell we rolled back Marx.
Now we're rolling back the new deal.

Gonna throw you to the sharks.
We've lost some battles but we've won the war
Cause we know what we're fighting for.

All my houses have incredible views.
Except for the classics all my cars are new.
We deserve all we got.
And we've really got a lot.

We're rich folks.
Really rich folks.
You have lost and we have won.

We're rich folks.

Filthy rich folks.

We've got a future and you've got none.

Conclusion

The San Francisco Mime Troupe is not radical anymore. They are not post-modern. They are not cutting edge. Like the title character in their *Ripped van Winkle*, they are an anachronism: a throwback to the 1960s. Yet they draw thousands of spectators to their free shows in San Francisco Bay Area parks every summer and are invited to perform in colleges and communities around the country and festivals around the world. Why?

For one thing, they provide an event that brings politically active people together. The troupe has been a magnet for leftist political activism at least since 1965 when R. G. Davis was arrested. Their commedias did not threaten the park commissioners as much as their ability to draw together a crowd of counterculture individuals and groups. They became an essential part of a political network in San Francisco that keeps many activist groups connected and celebrates their efforts. The same principle extends beyond their local role to national and international popular movements where networking and convening are difficult and essential. Social change can only be accomplished by people working together. The more people, the more the potential for change.

The Mime Troupe also remains important and popular because the plays tell the truth about politics, power, and the economy. We have grown accustomed to media propaganda obfuscating the power dynamics at play in the world around us, diverting our attention with sensationalism, and cloaking the government's dirty work in secrecy. Noam Chomsky has said that government secrecy is not for security but "to prevent the population here from knowing what's going on."[1] Troupe shows cut through the subterfuge and simplify what's going on (the California energy crisis, genetically engineered food, urban gentrification, managed health care, globalization, etc.) by revealing who's profiting and who's being exploited. And, like *Doonesbury* or Michael Moore's guerrilla documentaries, they reveal in a direct way by showing.

Troupe shows are deceptively simple because the underlying power dynamics in most shows are basic and usually the same: rich people in power marginalize the rest of us in order to stay in power and get richer. The simplicity of this message gives the troupe's shows clout, but the message can only be crafted into a play through rigorous investigation of the issues. Troupe members become extremely well informed about their subjects. Bertolt Brecht's observation that the play teaches the actors who in turn teach the audience always applies to the troupe's shows, even when spectators are already on top of the subject. Many people who have worked with the company describe it as a crash course in politics. Tom Hayden, former California state senator and one of the Chicago Seven, convicted of inciting riots at the 1968 Democratic Convention in Chicago, toured with the Mime Troupe in 1970 when they performed their play about the trial of Black Panther Bobby Seale. He described their collaboration:

> After the performances of *Seize the Time*, I would speak about the Panthers, Nixon's repression, and the trails scheduled for New Haven, and have dialogue with the audience. What was refreshing in retrospect is how the cast could come out from behind the masks and costumes and engage as real people in dialogue about the war, racism, social activism, and so on. There was no boundary between the performance and politics, acting and activism.[2]

This merging of politics and performance, life and theater, that Peter Berg named "guerrilla theater" in 1965 is still the core impulse in the troupe's work and of activist performance work all over the world. And it is as necessary today as it was during the 1960s. Then it was the war in Vietnam and the civil rights movement; now it is the future of the earth. The demonstrations at the World Trade Organization meetings in Seattle and Quebec, the World Bank and International Monetary Fund meeting in Washington, D.C., the Group of 8 summit in Genoa, the street demonstrations at the 2000 Democratic Convention in Los Angeles and the Republican Convention in Philadelphia, suggest that we are experiencing a burgeoning of activism that is bringing disparate groups together who share a growing understanding about the catastrophic future we all face if the value of individual life and the planet are not honored. Activist theater like that of the San Francisco Mime Troupe has a crucial role as a model in the people's theater movement and as a participant in the larger international movement joining thousands of groups and millions of individuals who are bringing about social change.

Notes

1. Noam Chomsky, "Weekend Teach-In: Opening Session, 15–16 April 1989," in *Understanding Power: The Indispensable Chomsky*, ed. Peter Mitchell and John Schoeffel (New York: New Press, 2002), 10.

2. Tom Hayden, email to Susan Vaneta Mason, 5 August 2002.

References

Articles, Books, and Other Sources

Aaron, Jules. *Frijoles (Beans to You). Educational Theatre Journal* 27 (December 1975): 557–58.

Bagby, Beth. "El Teatro Campesino: Interviews with Luis Valdez." *Tulane Drama Review* 11 (summer 1967): 70–80.

Barthol, Bruce. "In the Face of Fear and Struggle, Art." *American Theatre* 4 (June 1987): 26–29.

Berson, Misha. "Cabin Fever." *American Theatre* 8 (May 1991): 16–23, 71–73.

Brooks, Peter. *The Melodramatic Imagination: Balzac, Henry James, Melodrama, and the Mode of Excess.* New Haven: Yale University Press, 1976.

Browning, Frank, and Banning Garrett. "The New Opium War." *Ramparts,* May 1971, 32–39.

Chumley, Daniel. "Going South: The San Francisco Mime Troupe in Nicaragua." *New Theatre Quarterly* 3 (November 1987): 291–302.

Cohn, Ruby. "Joan Holden and the San Francisco Mime Troupe." *Drama Review* 24 (June 1980): 41–49.

Conner, Kim S. "*13 Días/13 Days:* How the New Zapatistas Shook the World." *Theatre Journal* 50 (March 1998): 97–98.

Coyote, Peter. *Sleeping Where I Fall.* Washington, D.C.: Counterpoint, 1998.

Davis, R. G. "Cultural Revolution U.S.A." In *Guerrilla Theatre Essays: 1.* San Francisco: San Francisco Mime Troupe, 1970.

———. "Guerrilla Theatre." *Tulane Drama Review* 10 (summer 1966): 130–36.

———. "Guerrilla Theatre: 1967." In *Guerrilla Theatre Essays: 1.* San Francisco: San Francisco Mime Troupe, 1970.

———. "Method in Mime." *Tulane Drama Review* 6 (June 1962): 61–65.

———. "On the San Francisco Mime Troupe." *Arts in Society* 6 (1969): 407–14.

———. "Politics, Art, and the San Francisco Mime Troupe." *Theatre Quarterly* 5 (June–August 1975): 26–27.

———. "Radical, Independent, Chaotic, Anarchic Theatre vs. Institutional, University, Little, Commercial, Ford, and Stock Theatres." In *Guerrilla Theatre Essays: 1.* San Francisco: San Francisco Mime Troupe, 1970. n.p.

———. "The Radical Right in the American Theatre." *Theatre Quarterly* 5 (September–November 1975): 67–72.

————. *The San Francisco Mime Troupe: The First Ten Years*. Palo Alto, Calif.: Rampart Press, 1975.

Davis, R. G., and Peter Berg, "Sartre through Brecht," *Tulane Drama Review* 12 (fall 1967): 132.

Dilday, Laurence Michael. "Experiment in Collectivity: Revolution and Evolution in the San Francisco Mime Troupe." Ph.D. diss., University of California, Davis, 2000.

Drescher, Timothy W. *San Francisco Bay Area Murals: Communities Create Their Muses, 1904–1997*. Hong Kong: Everbest Printing Co., 1998.

Edelson, Mary Elizabeth. "The San Francisco Mime Troupe as Radical Theater." Ph.D. diss., University of Wisconsin, 1975.

Foster, Rick, ed. *West Coast Plays 10*. Berkeley: California Theatre Council, 1981.

Gelb, Hal. "Theater." *The Nation*, 15 October 1990, 428.

Gordon, Mel. *The Mother. Tulane Drama Review* 19 (June 1975): 94–101.

Hartman, Chester W. *Yerba Buena: Land Grab and Community Resistance in San Francisco*. San Francisco: Glide Publications, 1974.

Holden, Joan. "An Answer to the Question, 'When Are You Going to Try Writing a *Real* Play?'" *Theater* 20 (winter 1988): 72.

————. "Collective Playmaking: The Why and the How." *Theatre Quarterly* 5 (June–August 1975): 28–36.

————. "Comedy and Revolution." *Arts in Society* 6 (1969): 415–20.

————. "Humor: Revenge of the Powerless." *Callboard* 24 (December 1999). 22.

————. "In Praise of Melodrama." In *Reimaging America*, ed. Mark O'Brien and Craig Little, 280–81. Santa Cruz, Calif.: New Society Publishers, 1990.

————. "The Melodrama Is the Message." *American Theatre* 6 (October 1989): 42–43, 122.

————. "Satire and Politics in America; or, Why Is That President Still Smiling?" *Theater* 10 (Spring 1979): 104–7.

————. "Up Front." *Theater* 29 (1998): 7–9.

Hurwitt, Robert, ed. *West Coast Plays 15/16*. Berkeley: California Theatre Council, 1983.

Isenberg, Barbara, ed. *California Theatre Annual, 1981*. Beverly Hills: Performing Arts Network, 1981.

————. *California Theatre Annual, 1983*. Beverly Hills: Performing Arts Network, 1983.

Jencks, Lance. "The San Francisco Mime Troupe in Its Social Context." Ph.D. diss., University of California, Davis, 1978.

Kerouac, Jack. *The Dharma Bums*. New York: Penguin, 1976.

Kleb, William. "*Hotel Universe*: Playwriting and the San Francisco Mime Troupe." *Theater* 9 (spring 1979): 15–20.

————. "The San Francisco Mime Troupe a Quarter of a Century Later: An Interview with Joan Holden." *Theater* 16 (spring 1985): 58–61.

Kolodney, David. "San Francisco Mime Troupe Ripping Off Ma Bell." *Ramparts*, August 1970, 26.

Kroll, Jack. "Pratfalls and Politics." *Newsweek*, 22 January 1973, 65.

Landahl, Rhonda R. "*I Ain't Yo' Uncle.*" *Theatre Journal* 44 (October 1992): 397–98.

Mason, Susan Vaneta. "*City for Sale.*" *Theatre Journal* 53 (May 2001): 317–18.

————. "The San Francisco Mime Troupe's *Spain/36*." *Theater* 18 (fall–winter 1986): 94–97.

McConachie, Bruce, and Daniel Freidman, eds. *Theatre for Working-Class Audiences in the United States, 1830–1980*. Westport, Conn.: Greenwood Press, 1985.

Mitchell, Peter, and John Schoeffel, eds. *Understanding Power: The Indispensable Chomsky*. New York: New Press, 2002.

Morris, Ardith Ann. "Collective Creation Practices." Ph.D. diss., Northwestern University, 1989.

Norton, Clark. "The S. F. Mime Troupe Turns Twenty-Five." *Mother Jones*, April 1984, 5.

O'Brian, Mark, and Craig Little, eds. *Reimaging America: The Arts of Social Change*. Philadelphia: New Society, 1990.

Ohanian, Bernard. "Fighting That Bushed Feeling," *Mother Jones*, January 1989, 49.

Orenstein, Claudia. *Festive Revolutions*. Jackson: University Press of Mississippi, 1998.

Perry, Charles. *The Haight-Ashbury: A History*. New York: Random House, 1984.

Petley, H. C. "The San Francisco Mime Troupe." *Cavalier* 17 (May 1967): 94–101.

Reid, Kerry. "Forty Years with the San Francisco Mime Troupe." *Callboard* 24 (December 1999): 21–23.

Reinelt, Janelle. "Approaching the Sixties: Between Nostalgia and Critique." *Theatre Survey* 43 (May 2002): 37–56.

Rich, J. Dennis. "An Interview with the San Francisco Mime Troupe." *Players* 46 (December–January 1971): 55–64.

San Francisco Mime Troupe. *By Popular Demand: Plays and Other Works by the San Francisco Mime Troupe*. San Francisco: San Francisco Mime Troupe, 1980.

———. *Guerrilla Theatre Essays: 1*. San Francisco: San Francisco Mime Troupe, 1970.

———. "Proceedings." *Radical Theatre Festival*, San Francisco State College, 1968. San Francisco: San Francisco Mime Troupe, 1969.

Savran, David. *In Their Own Words: Contemporary American Playwrights*. New York: Theatre Communications Group, 1988.

Schechter, Joel. "The Arrest of the Anarchist Keith McHenry." *Theatre Journal* 47 (December 1995): 541–42.

———. *Durov's Pig: Clowns, Politics, and Theatre*. New York: Theatre Communications Group, 1985.

———. "Zapatistas Take the Stage." *American Theatre* 14 (March 1997): 4–5.

Scheer, Robert. Introduction to *The San Francisco Mime Troupe: The First Ten Years*, by R. G. Davis. Palo Alto: Ramparts Press, 1975.

Shank, Adele. "The San Francisco Mime Troupe's *Americans, or Last Tango in Hauhautenango*." *Drama Review* 25 (fall 1981): 81–83.

Shank, Theodore. *American Alternative Theatre*. New York: Grove Press, 1982.

———. "Political Theatre, Actors, and Audiences: Some Principles and Techniques." *Theater* 10 (spring 1979): 94–103.

———. "Political Theatre as Popular Entertainment: San Francisco Mime Troupe." *Drama Review* 18 (March 1974): 110–17.

———. "The San Francisco Mime Troupe's Production of *False Promises*." *Theatre Quarterly* 7 (fall 1977): 43.

Shepard, Richmond. *Mime: The Technique of Silence*. New York: Drama Book Specialists, 1971.

Silber, Glenn, and Claudia Vianello. *Troupers*. Catalyst Media, 1985. Videocassette.

Solomon, Alisa. "Both Sides Now." *American Theatre* 6 (January 1990): 16–21, 60.

Stuart, Jan. "S. F. Troupe in a Bind." *American Theatre* 2 (July–August 1985): 39–40.

Van Erven, Eugene. *Radical People's Theatre*. Bloomington: Indiana University Press, 1988.

Weiner, Bernard. "The Mime Troupe and the Critics." *Callboard* 24 (December 1999): 23.

Wolf, Stacy. "Politics, Polyphony, and Pleasure: The San Francisco Mime Troupe's *Seeing Double*." *Theater* 23 (spring 1993): 61–81.

Zane, Donna Jean F. N. "Satiric Melodramas and Sociopolitical Change: The Plays of the San Francisco Mime Troupe, 1980–1988." Ph.D. diss., University of Hawaii, 1990.

Zimpel, Lloyd. "Surprise in the Wings." *The Nation*, 7 March 1966, 276–78.

Plays by the San Francisco Mime Troupe

L'Amant Militaire. Adapted by Joan Holden. In *The San Francisco Mime Troupe: The First Ten Years*, by R. G. Davis, 173–93. Palo Alto: Ramparts Press, 1975.

The Dragon Lady's Revenge. By Joan Holden, Patricia Silver, Andrea Snow and Jael Weisman. Lyrics by Randall Craig, Barry Glick, and Joel Weisman. In *By Popular Demand: Play and Other Works by the San Francisco Mime Troupe*, 115–64. San Francisco: San Francisco Mime Troupe, 1980.

Eco-Man. By Steve Friedman. In *By Popular Demand: Play and Other Works by the San Francisco Mime Troupe*, 256–66. San Francisco: San Francisco Mime Troupe, 1980.

Eco-Man. By Steve Friedman. In *Guerrilla Street Theatre*, edited by Harry Lesnick, 252–58. New York: Avon, 1973.

Factperson. By Joan Holden, Andrea Snow, Bruce Barthol. Songs by Andrea Snow and Bruce Barthol. In *West Coast Plays 15/16*, edited by Robert Hurwitt, 98–126. Berkeley: California Theatre Council, 1983.

Factwino Meets the Moral Majority. By Joan Holden, with Brian Freeman, Tede Matthews, Peter Solomon, and Henry Picciotto. Songs by Bruce Barthol. In *West Coast Plays 15/16*, edited by Robert Hurwitt, 126–57. Berkeley: California Theatre Council, 1983.

Factwino vs. Armageddonman. By Joan Holden, Robert Alexander, and Henri Picciotto. Songs by Bruce Barthol and Glenn Appell. In *West Coast Plays 15/16*, edited by Robert Hurwitt, 158–84. Berkeley: California Theatre Council, 1983.

False Promises/Nos Engañaron. By Joan Holden. Songs by Andrea Snow, Bruce Barthol, Deb'bora Gilyard, and Javier Pacheco. In *By Popular Demand: Play and Other Works by the San Francisco Mime Troupe*, 11–84. San Francisco: San Francisco Mime Troupe, 1980.

Frijoles, or Beans to You. By Joan Holden, Sharon Lockwood, Patricia Silver, and Andrea Snow. Lyrics by Andrea Snow. In *By Popular Demand: Play and Other Works by the San Francisco Mime Troupe*, 208–31. San Francisco: San Francisco Mime Troupe, 1980.

Frozen Wages. By Richard Benetar, Dan Chumley, Joan Holden, and the cast. In *By Popular Demand: Play and Other Works by the San Francisco Mime Troupe*, 232–43. San Francisco: San Francisco Mime Troupe, 1980.

Ghosts. By Joan Holden, with Arthur Holden and Dan Chumley. Lyrics by Andrea Snow. In *West Coast Plays 10*, edited by Rick Foster, 31–40. Berkeley: California Theatre Council, 1981.

Hotel Universe. By Joan Holden with the cast, Daniel Chumley, and Melody James.

Songs by Bruce Barthol and Eduardo Robledo. In *West Coast Plays 10*, edited by Rick Foster, 1–30. Berkeley: California Theatre Council, 1981.

I Ain't Yo' Uncle. By Robert Alexander. In *Colored Contradictions*, edited by Harry J. Elam Jr. and Robert Alexander, 21–90. New York: Penguin, 1996.

The Independent Female, or A Man Has His Pride. By Joan Holden. In *By Popular Demand: Play and Other Works by the San Francisco Mime Troupe*, 165–93. San Francisco: San Francisco Mime Troupe, 1980.

Meat. By San Francisco Mime Troupe. In "The San Francisco Mime Troupe in Its Social Context," by Lance Jencks, 135–37. Ph.D. diss., University of California, Davis, 1978.

Meter Maid. By San Francisco Mime Troupe. In *Break Out! In Search of New Theatrical Environments*, edited by James Schevill, 111–14. Chicago: Swallow Press, 1973.

The Mozamgola Caper. By Joan Holden, John O'Neal, and Robert Alexander. Songs by Bruce Barthol. *Theater* 20 (winter 1988): 55–71.

Newsman—the Fourth Estate: A Puppet Play. By San Francisco Mime Troupe. *Arts in Society* 6, no. 3 (1969): 412–14.

San Fran Scandals of '73. Steve Friedman and Joan Holden, from a story by Andrea Snow, Melody James, and Sharon Lockwood, with Joe Bellan's jokes. Lyrics by Phil Marsh and Joan Holden. In *By Popular Demand: Play and Other Works by the San Francisco Mime Troupe*, 85–113. San Francisco: San Francisco Mime Troupe, 1980.

Seeing Double: A Middle Eastern Comedy of Error. By Peter Sinai, Joan Holden, Emily Shihadeh, Jody Hirsch, Nabil Al-Hadithy, and Nidal Totah, with Harvey Varga, Arthur Holden, and Nidal Nazzal. Songs by Bruce Barthol and Randy Craig. *Theater* 23 (spring 1992): 61–81.

Los Siete. By Steve Friedman. In *By Popular Demand: Play and Other Works by the San Francisco Mime Troupe*, 244–55. San Francisco: San Francisco Mime Troupe, 1980.

Los Siete. By Steve Friedman. In *The New Radical Theatre Notebook*, edited by Arthur Sainer, 257–66. New York: Applause, 1997.

Telephone. Steve Friedman. In *Guerrilla Theater: Scenarios for a Revolution*, edited by John Weisman, 122–25. Garden City, N.Y.: Anchor, 1973.

Telephone. Steve Friedman. In "Ripping Off Ma Bell." David Kolodney. *Ramparts*, August 1970, 26–29.